# ONE SHINING MOMENT

*To the memory of our fallen student warriors—co-conspirators in their*

- *rejection of the obsolete nation-state system;*
- *defiance of Jim Crow and McCarthyism; and*
- *stubborn refusal to succumb to the inevitability of nuclear war*

*For much of the Twentieth Century they left their marks on the human condition and the world is better because of them.*

*This book is dedicated to the memory of:*

| | |
|---|---|
| *Ted Weiss* | *John Holt* |
| *Don McIntosh* | *Bernard Hennessy* |
| *Myron Weiner* | *Clare LindgrenWofford* |
| *Rob West* | *Erskine Childers* |
| *Allard Lowenstein* | *Helen Jean Rogers Secondari* |
| *Wilder Crane* | *Douglas Cater* |
| *James T. "Ted" Harris* | *Arnulf Pins* |

*John G. Kemeny*

# ONE SHINING MOMENT

### A HISTORY OF THE STUDENT FEDERALIST MOVEMENT IN THE UNITED STATES, 1942–53

### GILBERT JONAS

iUniverse.com, Inc.
San Jose   New York   Lincoln   Shanghai

**One Shining Moment**
A Short History of the American Student World Federalist Movement 1942-1953

All Rights Reserved © 2001 by Gilbert Jonas

No part of this book may be reproduced or transmitted in any form or by any means, graphic, electronic, or mechanical, including photocopying, recording, taping, or by any information storage retrieval system, without the permission in writing from the publisher.

Published by iUniverse.com, Inc.

For information address:
iUniverse.com, Inc.
5220 S 16th, Ste. 200
Lincoln, NE 68512
www.iuniverse.com

The information and material contained in this book are provided "as is," without warranty of any kind, express or implied, including without limitation any warranty concerning the accuracy, adequacy, or completeness of such information or material or the results to be obtained from using such information or material. Neither iUniverse.com, Inc., nor the author shall be responsible for any claims attributable to errors, omissions, or other inaccuracies in the information or material contained in this book, and in no event shall iUniverse.com, Inc. or the author be liable for direct, indirect, special, incidental, or consequential damages arising out of the use of such information or material.

ISBN: 0-595-13501-3

Printed in the United States of America

## Contents

Illustrations   *ix*
Prologue   *xi*

**Chapter 1   The Immaculate Birth**   *1*
    The Proposed Federation of the Atlantic Democracies   *3*
    Student Federalists Petition Voters in the 1944 National Election   *5*
    Student Federalists Rapidly Expand, Plan To Become National Organization   *6*

**Chapter 2   Becoming a National Organization**   *11*
    Easter Week, 1944: Students Convene First National Convention   *11*
    Second SF Convention Fashions Six-Year Plan for Growth   *13*
    Second Student Convention Abandons Atlantic Federation for Global Entity   *15*
    World Federal Government Receives Prominent Endorsements   *18*
    Returning War Veterans Help Spur SF Growth   *18*
    The Historic Concord Meeting, February 1946   *20*
    Education Programs Sparked by SF President Clare Lindgren   *24*
    Student Federalists Move into the International Arena   *25*
    Third Student Convention in 1946 Moves Toward Maximalist Position   *27*

**Chapter 3   A New Leadership Era Begins**   *33*
    Coke Prentice Becomes SF President   *33*
    Despite Aggressive Soviet Behavior, Student Federalist Movement Experiences Rapid Growth   *38*
    American Legion Calls for Global Armed Force Under U.N. Authority   *41*
    Process Begins to Unite American Federalist Organizations   *41*
    1946: The Greatest Federalist Growth in the Face of Stepped-Up Soviet Expansion   *43*
    The Great 1947 Asheville Compromise Produces the United World Federalists (UWF)   *44*
    SF Becomes UWF's Student Division   *47*

Student Division Participates in New National and International Organizations   49
Despite Soviet Rebuffs, UWF Demands UN's Transformation as Global Cop   50
Cord Meyer, Jr. Named UWF President in June 1947   53
UWF President Cord Meyer Urges State Department Proposals to Strengthen U.N.   54
Wofford and Lindgren Urge UWF 1947 Convention Delegates Not to Reject Montreux Proposals   54

CHAPTER 4   THE MOVEMENT PEAKS DESPITE A TENUOUS UNITY   59
Student Delegates Reach Emotional High: Fifteen Leave School to Volunteer for One Year   59
Despite Sizable 1948 Growth, Students Encounter Increasing Problems with Adults   61
Establishment Leaders Petition for United States Support of World Government   63
Soviets Complete East Europe Takeover; Kremlin Rejects Federalist Proposals   64
Intensive Volunteer Organizing Almost Doubles Student Membership to 9,500   66
Broad Coalition of National Membership Organizations Endorses World Federalism   68
As Cold War Heats Up, UWF Student Membership Plummets   68
Tensions Grow Within UWF Between Students and Adults   69
Federalists Victimized by Opponents of Free Speech; Students Seek Bar Against Racism Within UWF   73
Cross-Country Caravan by Student Federalists Highlights 1950   75
Student Federalists Fight Back Against Right-Wing Efforts to Silence Them   77
June 1950 Student Council Meeting Reveals Further Student-Adult Discord   82

CHAPTER 5   THE "REBELLION" OF THE STUDENTS   85
Wallerstein's Critique of UWF Policies Calls for Support of World Revolutionary Forces   85
October 1950 UWF Convention Further Reduces Student Authority   88
Student Leaders Become Major Force in U.S. Youth Delegation to World Assembly   90

*Contents*

Despite Student Objections, UWF Severs Relationship with World Government News   *93*
Wallerstein Resigns from National Executive Council, Charging UWF with Ineffectiveness   *96*
Stanford Student Body Votes to Send Delegate to 1951 Rome Congress on World Government   *97*
Showdown at Des Moines in 1951: Adults Reject Student Pleas, and Students Bolt   *101*
Students Form Interim Committee to Chart New Course   *103*
Last-Ditch Negotiations Fail to Produce Accord   *106*
ICAFY Issues Call to Student Activists for New Organization   *107*
American Students Federalists a Major Force in First World Assembly of Youth, August 1951   *110*

CHAPTER 6  AS THE COLD WAR HEATS UP, THE FEDERALIST CAUSE COOLS OFF   *115*
East-West Conflicts Increase in 1951 and 1952   *115*
American Student Leaders Convene in Philadelphia to Form WORLD   *116*
New Student Organization Gains Financial Subsidy   *117*
First WORLD Board Meeting Organizes New Entity in December 1951   *119*
Student Federalists Play Key Role in First Private Overseas Technical Assistance Agency   *120*
New Federalist Quarterly "World Frontiers" Launched   *124*
WORLD Launches American Campaign to Free Morocco from French Colonial Rule   *128*
Merger of WORLD and Students for Democratic Action Fails   *131*
WORLD—and Student Federalists—Quietly Fade Away   *132*

APPENDIXES   *135*
1  Program of the First Student Federalist Convention   *135*
2  Petition—to the Voting People of Our Country   *136*
3  Vote for Federalists in the Election of 1944   *138*
4  The Student Federalist Concord Charter   *141*
5  To America's Public Leaders   *142*
6  Marxism and Federalism   *144*
7  Opinion from Moscow   *161*
8  Delegates and Signers of the Concord Charter   *163*

9   Revised Concord Charter   *165*
10  Soviets Reject World Federation   *167*
11  Prospects for Concord   *168*
12  Student Federalist Chapter List, January 1947   *171*
13  What Happened at Asheville   *175*
14  Student Federalists: a List of Delegates and Observers to the Asheville Convention   *179*
15  United World Federalists, Inc. Policies and Programs   *181*
16  United World Federalists Student Chapters   *184*
17  The Talk of the Town, Notes and Comments, Dec. 8, 1945   *193*
18  Prominent Supporters of World Government During the Period Between 1943 and 1953   *196*
19  The Clark-Sohn Plan; the Draft Chicago Constitution   *198*
20  What About the Russians?   *202*
21  Suppose You Had No Cop on the Corner   *209*
22  On the Road: Student Caravan Reaches Washington   *211*
23  Participants in 1950 Student Federalist Caravan   *212*
24  Wallerstein's Resignation from UWF   *213*
25  The Wallerstein Credo: A Supplementary Credo for the Student Division   *215*
26  Revolution and Order   *217*
27  The Meaning of Revolution   *221*
28  Nationalism: Grand Illusions and Political Fact   *225*
29  Morocco and Tunisia—a Resolution   *229*
30  Fact Sheet on Morocco, 12/4/52   *231*
31  A Guide to Des Moines   *234*
32  The Interim Committee of American Federalist Youth   *238*
33  WORLD—a Youth Organization for a Just World Community under Federal World Government   *241*
34  Where We Stand   *247*
35  A Globalist Glossary   *251*
36  Internal Security in America   *252*
37  The Wiggins Case: Academic Freedom in Jeopardy   *260*
38  Point Four: Another American Tragedy?   *265*
39  To Train These Hands   *271*

Index   *275*

# Illustrations

Harris Wofford, Jr., founder of the Students Federalists   2
Student Federalist convention in Chicago, 1944   12
Student Federalist Leaders: Thomas Hughes, Harris Wofford Jr., Jerry Miller, Mary Ellen Purdy, Clare Lindgren   14
Clare Lindgren   16
Pvt. Harris Wofford, Jr.   17
Thomas Hughes   17
Gilles Corcos   19
Virginia Lastayo   20
Trudy Schneider   26
Steve Benedict   27
Joe Wheeler   29
Curt Farrar   29
1946 Student Federalist Convention in Chicago   30
1946 Chicago convention delegates   31
Student Federalist delegates at the University of Chicago in 1948   35
Dick Glascow, Natalie Rogers, and Larry Fuchs   36
Harris Wofford at Columbia University,1948   37
Patricia Kimball, Clare Lindgren, and Helen Ball   39
1948 UWF Student Division convention in Minneapolis   45
Student Federalist leaders and Carl Van Doren   48
"The Cop on the Corner"   51
Helen Ball, Justice Owen Roberts, Emory Reves, and Mary Ellen Purdy   52
Larry Fuchs, Alan Green, Upshur Evans, Abe Wilson, Cord Meyer, Jr., Cass Canfield, Mildred Blake, Randolph Compton, and Sam Levering   55
Larry Fuchs and Phyllis Barnhill   60
Natalie Rogers with student members in 1948   63
Ralph Fleming and Murray Frank at 1948 UWF Student Division convention in Minneapolis   67
Lord Boyd Orr at the Third Annual Conference of the World Student Federalist in Amsterdam, 1949   71
Murray Frank addressing plenary in 1949   72

Conclusion of student caravan in 1950; William Friedlander hands petitions to Secretary of the U.S. Senate Leslie Biffle   *77*
World Citizen's identity card   *79*
Mary Coleman   *87*
Herb Weiss   *87*
Don McIntosh   *88*
Bill Friedlander   *88*
Fritjof Thygeson   *94*
Immanuel Wallerstein   *95*
Shane Riorden   *98*
Gil Jonas   *98*
Des Moines all-nighter, 1951, Gil Jonas, Jerry Voorhis, Bonnie Palace, Neil Parsons, Herb Weiss, Duke Robertson, Immanuel Wallerstein, Elaine Klein, Nonie Clark, and Virginia Riorden   *102*
World Assembly of Youth at Bailey Hall, Cornell University   *108*
World Assembly of Youth assembly hall   *108*
Cartoon from the *St. Louis Post-Dispatch*   *109*
Herb Weiss, Duke Robertson, Immanuel Wallerstein, and Elaine Klein at WAY assembly   *111*
WAY delegates listening to simultaneous translations   *113*
Helen Dale and Gil Jonas at WAY steering committee meeting in Berlin   *122*
At WAY Congress in Berlin, Immanuel Wallerstein, Gil Jonas, and Gerrit Kreveld   *126*
Lucy Law (Webster) departing from New York harbor in 1953   *129*

# Prologue

This book was not planned. It grew out of a Fiftieth Plus Anniversary of the Student Federalist leaders that I had organized for November 1997 at the Princeton Club in New York City. To provoke a suitable degree of nostalgia, I asked those who had agreed to attend whether they had any printed, written, or graphic material from their Student Federalist days, which I then proceeded to organize on large sheets of fiberboard as displays along the walls of the meeting room.

Much to my surprise, a considerable amount of material turned up from Tom Hughes, Steve Benedict, Virginia Fleming, Bill Friedlander, and Immanuel Wallerstein, who sent me a full carton, organized in file folders, covering both Student Federalist and UWF Student Division years. The material was sufficient to provide a clear line of development and continuity for the entire movement, from its 1943 beginnings until the demise of WORLD in 1952.

By coincidence, Gene Schwartz, who was also an early leader of the United States National Student Association, attended the November 1997 reunion. Gene and some of his USNSA alumni had been working on a history of the student organization's first five years. Intrigued by the materials he saw on display and aware of the cross-overs between Student Federalists and USNSA leaders, he suggested I write a chapter on the Student Federalists and their relationship to not only USNSA but also some of the other student organizations of the period. I agreed, but because I was involved in several other projects at the time, I was unable to undertake any sustained outside research to fill the gaps not covered by the materials in hand. Fortunately, so many of the participants are still around, and some were able to describe events not covered by the written materials. Nevertheless, the text of this book is not meant to be the definitive history of the Student Federalist movement. Because the length of my draft was much too long for the USNSA book, a substantially shortened version appears in that study. On the other hand, the text I have written is barely long enough to be called a book; it is more likely a long article. And it is meant to be an *aperitif*—enough to stimulate the appetite, I hope, of some young doctoral students who might attract the resources and find the time to search for the elusive official files of the Student Federalists and of the Student Division of the United World Federalists. Then, and only then, can a fully developed history of this unique phenomenon be researched and written. If we are lucky, this written history will transpire in the immediate future, while most of the active players are still with us and can recall the events and personalities that carried the Student Federalists to the mountain top and back down again in the decade whose parameters were marked by the Allied invasion of Italy, on the one hand, and the end of the Korean "police action," on the other.

The most enjoyable aspect of this project was collecting and reading the relevant documents, letters, and articles, a selection of which appears in this book's appendices. I was frequently struck by both the wisdom and prescience of such young and relatively inexperienced Americans who, it appears in retrospect, anticipated many of the grave problems and challenges that mankind was to face in the decades ahead. The values and the methods of analysis that these young men and women applied, many of whom were World War II veterans, whereas others were to become Korean War veterans, display both a profound love of country and a deep commitment to the concept of world citizenship. As we enter the next millennium and experience the painful transition from a world dominated by the Cold War to a world increasingly anarchic and incapable of sustaining both justice and order, many of the concepts that intrigued young federalists half a century ago are ineluctably resurrecting themselves as possible alternatives to the rapidly diminishing nation-state system. Who knows: We may even again witness courageous political leaders unafraid to utter such threatening words as "sovereignty" and "federalism."

I owe special thanks to those former Student Federalist leaders (now all septuagenarians) who took the time and trouble to read this text and correct

*Prologue*

the facts. They include Steve Benedict, Bill Friedlander, Murray Frank, Virginia Fleming, Fritjof Thygeson, Lucy Webster, Harry Lustig, Elaine Klein, and especially, Thomas L. Hughes, who also challenged his eyesight by editing each line as well. In addition to the individual portrait photos and snapshots that the subjects sent, I am also indebted to Tom Hughes, Herb Weiss, Joseph Wheeler, and especially Virginia Lastayo Riorden, who has a major collection, for the photos that appear in these pages. I apologize to those still alive who appear in some of these photos and whom we were unable to identify fifty years later.

—Gilbert Jonas
New York City, August 3, 1999

# 1

# THE IMMACULATE BIRTH

*The New Yorker's* essayist and social critic E.B. White wrote in the years following World War II that foreign policy was the "top hat" of domestic policy. On a parallel plane, the Student Federalist movement for world government was the postwar "top hat" of the American democratic student movement, whereas the United States National Student Association (USNSA) comprised the closest thing to a mass student movement in the nation.

As a postwar student activist who bridged both movements during the period, I was presented with an interesting and singular perspective during the years that form the ideological cusp that introduced the decline of one movement and the irresistible growth of the other. The "cusp" years to which I refer are 1949 through 1951, but before addressing them, I want to turn the clock back to late 1942. During that year, the United States and its dwindling allies had suffered massive military and territorial losses in Europe (especially in the Soviet Union) and the Pacific (where Japanese forces had conquered all of the European and American colonial territories east of India and north of Australia after destroying most of the American fleet at Pearl Harbor).

The British Isles, under a stubborn Churchill, were bravely fighting off total collapse under the most destructive air assault theretofore known to human kind, as the Luftwaffe pounded civilian and military targets indiscriminately. Only the dauntless RAF stood between Britain and Nazi victory.

The year 1942 was the grimmest of the war and quite possibly the grimmest of the century for America's prospects.

On a wintry Saturday night early in 1941, a 14-year-old Scarsdale, New York, boy was having his bath, reading his Latin lesson, and listening to the radio. In a sudden luminous moment, the youngster's attention was captured by the speaker, Clare Booth Luce (a later revisionist version designates Clarence Streit as the speaker), who was convincingly delineating Streit's already well-known commitment to the notion of an Atlantic union of democratic nations federated along lines similar to those that bound the American states.

Harris Wofford Jr., founder of the Students Federalists.

In that very dark hour of American fortunes, the youngster, Harris Wofford, Jr., began to formulate a plan to organize his young peers across the land to support this very grand and luminous concept. The plan, however, gestated in Wofford's mind for a full year before he bicycled throughout Scarsdale, seeking to persuade some of his close friends and fellow students at Scarsdale High to join with him in what he would later envision as a crusade. The Scarsdale group was officially formed in April, 1942. Those of us who would later come under Wofford's charismatic spell for this and other causes know full well how difficult it must have been for his peers to resist him.

In this way, the Student Federalist idea was born in the United States. In retrospect, it came as no surprise that the idealism unleashed by World War II, in which evil personified sought to destroy that which remained free (and good), held sway over so many young and impressionable minds. After sheer survival, the most common impulse generating support for the American war effort was the genuine belief that "we" were fighting to preserve democracy, to defeat the totalitarian hordes that, if not defeated, would eradicate everything democratic, virtuous, and beautiful in the world. Franklin Delano Roosevelt's patrician rhetoric and the thrilling war-time inspirationals of Winston Churchill effectively captured the hearts and minds of both Americans and Britons, especially of the younger generation.

## THE PROPOSED FEDERATION OF THE ATLANTIC DEMOCRACIES

Although idealism was the spur of this unprecedented student initiative, it needs to be noted here that the initial wave of high school student participants was exclusively white, Protestant, and upper-middle to upper class. They had not yet discovered that the majority of the earth's peoples were non-white, non-Protestant, and mostly very poor. Nor were they much troubled by the decisive fact that almost two thirds of the human race lived under some form of despotism and could not have given a fig for the imperatives of democracy. That is why they found such philosophical comfort in the notion of an Atlantic democratic federation: It encompassed Britain, Canada, France, Denmark, Norway, the Netherlands, Belgium, and Luxembourg—hardly the critical mass defined as the majority of humanity.

Clarence Streit had put forth this radical notion as early as 1939, when the Nazi and Fascist hordes had begun to march toward their openly acknowledged objective to swallow Europe whole. (The earlier degustations in Danzig, Austria, and Czechoslovakia turned out to be easily digested *hors d'oeuvres*.) Before sweeping into Poland, Hitler had negotiated an infamous pact arranging for the cynical collusion of Stalin in the division of Poland. That triggered the French and British, however reluctantly, to come to the aid of their Polish ally. By the time they moved, Poland was gone and France was in mortal jeopardy. The Nazi blitzkrieg soon demolished the Low Countries without stopping for breath.

It is remotely possible that adoption of Streit's proposal in 1939 might have forestalled the Nazi invasion of Poland, but only remotely. There is little doubt that the Allied governments were much too unprepared to offer serious resistance to the Nazis at any point in 1939. And the keystone of the Atlantic alliance—the United States—was far from committed to joining the war, even though FDR believed that American involvement on the side of Britain was both desirable and necessary.

What is difficult to explain is the failure of the Federal Union adherents to include our two other vitally important allies, the Soviet Union and China, in the grand plan. Nevertheless, in April, 1942, Wofford persuaded six other Scarsdale High students to join him in forming the first chapter of the Student Federalists (SF). In September, the Scarsdale chapter members participated in the Shawnee Leadership Institute and signed up fifty new members from twenty schools. Over the next four months, new chapters were formed in New Rochelle and Roosevelt, New York, Chatham, New Jersey, and Concord, Massachusestts. Students throughout New York City formed a Metropolitan Council.

Wofford thereupon reached out to Streit to "affiliate" the Student Federalists with the adult organization, Federal Union (FU), without seeking any financial or other assistance from the adult organization. (In fact, a portion of the students' dues went to support FU's national office.) By so doing, he preserved the students' independence, both in terms of policy and program. By the first half of 1943, after word had penetrated the hinterlands, the SF Council's minutes acknowledged receiving a letter from Tom Hughes of Minnesota regarding his advocacy of the federalist idea in debate, oratorical contests, and conferences of the National Forensic League. Hughes had organized the Mankato, Minnesota, Student Federalist chapter, the first in the Midwest, which was quickly followed by the South St. Paul High School chapter, organized by Emmy Lou Lindgren, Hughes's frequent debating opponent and later, as Clare Lindgren, the wife of Harris Wofford. These three—Wofford, Hughes, and Lindgren—were to dominate the Student Federalist leadership until 1946, when Wofford and Lindgren entered graduate school (they were married in 1948) and Hughes went to Oxford as a Rhodes scholar.

During the summer of 1943, the SF Council launched its first fundraising campaign with a goal of $500. The Council provided each chapter with a fundraising kit, announcing that the following year the Council expected to organize a model "World Constitutional Convention to dramatize the problems of world government." The campaign flyer listed two other objectives: printing—as opposed to mimeographing—the organizational newsletter and garnering 5,000 signatures on a student petition "to the voting people of our country." The first issue of the newsletter had a circulation of 500 in April 1943. By September, that circulation had jumped to 2,000.

## Student Federalists Petition Voters in the 1944 National Election

The student petition is a most compelling document when one remembers it was drafted and adopted essentially by high school students. (See Appendix 2.) It calls for "complete victory by the forces of freedom" because "man cannot exist half slave, half free." It describes the current state of affairs between nations as "anarchy" that makes inevitable that "ever-recurring disputes will always lead to war." To remedy this anarchic state, the world requires "international government." That by itself is, however, insufficient: "The Nazis demand this, too" and they can only be countered by "an even stronger idea: democratic world government, securing decency and freedom for all peoples." However, to avoid a global despotism, the government's form must be federal. "The federal form is the only form that holds power democratically, the only form that can unite the differences in race, language, and nationality that exist in the world."

Thus, as early as 1943, the high school students comprising the nascent organization had already encountered the verbal formula that would later become their policy—a universal world federal government open to every country.

During late 1943 and 1944, this student petition was widely circulated as the SF's first effort to influence the national election in November 1944. A campaign bulletin in August featured a new chapter in Sarasota, Florida, and another document indicated that part of the campaign's proceeds would cover the costs of the SF sending two delegates to the Federal Union convention in Peoria, Illinois. To everyone's surprise, 30 SF delegates attended the Peoria convention that November, during which the Student Federalists formed their own national organization and affiliated with Federal Union. The founding delegates elected Wofford as their first president and Hughes as Vice President.

Wofford won another election a half century later when he defeated Reagan Attorney General Thornton to fill the U.S. Senate seat in Pennsylvania of the late Senator John Heinz, who had earlier died in a plane crash. Among the posts he held during a long career were the first staff attorney of the U.S. Civil Rights Commission, professor of law at Notre Dame, White House counsel to President Kennedy, director of JFK's civil rights section during the 1960 campaign, President of Bryn Mawr College, and Peace Corps Director in Ethiopia. Like Wofford, Hughes had served as administrative aide to Rep. Chester Bowles. Hughes also held a similar position with Senator Hubert Humphrey. After leaving the State Department, Hughes became President of the Carnegie Endowment for International Peace, from which he retired in 1997.

In August 1943, Wofford visited Mrs. Roosevelt at the White House for a 30-minute discussion in which she encouraged the students to continue "educating themselves in terms of world affairs." She doubted that the present generation would effect such radical change as a world government but hoped it would come about in Wofford's generation. She subsequently memorialized the meeting in one of her daily nationally syndicated "My Day" columns.

Wofford also had supportive meetings with Minnesota's Senator Joseph Ball (sponsor of a Senate resolution calling for world union with an adequate police force), Rep. Will Rogers, Jr., and a young but impressive Rep. William Fulbright.

The year-end (1943) SF Board meeting in Scarsdale is a telling gauge of how quickly the federalist concept was catching on. Boasting 25 chapters in 8 states, 11 of the 15 Board members were present, including representatives from Yale, the University of North Carolina, and Queens College. This four-day Board meeting was convened to establish a structure, regional divisions, and a headquarters operation for the Student Federalists, who were about to go national.

## Student Federalists Rapidly Expand, Plan To Become National Organization

The result of the meeting was the basic outline of the Student Federalist apparatus for the remainder of its independent existence. The first problem encountered by the Board was that of a suitable headquarters. The volunteer-driven headquarters in Scarsdale had been outgrown by the rapid establishment of new chapters, many in the Northeast. However, the SF financial situation precluded an immediate change. Thus, Scarsdale was to remain the national office at least until the summer. The priority goal was to establish a national office in New York City with an adult executive secretary and one other employee, supplemented by weekend and holiday volunteers from the SF Metropolitan Council. (There was a vain hope that Federal Union would establish a New York office, which the SF could share. FU's national office remained in Washington until its demise.)

A three-person executive committee (all women) was named by the Board to run the national office. The next decision was to decentralize as much as possible by dividing the nation into four regions, each to have its own headquarters and chairman. Scarsdale was to remain the Northeast headquarters, with Sarasota under Board member Jerry Miller heading the South regional office and Tom Hughes heading the Midwest regional office in Minnesota. (No decision was made for the West region.) A considerable proportion of SF resources, especially literature, was invested in the South.

As the organization's supreme policy-making body, the Board authorized the calling of the first Student Federalist convention over the Easter break (March 31–April 2, 1944) in New York City. The NY Metropolitan Council was delegated responsibility for making the convention arrangements, including a world constitutional convention, a student mass meeting, and several working sessions of chapter delegates to choose a new president, establishing the final details regarding a national headquarters, and devising a summer project to enable students to play a greater role in the 1944 national elections. The Board authorized each chapter to receive one delegate for every ten members, hoping to stimulate both membership and attendance at the convention. To ensure that economic circumstances would not determine who attended the convention, it also voted that SF would pay a sizable share of each delegate's expenses.

Also authorized was the establishment of a permanent Speaker's Division. Harris Wofford was authorized to undertake a major speaking tour beginning on Feb. 1, 1944, immediately after his graduation from high school, as far south as Florida and as far west as Minnesota. Publication of a speaker's manual was also authorized, and each regional division was given permission to organize and train its own speakers and to book its own speaking engagements. SF would pay all expenses associated with these engagements, but emphasis, this being war-time, was placed on "bicycling federalists" who would cover high schools within day-time cycling distance, a pattern established by the Scarsdale chapter in 1943. In all essential details, these decisions formed the structure and modus vivendi of the Student Federalists for the next decade.

In addition, the Board was informed that a student federalist poll and petition had been printed and each chapter was assigned responsibility in its jurisdiction for both drives. The petition, already discussed earlier, was directed to young males under 21 who were eligible for the draft and service with the armed forces. (Females could concur by signing the reverse side.) The poll was devised to ascertain the views and attitudes of high school students toward world federal government. The NY Metro council set January 15, 1944, to commence polling all NYC high school students.

As will be demonstrated, reliance on and belief in education was the bedrock of the Student Federalist organizational strategy. The plan to hold world constitutional conventions was one example. A second was the bibliography of federalist literature approved by the Board in December 1943, the first of a long and ever growing list of books, articles, speeches, papers, periodicals, reprints, and films on the subject. Yet another was the essay contests proposed by the Board for high school students on a variety of related federalist subjects, with monetary prizes. Another key educational tool, the newsletter had grown exponentially, with a winter 1944 circulation of 5,000. Each of Federal Union's 45,000 members also received a copy. Major publicity appeared in *Newsweek, PM,* and the *New York Herald Tribune.*

The most difficult aspect of the new organization's first major board meeting was grappling with finances. High school students in 1943, even relatively affluent ones, had very little access to cash, although war-time opportunities for part-time work for older high school students were fairly good. In that era, parents were far less prone to give youngsters serious sums; weekly allowances for middle-class high school students above their school costs were in the range of 50 cents to $1.50. The finance committee determined that a sum of $5,000 was required to accomplish all of the SF's 1944 objectives. Because reaching that sum was considered unlikely, a budget of $3,000 to $3,500 was drawn to cover convention costs, including part of the delegate's expenses; speaking expenses, including Wofford's tour; literature; the poll; mailings; the petition; contest promotion; and secretarial help. Publishing the *Student Federalist* newsletter was estimated to cost an additional $1,000, but at least that sum was anticipated in earnings from subscribers. In addition to collecting dues and chapter contributions, a national fundraising campaign was authorized under Wofford's leadership to raise "large sums," for example, gifts in the $100 range. The first $100 came from ten Board members who contributed $5 each together with a $50 gift from the adult adviser, Margaret Blumenstiel. Harris Wofford then contributed the next $100 toward his speaking expenses, a sum he said he had been raising over an extended period.

The young federalists pressed their cause in connection with the national election (see Appendix 3), targeting the isolationists for defeat and seeking to elect a federalist president. Faulting President Roosevelt for lack of commitment to the federalist position, the first electoral statement called for consideration of Henry Wallace (whose later Communist backers in 1948 were unremittingly opposed to world federalism as "lackeys of the capitalists"). On the Republican side, the SF leadership (Wofford and Hughes) were totally supportive of Lt. Commander Harold E. Stassen of Minnesota, Senator Joseph H. Ball, and Supreme Court Justice Owen J. Roberts, who the author of the flyer termed the "three 'white hopes' of the whole world." Wendell Willkie was dismissed as without a plan for federation and undeserving of SF support. All of this became moot in the summer of 1944 with the nominations of Franklin D. Roosevelt and Thomas E. Dewey.

# 2

# Becoming a National Organization

### Easter Week, 1944: Students Convene First National Convention

During the 1944 Easter break, SF's first national convention was convened at Columbia University. Tom Hughes, Wofford's choice to succeed him as president, presided over the three open business sessions of the delegates and over the world constitutional convention. At the public mass meeting on Saturday night, Hughes led off with a "Challenge to the Elder Statesmen." Wofford, about to become an Air Force cadet, and Clarence Streit, together with Rep. Howard McMurray, provided other inspirational speeches. At an executive session Sunday morning, Hughes was elected president without opposition. During the concluding luncheon that followed, Wofford delivered his self-described "farewell address"—shades of George Washington—followed by Streit, who lauded Wofford and then anointed Hughes as the new president. The new Student Federalist board met immediately after Hughes's address. Then, as the printed program stated, the delegates and observers made a "pilgrimage to Scarsdale," just two years after Harris Wofford had organized the first chapter. To ensure maximum attendance, the program scheduled a party in Scarsdale following the "pilgrimage."

In all, 102 delegates from 75 chapters in 16 states (exactly one third of the states then comprising the nation) gathered in New York City at the first

*Tom Hughes, newly elected SF President, meets with the Board of representatives at the Student Federalist convention in Chicago on Sept. 30, 1944. The participants are Hughes, Steve Benedict, Clare Lindgren, L. D. Garinger, Gerald Tucker, Joy Naffziger, Chris Magee, Wilder Crane, and Steve Chadwick.*

independent Student Federalist convention to adopt their first policy statement, which appears in Appendix 1. The convention decided to move its headquarters to Washington, D.C., sharing space with Federal Union. Hughes agreed to spend his summer moving the office from Scarsdale and supervising the new D.C. operation as well as the summer projects. In addition to the Scarsdale and Sarasota offices, the convention voted to establish ten new regional offices, each manned by an activist leader, usually a Board member. These new offices were to be located in Concord, Massachusetts.; Washington, D.C.; Greensboro, North Carolina.; Cincinnati, Ohio, Terre Haute, Indiana; St. Louis, Missouri; Chippewa Falls, Wisconsin; South St. Paul, Minnesota; Mankato, Minnesota; and Missoula, Montana, which was expected to spearhead the drive to organize the Northwest.

More than half of the delegates pledged to devote the entire summer vacation period to advocacy work for the Student Federalists. Hughes's address,

"We Challenge the Elder Statesmen," was adopted as a resolution by the delegates, who also heard Wofford answer in the negative his own rhetorical question, "Shall We Have Fought in Vain?" The delegates raised or pledged $600, elected Jerry Miller of Sarasota their Vice President, and promised to devote extra effort during the summer to sell a forthcoming new book, *One World*, by Wendell Willkie, the Republican nominee for President. Thanks in no small measure to the New York City delegation, the white Protestant monopoly was breached by roughly a dozen Jewish delegates and a number of Catholics as well.

During the summer, in addition to setting up the new D.C. office, Hughes and newsletter editor Steve Benedict debated two other students on Ted Granik's "Town Meeting of the Air," over the national radio network owned by Mutual. Both defended the Federal Union strategy of a federal government of democracies, and their opponents called for an institution that encompassed "the entire world." Hughes also followed Streit in testifying before the resolutions committees of the Republican and Democratic party conventions, emphasizing the same strategy and asserting that the vast majority of students, who would soon be voters, feared another world war within 50 years. An eminent journalist, Emmet Crozier of the *New York Herald Tribune*, wrote in June: "It is doubtful whether any other teenage generation has ever thought so deeply or argued so vehemently about world affairs as the high school youngsters represented in the Student Federalist movement." Such passion and commitment were to remain for the rest of the decade as thousands of new recruits joined the young movement. The new development, however, was that the Student Federalists had begun to capture the imagination of college students as well.

## SECOND SF CONVENTION FASHIONS SIX-YEAR PLAN FOR GROWTH

The SF's second convention was held in Chicago from Sept. 28 to Oct. 1, 1944, during a period when the military draft was at its peak, accounting for the absence of a great many males 18 and older. Half the number of delegates who had attended the founding convention appeared in Chicago—a total of 51—according to the November issue of the newsletter. Undaunted, the delegates approved a six-year plan for growth, shooting for 250 chapters by the end of 1945, 500 in 1946, with annual increases such that by 1950, a total of

*Student Federalist Leaders: President Thomas Hughes, Founder Harris Wofford Jr., Vice President Jerry Miller, Board Member Mary Ellen Purdy, Secretary Clare Lindgren. (Photo from* Student Federalist.*)*

5,000 chapters was projected. In addition, the delegates called for establishment of a teachers' division with a first-year goal of 1,000 teachers signed up and a 1950 goal of 30,000 teachers!

The convention also established summer training camps, again setting a goal of 300 trained students in 1945 and, by 1950, 25,000 trained, out of a total projected membership of 100,000. In looking back, one might theorize that Chicago's water supply contained an unknown ingredient that produced temporary euphoria.

## Second Student Convention Abandons Atlantic Federation for Global Entity

More significantly, the convention, which had followed the Dumbarton Oaks meeting preparing the world for the structure and power arrangements of the forthcoming United Nations Organization, realized that the strategy relying on an Atlantic federation of democracies was no longer viable or relevant. Accordingly, the delegates voted to "shift the emphasis of the organization from the immediate uninclusive federation of democracies to an eventual Federal World Democracy," the official newsletter proclaimed in November 1944. The membership was advised to support the expected "comparatively weak United Nations organization [which] will come from this war" while urging "all free peoples to unite in a nuclear Federal Union that would cooperate with other governments as a member of the forthcoming United Nations League." Revealing the unresolved ambivalences that the Dumbarton Oaks conference results produced, an SF newsletter editorial also raised high a new standard, declaring "Wherefore, we Student Federalists now raise our sights to our long range goal of Federal World Democracy." These few words contained the seeds of virtually endless debates within SF and its successors, as well as the death knell for Federal Union.

Hughes undertook a speaking tour in Canada, appearing before an estimated 10,000 students. The result was the first decision by the SF to collaborate with federalist movements in other countries, starting with Canada, which ultimately led to the U.S. student federalist organization assuming a major role in the international grouping. By November, Vice President Jerry Miller had formulated a plan to establish a coordinating council of student federalist organizations from foreign countries together with the U.S. group. Perhaps the most important external development of the year was *Time* magazine's laudatory article on the Student Federalists and Wofford in the Nov. 20 issue. The writer describes the SF as "one of the few United States youth movements of recent years that did not spring from left-wing yearnings or promptings. . . . Convinced that their cause has no more than a half a century in which to save mankind from a third world war, they have set their sights" on extraordinary numerical goals, which have already been cited. Continuing the patrician bias, the writer observes: "As a group, the Student Federalists tend to be as well-bred as Harris Wofford, Jr.'s first recruits in wealthy Westchester County." Perhaps it was this "safe" image that impelled otherwise conservative *Time* to publish such a favorable commentary; more likely, it was the public support of the Federalist position by Clare Booth Luce, wife of the publisher, which predisposed the writer.

This Luce publication testimonial in no way protected the federalists from virulent attacks by the extreme right (and left). Professional hate-mongers such as Gerald L.K. Smith and witch-hunting members of Congress launched

*Clare Lindgren conducts SF meeting.*

vicious attacks on individuals associated with the various Federalist groups, as well as on the groups themselves, once World War II was concluded. As the Soviets began to reveal their true aims in Europe and the anti-communists stepped up their attacks, the heat on the federalists increased proportionately. Neither a Luce testimonial nor an equally poisonous attack from the Stalinists could provide sufficient cover from the professional right-wing rabble rousers.

The autumn brought the first Congressional investigation of the Student Federalists, when Rhode Island's Senator Green presided over an inquiry into campaign spending and sought to determine whether the SF was supporting any candidate in the November elections. High school graduate Wilder Crane of Chippewa Falls, Wisconsin, volunteered to serve as temporary National Director, running the national office in Washington until the SF Board was in a position to recruit a full-time executive director. In October, Private Harris Wofford appeared with Shirley Temple at the Herald Tribune Forum in New York, and presented the newly-revised Student Federalist position, which was broadcast over the CBS network. Before the year was out, the first California chapter had been organized in Los Angeles by Aaron Eshman. Other new chapters included St. John's College, Maryland; Montana State, Montana; Jacksonville, Florida; Wagner College, South Carolina; Pratt, Kansas; Central Missouri State Teachers, Missouri; and Silver State, Reno, Nevada.

Pvt. Harris Wofford, Jr., U.S. Army Air Force.

Thomas Hughes.

## World Federal Government Receives Prominent Endorsements

The overall concept of world federalism received a major boost when the Nov. 14 issue of *Look* magazine supported the evolution of the United Nations into a world federation that would control the peaceful decentralization of Germany. Actress Ingrid Bergman was recruited as a federalist by the South St. Paul chapter. According to an organizing folder issued the following year, at the close of 1944 the Student Federalists could boast 100 chapters and "several thousand members," an achievement of considerable weight for a group of teenagers and a budget of a few thousand dollars.

## Returning War Veterans Help Spur SF Growth

The year 1945 opened auspiciously with Supreme Court Justice Owen J. Roberts addressing a SF rally in Washington and scores of veterans publically declaring their support for the objective. The SF leadership urged veterans who belonged to SF to join the American Veterans Committee and began forming alliances with returning veterans and their groups. The newsletter proposed that President Roosevelt become the U.S. representative to the United Nations and be accorded the power to act on his own (without Congressional approval) to thwart aggression. After Roosevelt's death in April, the proposal was never revived.

In an attempt to restrict the consumption of petroleum and other sources of energy, the federal government in 1945 had ordered the prohibition of conventions involving more than 50 persons. The SF leadership decided to cancel its scheduled 1945 convention and, in its place, organize a major summer training camp for more than 100 students at American University in Washington, D.C. The camp was organized by Emmy Lou Lindgren who, later in the year, succeeded Tom Hughes as SF President. Under Lindgren, the educational emphasis continued, with training camps the preferred route.

Meanwhile, in April, the organizing conference of the United Nations had begun in San Francisco. Several Federalists attended the historic meetings, including Wofford, Hughes, California federalist Aaron Eshman, and SF Veterans Committee chairman Cord Meyer, Jr., who was an aide to Minnesota Governor Harold Stassen. The global scope of the new United Nations produced a permanent change in most of the Student Federalists, causing them to abandon partial federations and groupings and to emphasize the need for a government that encompassed every nation. The urgency of achieving this objective was underscored by the explosion of the two atomic bombs in August over Hiroshima and Nagasaki and the then unimaginable devastation wrought by these weapons.

The 1945 training institute was summarily transformed into a Student Federalist convention, recalls Virginia Lastayo Riorden, who attended the convention at the urging of Wofford. Wofford was stationed at the Selma, Alabama, air base and, although unable to obtain leave from the Air Force to attend the Washington gathering, peppered the organizers with his views on what the meeting should produce. When the two atomic bombs were unleashed upon the Japanese cities, Wofford strongly signaled the SF leadership to use the training meeting as the occasion for a national convention and to move the SF totally and finally into the universalist camp and away from the partial federation proposal of Federal Union. He also pressed the students attending the Washington meeting to begin a dialogue on arms control, especially in respect to the atomic bomb. After the convention, Lastayo returned to Alabama for her final college year while assisting Wofford with some editing of his book, *It's Up to Us*.

*Gilles Corcos.*

*Virginia Lastayo.*

For these reasons, as well as the growing distance between Federal Union and the Student Federalists over universality, and the ferment on campuses following the use of atomic weapons by the United States, Wofford successfully pressed the SF leaders to open their own New York office at 299 Madison Avenue and, with all the persuasive charm at his disposal, convinced Lastayo to forego her graduation (she had already garnered sufficient credits to graduate) to accept the one full-time "paying" job at the New York office. A squad of volunteers kept her from becoming lonely, including Wofford, Joseph Wheeler (who was then organizing the Concord Conference), Laura and Don McIntosh, Alvin and Steve Kaye, Mary Ellen Purdy, David Bauman, Ivan Abrams and Shane Riordan, who not only was promoted to a "paid" position but also eventually courted and married Virginia Lastayo in 1947.

### THE HISTORIC CONCORD MEETING, FEBRUARY 1946
Much of the second half of the year was invested in planning the single most important meeting in the history of the Student Federalists: the four-day Concord, Massachusetts, conference on February 8–11, 1946, to revisit and review the basic federalist positions to align them with the new postwar realities. Invited were representatives of both Student Federalist chapters and like-

minded student organizations interested in world law and order. Eighty-five delegates from 35 colleges and 25 high schools participated in this gathering. The most important result was the unanimous agreement that the ultimate objective was the formation of a world federal government—the universalist position—either by amending the U.N.'s charter or by other means. The Concord Charter, the full text of which is printed in appendixes 4 and 8, calls for the destruction of irresponsible nationalism while preserving national identity by transforming the U.N. into a "new world sovereignty." The charter recognizes "frankly that the United States and the Soviet Union are the two chief obstacles to such action. Either is powerful enough to take the lead." To overcome these obstacles, the charter insists that "We must make world citizenship (later the phrase "in a world community" was added) a political fact." The charter outlines the educational and advocacy techniques that SF had already developed in order to change public opinion in support of the goals of the charter. These include a study program for local chapters, camps, and training institutes, analysis of and commentaries on current issues bearing on world government through the pages of the newsletter, and the production and distribution of all forms of literature, polling, publicity, and related means. The charter continues such SF programs as the Teachers's Division; establishes a permanent international committee to promote likeminded groups abroad; establishes an autonomous Graduate Information Service to inform members of opportunities for work on behalf of world government in different fields, including government service; and calls for a Council of Advisors and for an adult auxiliary. The delegates pledged a total of $2,300 toward the support of the action program. Finally, the delegates "strongly urge[d] the unification of all adult federalist groups in a common movement for federal world government with *a minimum of doctrinal conflict* (my italics)."

Two leading war veterans spoke persuasively to the attending delegates— former Marine hero Cord Meyer, Jr., who had recently published a moving article in *Atlantic Monthly* entitled "A Serviceman Looks to the Peace," and his successor as SF Veterans Committee Chairman, Steve Chadwick, who described in vivid detail his front-line experiences against the Nazis.

As caller of the conference and temporary chairman, Wofford opened the gathering by drawing analogies between the minutemen of Concord in 1775 and those attending the 1946 Concord meeting. "We are here," he said, "to proclaim a world people's sovereignty. We assert our citizenship in the world. . . . We are here to plan our part in the long, hard fight to achieve the birth of a democratic world civilization, protected and promoted by a federal world government . . . and to unite in a common student movement for world federation with an effective program to carry to our generation and to the people of the world." See Appendix 11 for an article Tom Hughes wrote prior to the conference presenting the views of the SF leadership in respect to the prospects for the Concord meeting.

The original planning report of the SF Board's Committee on Delegates called for a total of no more than 80 delegates and stated that 50 to 75 would be sufficient for the Concord conference. It reserved 32 delegate places for representatives of the following student federalist groups (the number of delegates for each in parentheses):

- Yale League for World Government (2)
- Wellesley Committee for World Federation (2)
- Boston Council for World Federation (4)
- Wheaton Committee (1)
- Bennington, Smith College and Vassar College SF chapters (1 each)
- Southern SF Council (3)
- California SF chapters (2)
- Illinois and Ohio SF chapters (4)
- Colorado, Oklahoma and Texas SF chapters (4)
- Montana, Oregon and Washington state chapters (2)
- At-Large delegates (DC, servicemen, etc.) (3)

In addition, 25 delegate places were set aside for determination by the Invitation Committee and accredited by the SF Executive Committee. The report suggested that these positions should be filled by student leaders advocating world government from other colleges, like-minded veterans, AVC college leaders, young atomic scientists, and outstanding individuals of the "rising generation." In reality, the representation from both colleges and high schools proved to be less diverse: Nineteen, or almost one fourth of the total, came from the premier women's colleges; 11 from the Ivy League and the smaller Ivies (including 7 from Yale alone); 8 represented state or municipal colleges; and of the 18 high school delegates, only 2 were from large metropolitan cities. The participants were overwhelmingly privileged economically, white, Protestant, and apparently suburban or rural.

In addition to the already prominent SF leaders (Wofford, Hughes, Lindgren, Steve Benedict, Virginia Lastayo, Colgate Prentice, and Wilder

Crane), those attending included a sizable number of rising leaders who would carry the organization forward for the next three years or more: Helen Ball, Steve Chadwick, Curt Farrar, Pat Kimball, Laura and Don McIntosh, Charles Nelson, Cushing Niles, Eleanor Schneider, Foster Parmelee, Jr., Mary Ellen Purdy, Richard Shapiro, and Joseph Wheeler. (See Appendix 8 for a complete list of the student delegates to the Concord gathering.) Also among the Concord delegates were Daniel Patrick Moynihan of Tufts, later the multiterm U.S. Senator from New York, and Brooklyn high school student Stephen Schwebel, later the president of the International Court of Justice in The Hague. Schwebel was an advocate of the United Nations and a gradualist, never a Student Federalist, as he reiterated in a letter declining an invitation to attend an SF reunion in 1997. As to Moynihan's views on supra-nationalism, uncertainty currently prevails.

As a prestigious followup to Concord, SF's staff scheduled a dinner on February 12, which was postponed because of a city-wide transportation interruption. It was ultimately held at the Town Hall Club on March 18, 1946. Cord Meyer and Harris Wofford were billed as the main speakers who were reporting to "their elders" on the results of the Concord Conference and the "heartening process underway." (Cost of the dinner and meeting was $3!) What is most unusual (and, no doubt, surprising to an outsider) was the level and celebrity of the 20 adult sponsors. Among the 200 persons attending were Wall Streeters Harold Bache and Randolph Compton, former presidential adviser and law professor Grenville Clark, economist Leo Cherne, columnist and radio personality Clifton Fadiman, future Air Force Secretary Thomas K. Finletter, pollster Elmo Roper, writer Rex Stout, poet Mark Van Doren, and radio newscaster Raymond Swing. Most of them served as members of a council of advisors to the Student Federalists and to other adult federalist groups as well. In addition to Fadiman, Roper, Van Doren, and Finletter, other prominent intellectuals and public figures also joined the SF Council of Advisors, including Professor Mortimer J. Adler, the noted philosopher at the University of Chicago; Mrs. Raymond Clapper, wife of the late celebrated war correspondent; Russell Davenport, a leading editorial writer with *Fortune* and *Life*; Dorothy Canfield Fisher, author; Emery Reves, whose recently published "Anatomy of Peace" was the "bible" for most federalists; historian Carl Van Doren; and the ubiquitous Clarence Streit, who had fathered the federalist concept and was to witness its evolution to a larger concept without his own participation. (A list of many of the prominent Americans who publically supported the goal of world federal government appears in Appendix 18. Also, see Appendix 17 for the quotes of world statesmen in support of the idea as they appeared in *The New Yorker*'s "Talk of the Town" in 1945.) The SF leadership expected to increase the level of financial support from among those adults attending.

Shortly before the Town Hall Club dinner, an historic meeting of American leaders from science, business, religion, labor, and government conducted a week-long meeting (March 11–16) at Rollins College in Florida on world government and control of atomic energy. The conference issued a ringing statement, declaring that the discovery of atomic fission has placed the survival of the world in grave jeopardy and that the only rational way out is to transform the United Nations into a world federal government. The government would feature a representative legislature, with power to control weapons of mass destruction, the right to inspect for violations, the establishment of an adequate police force to enforce the civil and criminal sanctions that are legislated by the General Assembly, the creation of an independent judiciary with powers limited to adjudication of laws enacted by the General Assembly and questions concerning interpretation of the U.N. Charter, the adoption of a Bill of Rights to protect individuals, and the transformation of the Security Council into the executive branch of the world government to execute and enforce the laws under the direction of the General Assembly.

This was no longer a group of zealous but innocent teen-agers venting their understandable idealism. At Rollins, some of the nation's most important movers and shakers were calling for the most radical political transformation in modern times. The fall-out could only help to boost the stock of the Student Federalists. At Wellesley College, for example, Virginia Beech reported over 200 members. Its SF chapter conducted a poll among the students, in which 1,085 students (all females, of course) supported the world federalist concept.

## EDUCATION PROGRAMS SPARKED BY SF PRESIDENT CLARE LINDGREN

Under the energetic direction of SF President Lindgren, who replaced her original first name (Emmy Lou) with Clare, the organization and its chapters burst out into a panoply of educational activities. Between June 20 and September 7, 1946, four major summer institutes to train leaders were held: the Eastern institute at Phillips Exeter Academy (New Hampshire), June;

Southern Institute (Jacksonville, Florida), July; Western (Pomona College), August; and Mid-Western (University of Chicago), September. Bowdoin student Joe Wheeler, who played a major role in organizing the local arrangements for the Concord meeting, directed the planning and preparations for the four institutes. The total fee for the last two institutes, including meals, was $25. The Florida institute fee without meals was $5. Board meetings were held in conjunction with the June institute at Phillips Exeter and the September meeting at the University of Chicago, which was also the occasion for the SF's third national convention.

In late June, Harcourt Brace published Harris Wofford's highly personal four-year odyssey on behalf of world federal government, beginning with the bathtub episode and working its way through his Air Force experiences to a prescription for achieving world government. It was appropriately entitled *It's Up to Us*, the "Us" largely directed as young Americans. The book became a center piece of SF activity, both as an educational tool and as a means to raising funds.

Coordinated with the book's release was a Town Hall Meeting of the Air debate broadcast nationally on world government, with Wofford and Thomas Finletter representing the affirmative side. The debate also kicked off the Exeter Institute, where both were to speak later that week. Also in June 1946, five adults associated with the federalist movement, including Wofford's father and Margaret Blumenstiel, the devoted business manager of the SF, signed documents incorporating the Student Federalists under New York State law, which required men and women of voting age to incorporate. Afterwards, they met at Price Waterhouse's offices (Percival Brundage of that firm was one of the five signers) and resigned as the original Board in favor of the Board elected at Concord.

## STUDENT FEDERALISTS MOVE INTO THE INTERNATIONAL ARENA

The international dimension of Student Federalists took a major step forward that summer, sending two delegates to Oxford, England, to attend the 1946 International Conference of Christians and Jews. The two selected were Richard Shapiro of Yale and Foster Parmalee of Princeton. Of even greater significance for the future, two SF delegates—Curt Farrar of Yale and Eleanor Schneider of Mt. Holyoke—were selected to attend the Prague meeting of the

International Student Conference in mid-August, a meeting that would have long-term significance for both the United States National Student Association and the Student Federalists.

In late May, SF treasurer Foster Parmalee interviewed Professor Albert Einstein on the subject of world federal government in a broadcast heard by several million Americans. During the summer of 1946, a number of SF leaders attended student and youth institutes conducted by other organizations on both coasts and in between, further spreading the SF credo. War veteran Steve Chadwick of Yale persuaded the college's American Veterans Committee chapter to adopt a world government resolution, which was then promoted by the national organization of veterans, which joined federalists in urging Congressional support for a similar resolution. The June 1946 SF Board meeting authorized a $100,000 expansion budget over five years and moving its New York headquarters to a "whole floor in a new World Government House" at 31 East 74th Street, also in Manhattan.

In what was to become a defining decision, the Student Federalist leadership wrote to the other 11 American world government organizations, most of them adult, urging as an outcome of the Concord meeting that they unite in a common movement with one headquarters, suggesting that leadership for this salient step be taken by the stronger of the adult organizations. Within months, the students' proposal was not only received enthusiastically but also acted upon in a systematic and constructive manner. By fall, formal meetings

*Trudy Schneider.*

*Steve Benedict with Wilder Crane in the background.*

were taking place to feel out the positions of each of the groups. Meanwhile, SF leaders were exploring their own positions to agree on a formal position when actual negotiations were to take place. The summer board meetings and institutes no doubt witnessed a considerable amount of discussion on the subject. In the fall, it was announced that a council had been formed to work out the details of a merger at a conference on Nov. 28 and 29, 1946. Meanwhile, the SF and Students for Federal World Government began discussions to merge their organizations before joining with the adult groups.

## Third Student Convention in 1946 Moves Toward Maximalist Position

In September, SF held another national convention and amended the substance of the Concord Charter, no doubt after some criticism from the United Nations adherents and some reflection of their own. (The revised text of the

Concord Charter appears in Appendix 9.) The final text, which became the "Student Federalist Charter," inserted in the opening sentence the concept of "a world community" as a prerequisite for world citizenship. The called-for "new world sovereignty based on the principles of federalism" was no longer expected "to preserve national identity." Instead, a broader and more radical notion was inserted: The new federalism would "effectually attack the economic and social problems whose solution is essential to the creation of a world community." The addition of this clause was to have preeminent meaning for student federalists in the remaining years of its existence. It reflected a left-of-center influence by those who supported either democratic socialism or the general New Deal Fair Deal approach to government.

More importantly, it illuminated the vision of the preponderance of the students on two levels: The first was the commitment over the long term to eradicating colonialism, racism, the great disparities of wealth between the haves and have-nots, and the arms race and its sponge-like absorption of America's "surplus" wealth instead of ameliorating poverty and ignorance at home and abroad. Indeed, the mantra of the Student Federalists was a sentence from Emery Reves's recent book, *Anatomy of Peace,* in which he brilliantly summed up these views with the statement "Peace is not simply the absence of war; it is the presence of justice." Not every federalist agreed with that view.

Second, it opened the door wide to the opportunities for, and the need to find expression for, each of the more immediate issues and controversies facing American foreign (and occasionally domestic) policy. As the students were to learn, the movement's adults found neither approach attractive or necessary. In a major sense, this division shaped the vision each held for the ultimate federal government and the powers accorded it. A minority of the students—mostly conservative—agreed with the adults to the very end, arguing that every stand the student federalists took on more immediate issues warded off potential supporters of the more vague but noble notion of a world federal government.

Similarly, in the amended version of the charter, the drafters found it necessary to add that "We support the United Nations as the primary international organization attempting to achieve some of these aims of world government," and to insert in the operative paragraph dealing with the transformation of the U.N. into a world federation the need both for a "revisional convention" (one year after the U.N. Charter was adopted) or "by strengthening

Joe Wheeler.    Curt Farrar.

the U.N. through fundamental amendments under Article 108." No further mention was made of the U.S. or the Soviet Union being the "two chief obstacles" to such a transformation, nor was any mention made of the veto power of the Big Five and the unlikelihood that either would give up such a prerogative.

To further support the more gradual approach to the U.N.'s transformation, a penultimate paragraph was added to the charter, expressing the realization "that to lay the foundation for world government, the people of the world must awaken to their responsibility as citizens of the world community. To make world citizenship a political fact, we must work to create a world government dedicated to human rights and justice under law." The last two phrases, especially, underlay the immediate concerns of the students, concerns that they increasingly felt cried out for definition and advocacy. They also added highly important elements to the nature of the world government's powers, when it was to be finally realized.

These changes were not taken lightly, nor were they surreptitiously enacted by a small band of leaders. The 1946 Chicago convention was the largest to date in SF history with 160 delegates from 92 different colleges and secondary schools. The policy debates paralleled the week-long summer institute at

*The famous finger vote at the 1946 Student Federalist Convention in Chicago. The sleep-deprived delegate in the front row, left, is Girvan Peck of Yale. Also in the front row at right is Steve Chadwick of Yale. Identified in the second row, second and third from left, are Jim Stockman and Edith Reynolds. In the fourth row, to right of Miss Reynolds's upraised hand is Fritjof Thygeson of Stanford. The 1946 convention was the largest to that date, with 160 delegates from 92 colleges and secondary schools.*

the University of Chicago, where some of the nation's best minds were expounding on the very same subjects. Between the working business of the convention and the lectures and seminars at the institute, the delegates were putting in 18-hour days. To save time in the vote-counting, a *Life* reporter suggested the use of finger-counting, wherein a person in each delegation raises the appropriate number of fingers for each vote, rather than having each delegate recorded individually. This process was reported to have injected a needed degree of humor into the otherwise serious proceedings.

*The 1946 Chicago convention delegates found time to relax between sessions. Tom Hughes (at the piano) accompanies the delegates in songs from Broadway shows.*

# 3

# A NEW LEADERSHIP ERA BEGINS

### COKE PRENTICE BECOMES SF PRESIDENT

One further change took place at the September convention: the end of the reign of the original triumvirate (Wofford, Hughes, Lindgren) with the election of Colgate "Coke" Prentice as SF President. A Swarthmore junior and Air Force combat veteran who flew 19 missions and received the Air Medal, Prentice immediately embarked on a 5,000-mile, three-month speaking tour through New England, the Midwest, Pennsylvania, the Mountain states, and California, appearing before an estimated 24,000 students in a dozen colleges and 16 secondary schools, the SF California regional meeting, the Junior Statesmen of California, and a number of religious denominations as well as a unit of the Lions. Sandwiched between these engagements were scores of newspaper and radio interviews, in what was probably the warmest media reception for a student federalist leader to date.

At the same meeting, Helen Ball was elected National Chairman, Richard Shapiro, College Chairman, David Bauman, High School Chairman, and William Lynch, Prep School Chairman. Steve Chadwick, who lost the election for president to Prentice, was chosen as Secretary-Treasurer. Also rising to the fore were such new leaders as Robert Bennett of Stanford, Girvan Peck of Yale, and Fritjof Thygeson of Sequoia Union High School. Virtually every post was challenged at this election: The ballot for the 15-person Board of Representatives, evenly divided among three groupings—college, secondary school, and at-large representatives—consisted of almost three times that number of nominees, a total of 42. For the first time, the SF was experiencing a plethora of leaders willing to make the sacrifices incumbent in the jobs.

The convention delegates also received a report on the Prague meeting of the World Student Congress held in August 1946, and attended by three Student Federalists: Curt Farrar, Foster Parmelee and Lt. Samuel Lessey of the U.S. Army on furlough. Farrar was instrumental in securing passage, with Soviet support, of a "recommendation: that the students support the United Nations" and "take steps to strengthen it by working for the establishment of a democratic world system of government . . . preserv[ing] the identity of member nations while introducing the concepts of world law and world citizenship." The resolution passed by 90 to 35 with 4 abstentions. The report on the Congress that was published in the October SF newsletter illustrates how the Soviets exploited the idealism of American and other students on behalf of the Kremlin, while moving covertly, as it later turned out, to control the International Union of Students (IUS) and the World Federation of Democratic Youth (WFDY), with which the IUS voted to collaborate in Prague. A glaring example of wishful thinking, if Farrar's report on the prospects of American participation in the IUS were read today, it would make the most zealous idealist cringe. However, it was written 53 years ago when we still had a great deal to learn both as a nation and as federalists.

As a footnote to the September gathering at the University of Chicago, the institute held in conjunction with the meetings was one of the most memorable, highlighted as it was by lectures by Dr. G.A. Borgese, noted antifascist historian and the architect of the Chicago draft for a world constitution, and Prof. Mortimer Adler of the University of Chicago. Based at the University of Chicago and blessed by support from that institution's renowned Chancellor Robert Hutchins, the Committee to Frame a World Constitution included Robert Redfield, Stringfellow Barr, and Professors Adler and Borgese, four of the outstanding intellects of their time. In 1948, they published a maximalist draft constitution for a world federal government after two years of study and debate as well as a superior monthly periodical on the subject, *Common Cause*. (A summary of the provisions of the world federal government constitution proposed by the University of Chicago committee appears in Appendix 19, together with the draft proposed by Grenville Clark and Professor Louis Sohn of Harvard Law School, which includes examples of weighted systems of

*Student Federalist delegates take a break from the 1946 plenary sessions to sit for a photo in front of Wyoming Union of the University of Chicago.*

representation.) The Draft Constitution impacted heavily on many of the student federalists.

The SF institute also heard two lectures on "Marxism and Federalism" by Carleton College student and former SF president Tom Hughes, who asserted that "Marxism . . . has been subverted by nationalism to serve nationalistic ends." Nevertheless, Hughes, who was later to become the State Department's Director of Intelligence under Presidents Kennedy and Johnson, found in his examination of Marxism grounds for hope that the Marxists would some day agree to support the idea of world federal government. (An abridged version of Hughes's 1946 article on "Marxism and Federalism," which appeared in the Yale Political Review, appears in Appendix 6. Virginia Lastayo Riorden performed the abridgement.) Many federalists in 1946 shared this view. Both they and Hughes were to revise their optimism as events of the next three years unfolded.

*Delegate Dick Glascow of Oak Ridge, Tennessee, makes a telling point during a Student Federalist convention policy debate as Natalie Rogers and Larry Fuchs listen intently.*

A highly critical news article in *Time* (Sept. 16) of the Student Federalist convention, which in retrospect proved a barometer of radically shifting views based on the perceptions of Soviet behavior, was answered by SF President Prentice. The *Time* writer (or editor) chided the students for not providing either a timetable or a structural outline of the proposed world government. Defensively, Prentice stated that the students believe they must work for world government *now*, that the framers of the world constitution have the job of establishing the structure, and that the job of today's students is to educate the populace on behalf of world federation. Responding to a needling comment that the role of the U.N. was hotly debated among the delegates, Prentice repeated the words of the revised Concord charter, supporting the U.N. but urging that it be changed at the same time. That the magazine chose to single out these points for criticism two years after it had warmly comforted the same group under the similar circumstances was a warning shot across the bow—the tide was beginning to turn. Shortly, Mrs. Luce would leave the ship; her husband Henry would begin to back the anti-communist vessel.

*Harris Wofford addresses SF regional meeting at Columbia University, Dec. 18, 1948 (photo by John Grifalconi).*

## Despite Aggressive Soviet Behavior, Student Federalist Movement Experiences Rapid Growth

However, the momentum at the moment was still with the Student Federalists, which experienced its greatest one-month growth since its inception: Twenty new chapters were officially chartered during the month of October, with every region represented, in a report given by SF Chapter Secretary Virginia Lastayo. The new chapters included Brothers (New Jersey), Brown, Bryn Mawr, Carleton, New Paultz Teachers (New York), Smith, Swarthmore, and University of Wisconsin, at the college level, as well as secondary school chapters in three New York schools—Brearley, Bronx and New Rochelle Highs; three New Jersey schools—Madison, Perth Amboy, and Pingry; two California schools—Deep Springs and Humboldt; Culver Military, Indiana; Humbolt High, Iowa; Rutland High, Vermont; and Winsor, Boston. The SF newsletter proclaimed the Yale chapter as SF's largest with 175 members, apparently having forgotten an earlier article in which Wellesly was reported to have more than 200 members.

NYU volunteer Larry Fuchs undertook to organize the New York City schools, producing the first Bronx chapter and appearing at Hunter College, New York University Uptown, four assemblies of 1,900 each at DeWitt Clinton High, and the National Christian Youth Conference. He also drew representatives from Barnard, Brooklyn, City, and Columbia Colleges together to plan a city-wide federalist rally. At Yale, the Federalist Party was the second largest in the Yale Political Union and its president, Richard Shapiro, was elected the Union's president.

In October, at the pioneering Luxembourg Convention, world government organizations from 14 nations formed the Movement for World Federal Government. Treasurer Foster Parmelee was SF's official representative at the founding meeting, one of seven American delegates present. Tom Griessemer, Executive Director of World Federalists, USA, was named temporary Secretary of the Movement, which was to be initially housed in World Government House, New York City. In all, 76 delegates participated in the founding world congress, including a 14-person French delegation and a British delegation headed by three M.P.s.

Sensing the rise in public awareness, at a SF Board meeting on Nov. 17–18, 1946, the members adopted a resolution to make world government a political issue, enabling the SF and its chapters to seek to persuade state legislatures to support the "Humber resolution" calling for world federation. (North Carolina State Senator Richard Humber had led a national campaign to persuade state legislatures to endorse world government or to adopt his resolution calling for the establishment of a world federal government. By that point in time, 14 state legislatures had adopted such resolutions. Later, when the "Red" scare took hold, most of the legislatures renounced their support for the Humber resolution.)

In addition, the new stance enabled units to work to place world government resolutions on state ballots, to have world federation planks in each party's platforms in 1948, and to support federalists for political office. This resolution effectively moved the SF units out of the isolation of the academy and squarely into the rough-and-tumble world of politics.

*Patricia Kimball of Pomona College, California, Clare Lindgren of the University of Minnesota, and Helen Ball of Wheaton College, Massachusetts demonstrate the geographical division at Concord. Another California delegate, Charles Norris of Van Nuys, came all the way and returned by bus. A leading high school delegate, Ernest Johnson, came from Selma, Alabama. Altogether, 26 states were represented. (Photo from* Student Federalist.*)*

Of longer-term significance was another Board resolution for the Student Federalists to act on behalf of "non-controversial, non-political, international projects furthering the world community (i.e., UNESCO and the U.N. Social and Economic Council.)" In a few years, student federalists would be devising imaginative implementations of this decision.

That same Board meeting ratified a committee outline for the prospective merger of the Student Federalists and the Students for Federal World Government and heard an off-the-record report on progress toward the merger of all of the world government groups. The Board took one other action that readers of this book will find relevant: It chose Curt Farrar as one of two representatives (Eleanor Schneider was later named the second delegate) to be its delegates at the founding meeting of a National Union of American Students in Chicago, Dec. 27 to 29, 1946. Several hundred university and college delegates were expected to attend the meeting to hear a report on the Prague meeting of the International Union of Students and to choose a planning committee for a constitutional convention to be held the following summer to set up the American student association (which would ultimately become known as the United States National Student Association).

Following the Board meeting on Monday night, Nov. 18, a critically important dinner was organized for most of the group's Council of Advisors, a number of wealthy potential donors and the Board members and staff of SF at the Cosmopolitan Club on East 66th Street. The advisers strongly urged the SF to concentrate its energies on the single issue of world federal government. This was the singular message of Supreme Court Justice Roberts, and it was reenforced by comments from Emery Reves, R.H. Macy Chairman and tax expert Beardsley Ruml, Clifton Fadiman, and St. John's College President Stringfellow Barr. Other comments were made by *Saturday Review* editor Norman Cousins, Elmo Roper, and Clarence Streit, as well as SF officers and staff. The latter departed with a sense of optimism both in respect to the prospects of financial support and of the pending merger.

That optimism was further fed by the rash of public pronouncements endorsing world federalism during the last few months of the year. On Nov. 16 Philippine United Nations delegate Carlos P. Romulo unequivocally supported world government, endorsing a Cuban proposal for a convention to revise the U.N. Charter. A few days earlier—on Nov. 12th—British Prime Minister Clement Atlee told the House of Commons that world government was "the ultimate aim of Great Britain's foreign policy."

The November installment of the SF Forum-Poll produced a mild surprise: Of 4,700 students polled, 35 percent favored the Baruch proposals, in which the U.N. would be given a monopoly on atomic weapons, over changing the U.N. into a limited world government to control weapons of mass destruction or into a world federation with power to attack economic and social problems. The two federalist options together polled only 30.25 percent. Seven percent preferred controlling atomic weapons by the Security Council, 14 percent were in favor of treaties banning the use of atomic bombs, and 13.5 percent wanted the U.S. to keeps its atomic weapons and knowledge while working to maintain its advanced position over all other nations.

## American Legion Calls for Global Armed Force Under U.N. Authority

Even more startling was the vote on Nov. 23 by the American Legion executive committee calling for a world army under U.N. authority and eliminating the veto in the Security Council. The Legion advocated establishment of a highly professional military force that could deal "instantly" with any nation judged by the World Court "to be preparing for aggression." The authority of the military force would include inspection of member nations so judged. The Legion expressed the hope that the standing army would consist of soldiers from small nations that could be supplemented by "national contingents" from the Great Powers. The Legion resolution also called for a ten-member Security Council that could act on the affirmative vote of six members, effectively eliminating the veto. Also in late 1946, 14 members of the newly elected Congress were revealed to favor changing the United Nations into a world federation. Finally, Chapter Secretary Lastayo, having produced the SF's first chapter bulletin, announced that 12 more chapters were chartered in November.

## Process Begins to Unite American Federalist Organizations

With what must have seemed like a full head of steam, the Student Federalist officers and Board called a third Board meeting at year end (Dec. 21–22) 1946, to discuss and ratify a call to organize a convention "to effect the corporate merger or consolidation of all groups working for world government under a common name and with complete integration of personnel and equipment. In any consolidation, *the student organization shall remain autonomous, but a formal connection between student and non-student consolidation can be made.* (my italics)."

A four-person committee, including SF's National Chair, Helen Ball, had developed plans under a mandate of the U.S. Council of the Movement for World Federal Government to convene in Asheville, North Carolina, Feb. 21 to 23, 1947, for this purpose. They and the other parties agreed that the voting power at this convention would be apportioned to all groups working for world government on the basis of one vote for each 50 members or majority fraction thereof. The SF Board approved the plan and the prospective merger unanimously.

The Board took a series of actions to amend its bylaws and charter to permit merger with the Students for World Federal Government as well as with the adult federalist groups. It created an interim governing committee comprised of the officers of both organizations. It devoted considerable time to the most pressing structural issue—the autonomy of local chapters. For the time being, the Board decided to permit local chapters to take positions on any foreign policy issue that its membership believed would "lead to a world government policy." Chapters were barred from endorsing political candidates, but members were urged to participate in politics "to advance world government principles." Further, the Board decided that it would refrain from foreign policy positions, but until a national convention determined SF's "position of foreign policy and political activities," the chapters possessed the right to take such stands.

Farrar offered the financial report that revealed that during the last six months of the year 1947, minus the final 10 days, the organization had received slightly more than $18,000, of which membership dues constituted only $1,426, or less than 8 percent. The minimum dues for a student (or teacher) in 1946 was $1, of which 50 cents was allotted to the newsletter. The expenditures during the same time frame came to $16,684. The cash remaining in the bank account was slightly more than $1,000 after allowance for unpaid bills. That bleak financial situation may have been behind the decision to consolidate all speaking tours, even by volunteers, in the national office. At the same time, the Board decided to try to mount between five and ten summer institutes in 1947, as compared to four in 1946. All of the institutes had been paying for themselves.

At year's end, the total number of recognized chapters had risen to 111, of which 53 were college or university chapters and several were area-wide, including colleges and secondary schools.(A list of college and high school chapters chartered by the Student Federalists in January,1947, appears in Appendix 12.) The estimated membership by year's end was between 4.000 and 5,000, in all probability the largest single world federalist organization in the nation and the largest student federalist group in the world.

## 1946: The Greatest Federalist Growth in the Face of Stepped-Up Soviet Expansion

During 1946, a year when the federalists had experienced their greatest growth to date, other sinister forces were moving in the opposite direction. With the Red Army acting as enforcer, the Communist parties of the East European nations occupied by the Soviets began to consolidate power and take over their regimes, eliminating by violent means whatever democratic opposition chose to resist. At the same time, the Communist parties of Italy and France were moving electorally and by non-democratic methods to gain control of *their* governments. The Soviets were backing an armed revolution in Greece while seeking to destabilize the Turkish regime. It was becoming apparent to all but those bedazzled by the Soviet's disingenuous declarations on behalf of world peace that a new and terrible global confrontation was developing. The development of the atom bomb produced perils of a magnitude never before experienced by humankind. By the end of 1946, the Soviet Union had accomplished most of its territorial objectives. Meanwhile, the Chinese Communist insurrection was beginning to make serious inroads against Chiang Kai Shek's Nationalist regime.

On the weekend of Washington's Birthday in 1947 in Asheville, a merger was effected of the five most important world government groups in the nation: Americans United for World Government, Massachusetts Committee for World Federation, World Citizens of Georgia, World Federalists, U.S.A., and the Student Federalists. The first organizing folder of the new entity—the United World Federalists (UWF)—claimed the merger produced more than 200 local chapters (quite probable, considering the student total alone was 111). It also claimed "active adherents . . . topped the hundred thousand mark." If "adherents" was meant to imply "members," the claim had little merit, however. As many as 500 delegates and member/observers from 33 states attended the Asheville meeting. Because most of the ground work had been done in the previous months, the key decisions before the delegates were made with a minimum of conflict.

## THE GREAT 1947 ASHEVILLE COMPROMISE PRODUCES THE UNITED WORLD FEDERALISTS (UWF)

The delegates made a significant policy decision by adopting a subtitle to appear after the new UWF name: "for world government with *Limited* Powers Adequate to Prevent War (my italics)." This represented the so-called minimalist school of federalists, those who believed that the sole purpose of a world government was to maintain peace (and the status quo), while ignoring poverty, colonialism, racial and ethnic conflict, and domestic tyranny, or those who believed that the best strategy for gaining popular American support for the federalist proposal was to limit the purpose of a world government to the prevention of war, while ignoring the reality that few nations outside the so-called "haves" would find such a formula to their self-interest. The policy statement adopted by the delegates was deliberately brief in order to merit the widest possible support. (The complete text appears in Appendix 15.) It further emphasized the minimalist position that the student delegates felt compelled to swallow in the interest of organizational unity:

> Statement of beliefs: We believe that peace is not merely the absence of war, but the presence of justice, of law, of order—in short, of government and the institutions of government; that world peace can be created and maintained only under world law, universal and strong enough to prevent armed conflict among nations.
>
> Statement of purposes: Therefore, while endorsing the efforts of the United Nations to bring about a world community favorable to peace, we will work *primarily to strengthen the United Nations into a world government of limited powers adequate to prevent war* and having direct jurisdiction over the individual in those matters within its competence.

There is no doubt that this word formulation was conceived in the expectation that it provided the public with the most "salable product" that the federalist movement was capable of putting forth. (A sympathetic interpetation of the Asheville convention was published in *World Government News* in March

1947. A condensed version was reprinted by the UWF and appears in Appendix 13.)

The initial constitution was, in their own words, "broadly democratic, encouraged grassroots organization, and left room for local autonomy." All three characteristics were of major concern to the Student Federalist delegation. Between 80 and 90 Student Federalists participated in the Asheville convention, of whom 29 were voting delegates and the remainder officially observers. (The official list of Student Federalists, both delegates and observers, attending the Asheville convention appears in Appendix 14.) Most of the past and present leadership attended, including staff. SF was represented by the second largest delegation after World Federalists, U.S.A. Those students present who advocated a world government with powers broader than that proposed by the minimalists took heart with the inclusion of the phrase "peace is not merely the absence of war, but the *presence of justice,*" which had come

*The standing-room-only sign was up for the delegates assembly at the 1948 UWF Student Division convention in Minneapolis (photo by Hugh Nash).*

to mean, in federalist code, economic and social advancement, human rights, and the eradication of colonialism and racism.

As an interim measure, the convention chose 30 members from a slate of 79 to form a governing Executive Council, the latter then choosing an additional 8 from among the most prominent names available. The students appear to have accepted significant underrepresentation, considering that their membership comprised at least one third and perhaps 40 percent of the groups merging. Out of the 38 on the Executive Council, only 6, about 16 percent, were students. Further, of these six, several were past student age and ready to be called adults. The six SF members elected were Helen Ball, Virginia Lastayo, Clare Lindgren, Cord Meyer, Jr., Colgate Prentice, and Harris Wofford. None of the students were among the seven celebrity vice presidents: Grenville Clark, Norman Cousins, Thomas K. Finletter, W.T. Holliday (Standard Oil Of Ohio CEO), Robert Lee Humber, Raymond Swing and Carl Van Doren. The more prominent names on the Council, in addition to the Vice Presidents, included Henry B. Cabot, Cass Canfield, Mrs. J. Borden Harriman, Edgar Ansel Mowrer, and Mark Van Doren. For all intents and purposes, the initial UWF governing council was 100 percent white and almost totally Protestant. Its only claims to representativeness were geographic and organizational.

These selections were the product of a six-person nominating committee, including SF National Chairman Helen Ball as Recording Secretary. This group had unanimously agreed on the eight persons to be added to the Executive Council, on the seven Vice Presidents, and on the persons they most preferred for advisory council membership from a list of more than 120 names. Newscaster Raymond Swing reported that former War Secretary Henry Stimson had been invited to serve as UWF's Honorary President and was considering the offer. (He subsequently declined.) The most difficult issue before the nominating committee in its second session, at the beginning of which Colgate Prentice replaced Helen Ball as the SF "representative," was the choice of executive chief, the CEO in today's terms. Initially, the committee talked about employing a prestigious full-time president who would be "highly paid—perhaps in the $20,000 to $25,000 a year bracket." In what might be regarded as an epidemic of group hubris, the committee recommended nine well-known figures for this position, in the following order of preference: Supreme Court Justice William O. Douglas, John Winant, Senator William Fulbright, Supreme Court Justice Robert Jackson, Dr. Irving Langmuir, Chester Bowles, W.T. Holliday (the Standard Oil CEO!), Robert Watt, and former Office of Price Administration Administrator Paul Hoffman.

Then, the committee was compelled to face the hard decision about hiring a capable individual who could actually run the organization—in short, an executive director. As the discussion proceeded, it became clear that the new organization could not afford two highly paid executives, at which point the committee decided to wait to see whether any of the celebrated nominees would accept the presidency *and* serve without pay, which would then permit UWF to employ an executive director. In the interim, the committee nominated Mildred Blake, formerly a leader of World Federalists, U.S.A., to serve in the post "without regard to salary."

## SF Becomes UWF's Student Division

The membership of the Student Federalists, as well as student chapters of other merging groups, became the Student Division of the United World Federalists. For the time being, a wide degree of autonomy was permitted the Student Division and its local chapters. However, the burden of financing its activities fell largely on the students themselves. The initial governing body of the student division was designated the National Student Council (NSC), which met on March 24 to determine its rules of procedure. It continued the $1 annual dues that included a subscription to the newsletter. The entire sum was to be paid to the national student headquarters in New York, which meant that the local units needed to seek a larger sum or exist solely on contributions. It set a floor of ten students as the minimum for eligibility to become a recognized chapter.

Student chapters had the same status as adult chapters except that they fell under the direction of the NSC. The NSC retained the power to charter new chapters and to "discontinue" existing chapters for cause by a two-thirds vote. Any student in school or college was eligible for membership, as well as any resident of the U.S. not in school and under the age of 22. The local student chapters' purposes and activities were forbidden from conflicting with the UWF's policies and purposes, but in all other respects, the student chapters were autonomous. In states with three or more student chapters, the latter were authorized to set up a state student council. Student chapters were, in a somewhat ambiguous arrangement, directed to work through the national student headquarters *and* to participate as chapters of the state branches of UWF (all of which were adult-dominated).

The students were authorized to hold their own annual convention (in tandem with the adult General Assembly), establish the procedures for selecting delegates, develop action plans for the student arena, and elect the following year's Student Council. The latter was to consist of 35 members, at least 10 of which were from secondary schools. The NSC, in addition to serving as the link between the Executive Council and the students, had the power to initiate and direct student projects, to decide on literature and other publications, and to appoint the student staff.

Overseeing the Council's work was an administrative committee consisting of Helen Ball, Abe Bargman, Lewis Berger, Diane Duke, Katherine Fox, Larry Fuchs, Virginia Lastayo and an as-yet-named member of the Yale chapter. (It is unclear who appointed this committee. Ball, Fox, and Lastayo were paid staff. The others were all Council members.) The Council itself included 12 secondary school members, all but one from the Northeast. The exception was Sherwin Montell of Clayton, Missouri. Nineteen college and graduate

*Student Federalist leaders meeting with historian Carl Van Doren of Columbia University, who was himself an outspoken federalist.*

students were elected, including more than half from the leadership developed in the early years: Wofford, Lindgren, Benedict, Chadwick, Farrar, Minot, Parmelee, Peck, Wheeler, Schneider, and Kimball. The new wave of leadership was represented by Larry Fuchs, Abe Bargman, James Compton, and Tom Farr, as well as most of the high school members. In addition, two representatives from World Republic, an Evanston, Illinois group that was exploring merger, were elected to the Council: Fred Carney and Phil Ruopp. Colgate Prentice, who had been Student Federalist President at the time of the merger, was named Chairman of the NSC with California high school activist Fritjof Thygeson as Vice Chairman.

The same month that the first NSC meeting took place, a Princeton unit was organized. Although it was considering affiliation with UWF's Student Division, Albert Einstein publically chose to join the chapter, providing a major morale boost to the students. At the end of March, Chapter Secretary Virginia Lastayo announced that seven student institutes were planned for that summer. The locations were Carleton College, Minnesota; St. John's College, Maryland; Yale University, Connecticut; Wellesley, Massachusetts; St. Louis, Missouri; and Asilomar, California. A planned institute for New Jersey was subsequently dropped. The *New York Times* published an interview with British historian Arnold Toynbee, who strongly endorsed the possibility that world government would gradually evolve from the United Nations.

The Student Division announced the formation of 28 chapters during the month of March, the highest single-month total, raising the overall number to 143 units. Among the major colleges affiliating were chapters from Duke, Iowa State, Texas Christian, Texas Tech, DePauw, and the Universities of Connecticut, Michigan, and Virginia, as well as 13 new secondary school chapters. The national office revealed that a new speakers' bureau had been established, that a popular radio show produced by one of the adult organizations in the merger was broadcast on ABC network, that a new film "One World or None" narrated by Raymond Swing had been produced for chapter use, and that as a result of intense federalist lobbying, the Massachusetts legislature had approved a world government resolution.

## Student Division Participates in New National and International Organizations

At the same time that the students were preoccupied with the mechanics of the merger, they were also reaching out to the larger constituency at home and to the international venues. Student chapters were encouraged to participate in the drafting of the constitution of the new National Student Organization in early September in Madison, Wisconsin. Student Federalists were alerted to the fact that delegates to the Madison meeting were being elected on campuses throughout the country. The convention, which was to produce the U.S.N.S.A., was expected to last ten days.

Meanwhile, federalists were being urged to take part in the World Youth Festival scheduled for Prague from July 20 to August 17, 1947, with the suggestion that the expected 300 American delegates would help to provide a democratic (and even federalist) balance to the event. The European Union of Federalists had invited students to spend time at their planned international centers to discuss federalist ideas and ideals. The first center was to open at Heyst sur Mer, near Bruges, that summer.

Despite these temptations and distractions, the new entity faced the daunting task of merging staffs, memberships, offices, equipment, and supporters, while finding a new executive leader. As these difficult and time-consuming efforts were proceeding, Soviet Foreign Minister Andrei Gromyko told the United Nations that his government totally and flatly rejected the U.S. proposal, known as the Baruch Plan, to give the United Nations the power to control atomic power and weapons. Shortly thereafter, in response to America's perception of Communist subversion in Greece and Turkey, the U.S. President pronounced the "Truman Doctrine" to resist Communist subversion and aggression, starting with military aid to Greece and Turkey. In so doing, Truman stated that the United Nations was incapable of handling the problems for which it had been established, especially resisting aggression, requiring the United States to act unilaterally.

## Despite Soviet Rebuffs, UWF Demands UN's Transformation as Global Cop

The UWF response was to reassert the urgent need to revise the United Nations charter so that it could be transformed into a world government capable of preventing war—and only that. In one of its most memorable organizing folders, UWF compared the United Nations's shortcomings to the absence of effective local law enforcement. The cover page featured a line drawing of a police officer directing traffic, under which the legend stated "Suppose You Had No Cop on the Corner...."

# A New Leadership Era Begins 51

*Cover page of UWF's "Cop on the Corner" organizing leaflet. Text of the leaflet appears in Appendix 21.*

**Suppose you had no Cop on the Corner...**

The inside pages asked the reader how safe he would feel without law and police at the local, county, or federal level. It pointed out that originally all of our levels of government were, in effect, "leagues" that could only recommend "that certain laws be obeyed." It asked further: "Would the strong respect the rights of the weak? Would order and peace be possible? How long would you and your family be safe?" The text then invited the reader to join with UWF "to awaken the American public to the need for a greatly strengthened U.N.—that will make laws, interpret laws, and enforce laws binding on all people." (The text of the folder appears in Appendix 21.) The "Cop on the

*Helen Ball, Student Federalist Chairman, reading citations to Supreme Court Justice Owen Roberts and Emory Reves (second and third from left) as Board member Mary Ellen Purdy looks on.*

Corner" folder was regarded as one of the most effective, and successful, in the history of the movement.

## CORD MEYER, JR. NAMED UWF PRESIDENT IN JUNE 1947

In June 1947, both the UWF Executive Council and the National Student Council held meetings, the latter in conjunction with the training institute at Maryland's St. John's College. The Executive Council solved the salary dilemma and hired both a paid Executive Director and a paid President. The latter was Cord Meyer, Jr., a former combat marine in the Pacific and a graduate of Yale who had also served as the Student Federalist's veterans chairman. An articulate speaker and seasoned writer, Meyer served as Governor Harold Stassen's aide at the founding United Nations Conference and played a major role in the affairs of the American Veterans Committee. Chosen by the Council as Executive Director was an oil company executive who had served as a "combat intelligence officer" in Southeast Asia during World War II (most probably with the Office of Strategic Services)—Upshur Evans. (Meyer left the UWF presidency a few years later to play a significant role in the CIA in providing support to a sizable array of private organizations within the democratic spectrum, both at home and abroad.) Presumably, both executives accepted less than the "high salary" originally contemplated by the nominating committee. They began their tenures together as July 1947 neared.

The Student Council launched a nationwide membership drive by assigning a quota to each chapter to build its membership to equal ten percent of its student body. Further, each chapter was charged with obtaining signatures from half the student body on "I am for world government" cards. CCNY chapter president Abe Bargman was commissioned to write a report for UWF President Meyer on student political action.

The growth of the summer institutes had been so rapid that the Council recommended the hiring of a full-time education secretary, who would also organize the institutes. Because Chapter Secretary Virginia Lastayo had resigned to marry Harvard federalist Shane Riorden in Boston, Eleanor "Ellie" Schneider was named as her replacement. A Mount Holyoke graduate with an M.A. in international affairs, the Vienna-born Schneider and her family had fled from Austria after the Nazi *Anschluss* in 1938. Schneider and Student Division Chairman Colgate Prentice were appointed by the Council to be its representatives at the founding constitutional meeting in Madison, Wisconsin, of the National Student Organization. Three members of the NSC were among the seven Executive Committee members elected at the founding meeting of the World Student Federalists—Gilles Corcos, Trudy Schneider, and

Fred Carney. They participated as well in the first world convention for world government in Montreux, Switzerland, in mid-August 1947.

The Montreux conference called both for the strengthening of the U.N. into a world government and the calling of a world constituent assembly to draw up a constitution for a world federal government. The latter proposal appears to have sent shivers down the spines of most adult members of the UWF, appearing as it did to be a populist proposal that would base the proposed federation's political power on population. Such a formulation would give the poor, non-white nations of the world the overwhelming legislative majority, but the white, prosperous (and often democratic) nations would constitute a relatively small minority. When Henry Usborne, a British M.P. and the leading advocate of the constituent assembly route came to the United States in September, UWF leaders instructed the staff to ignore his presence and to discourage chapters from providing him with a platform. A major controversy was brewing with UWF over the Montreux recommendations.

## UWF President Cord Meyer Urges State Department Proposals to Strengthen U.N.

In September 1947, after the second General Assembly of the U.N. convened in Lake Success, New York, UWF President Cord Meyer wrote to Secretary of State George Marshall, indicating that the proposals submitted by Marshall to amend the Charter were grossly insufficient. He transmitted the recommendations of UWF to transform the U.N. into a limited world government. Barring this, Meyer wrote General Marshall, the U.S. should refrain from pressing any proposals not presented in advance for consultation with the permanent members of the Security Council, having in mind the Soviet Union. Because the Soviets had never been offered a world government proposal, Meyer observed, we cannot claim to have "exhausted all possibilities of joint agreement."

## Wofford and Lindgren Urge UWF 1947 Convention Delegates Not to Reject Montreux Proposals

Harris Wofford and Clare Lindgren, returning from Montreux, prepared an open letter to the delegates attending the UWF assembly in St. Louis Nov. 1–2, 1947, attempting to disabuse them of the mistaken notion that the World Movement was advocating an end run around the United Nations (and even

*Newly elected president of UWF Student Division Larry Fuchs briefs the UWF Executive committee regarding his plans for the coming year. Seated, left to right, are Alan Green, Executive Director Upshur Evans (who was not a committee member), Abe Wilson, President Cord Meyer, Jr., Cass Canfield, Mildred Blake, Randolph Compton, Sam Levering, and Fuchs, who had taken a year off from NYU for speaking tours and organizing new student chapters.*

its member nations) by seeking to organize a private peoples convention to choose delegates who would participate in a world constitutional convention. Wofford and Lindgren stated that the actual plan, formulated and led by Usborne and supported by 80 members of the British Parliament, was to convene an *unofficial* global convention of leading "world citizens from all countries who would draw up a specific charter for world government that federalists everywhere could rally around."

Noting that most European federalists had given up the notion that the U.N. Charter could effectively be revised because of their expectation that the Soviets would in the end reject serious efforts to amend the Charter to provide limited world government (of the kind advocated by UWF), Lindgren and Wofford pleaded with the UWF delegates to keep an open mind toward

Usborne's strategy as one of a number of possible approaches. Reminding UWF that Sir William Beveridge and Lord Boyd Orr had already announced as candidates for the constitutional conference in Britain, the writers suggested that the Europeans were going forward with this strategy regardless of UWF's position. That being the case, they argued, it would be better that UWF should direct the effort to select the 130 American delegates to the world conference in 1950.

Wofford and Lindgren went several steps further in their open letter, virtually challenging the adults to a duel: They insisted upon a universal world government, which necessarily must include the Soviets; they asked UWF to reject any U.N. Charter amendments less than world government that could drive away the Soviets; and they demanded that UWF "find a way to take active federalist-oriented stands on current world issues so that we become the vanguard of the internationalist one world movement." Examples of the latter were support for economic aid to Europe to avoid collapse and support of a policy of working through the U.N. and its agencies to solve economic and social problems. The writers also castigated the Executive Council for "policy dogmatism and organizational domination." They called for a greater grass-roots base, with more activist local leaders elected to the national council instead of celebrities who did nothing but lend their names. They vigorously opposed giving each Council member and officer a convention vote, making them equal to a working chapter. (There were by then almost 50 council members and officers.)

On November 1, 1947, more than 200 delegates participated in the first UWF national convention in St.Louis and almost half of them were card-carrying students. That more than any other factor explains the rather liberal new statement of principles and purposes adopted by the assembly. Indeed, the final adopted draft very much resembles that which Student Federalists adopted in 1946. Most of the positions urged by Wofford and Lindgren were in fact adopted by the delegates, starting with the UWF's affiliation with the World Movement for World Government. Under "Principles," the new UWF statement called for membership open to all nations with the right to secede; a provision that all powers not delegated to the world federation were reserved to the nations that also retained the right to their own domestic political, economic, social, and religious institutions; enforcement of world law upon individuals; a bill of rights assuring individuals affected by world law of equal and adequate protection; the power to tax by the federal government for "carefully defined and limited" purposes; and reasonable provision for amendment.

Under "Purposes," the statement called for legislative and judicial powers to prohibit any nation from possessing armaments and forces beyond "an approved level required for internal policing"; assigning to the world government power to control dangerous aspects of atomic development and of other weapons of mass destruction; granting to the world government the power to inspect and the ability to organize police and armed forces sufficient to enforce the law and maintain world security—in short, the basic peace-keeping powers that UWF and others considered the minimum for a limited government.

In addition, the conflict between the maximalists and minimalists, often the liberals and conservatives, and not infrequently the students versus the adults, over what other powers would be accorded the new world federation was temporarily resolved with the following formulation, a classic compromise: "We recognize that although some world federalists believe that such limited powers would be sufficient as a beginning, others are convinced that any world organization to be effective, even at the start, must have broader powers to bring about peaceful change in the direction of a free and prosperous world community. Such differences as exist among world federalists on this point *are mainly questions of timing* (my italics). There is full agreement that we should move as rapidly as possible to a world federal government with authority and power to legislate on other basic causes of international conflict."

It would appear that, for the time being, a modus vivendi had been found in which each of the sides could find room to maneuver. The magnitude of the student accomplishment was better demonstrated in the policy statement adopted on Nov. 2, in which the methods of achieving world government were expanded to include not only "the amendment processes of the United Nations" but also participation in world constituent assemblies, "whether of private individuals, parliamentary or other groups, seeking to produce draft constitutions for consideration and possible adoption by the United Nations or by national governments in accordance with their respective constitutional processes."

# 4

# The Movement Peaks Despite a Tenuous Unity

### Student Delegates Reach Emotional High: Fifteen Leave School to Volunteer for One Year

The 1947 student convention was perhaps the most exciting in its history. Almost a hundred delegates elected Larry Fuchs, a Navy veteran and a New York University junior, its first non-Protestant chairman. The appointment of Charlotte Hanna as Education Director was announced. During an emotional exchange, 15 students from 10 states stood up and announced they were taking off from school for the winter semester to undertake regional organizing for the student division. They pledged to raise their own support funds; each needed about $150 a month. The "epidemic" of volunteers began when CCNY chapter President Abe Bargman made an impassioned speech "on the need for regional field workers, then offered to leave school himself, for a semester. Fourteen other students rose to join him." They were Larry Fuchs, New York University; Benjamin Weiner, Syracuse; James Burns, Princeton; Anna Buel, Morristown, New Jersey; Phyllis Barnhill, Connecticut College; Natalie Rogers, DePauw; Lou Zamorsky, Cornell College (Iowa); George Shepherd, University of Michigan; Donald Knoerr and Richard Koppenaal of Wauwatosa, Wisconsin; John Shelton Davis and Melvin Jashchke of the University of Texas; Donald Irion of St. Petersburg Union College, Florida; and Jack Matlock, Duke University (who was later to become Ronald Reagan's Ambassador to the Soviet Union). Shortly thereafter, John Logue of

*Student Federalist Chairman Larry Fuchs signs correspondence to chapters prepared by staffer Phyllis Barnhill, formerly of Connecticut College and soon to be Field Director.*

St. John's followed suit, serving in the Pennsylvania State conference office. Student members were asked to contribute $1 each to help fund these volunteers.

Over the Christmas holidays, the Student Division held workshops in Clearwater, Florida; Princeton, New Jersey; and Chicago. (The Princeton chapter formally affiliated with UWF, which meant that Albert Einstein was a member of the Student Division.)

Having papered over their differences for the sake of unity, the Student Federalists concluded a year of its greatest growth, outreach, and presence, both nationally and internationally. More than 150 local chapters dotted the American landscape. There were so many secondary school chapters that the Student Council felt compelled to authorize the formation of a Secondary School National Council under its jurisdiction. At the St. Louis convention, eight students were elected to the UWF Executive Council and, for the first time, none of the original founders were chosen. The most veteran "student" was Steve Benedict, now with the *Common Cause* magazine. The others were

James Burns, Gilles Corcos, Philip Leserman of Yale, Coke Prentice, Shane Riorden of Harvard, Larry Fuchs of New York University, and Fritjof Thygeson, about to enter Stanford, who had in September embarked on a four-month speaking tour of secondary schools that took him to almost every region of the nation.

All eight of these students were also elected to the Student Council, along with some new leadership arising from the ranks: Eugene Berman of Nebraska; Brent Bozell of Yale (later to become the close associate of William F. Buckley); Howard Lord of Chicago University; Donald McIntosh of Columbia; high schoolers Paul Priest, Don Irion, Donald Knoerr, and Donald Levine, as well as Stanford's Richard Kelton, the West Coast Chairman of U.S.N.S.A. (and my own mentor as his West Coast successor in U.S.N.S.A. two years later). Among the new adult members of the Council were Professor Reginald Lang of Carleton (who was much revered by the students); Cass Canfield, Chairman of Harper & Brothers; and Thomas Dodd, then a candidate for governor of Connecticut who would later become that state's U.S. Senator. With greater numbers and new blood, the prospects from within the organization, including the Student Division, appeared to be the best to date.

## Despite Sizable 1948 Growth, Students Encounter Increasing Problems with Adults

The decisions made in St. Louis, including the compromises embodied within the UWF Policy Statement, failed to resolve what were fast becoming serious philosophical schisms. On Jan. 19, 1948, Student Director Helen Ball wrote to Steve Benedict that "a heated and healthy debate . . .is going on concerning UWF policy" of which "very few people in the Eastern chapters" are aware or fully briefed. She expressed the view that "there is a real need for informal discussion on the various points . . ." These were the same points raised in the Wofford-Lindgren open letter in October and by the students and liberals at the St. Louis convention during the policy debates.

In brief, only a sightless optimist could sit back after Asheville and St. Louis under the impression that the UWF positions were now fixed for a reasonable period of time. Still being contended by many was the serious student concern that stands could be taken, either by the national council or, in its absence, by the local chapters on issues relating to the eventual achievement of world government or world community. The concept of a people's constitutional convention was being met by hardened opposition within the adult sector. The differing views regarding the powers of the ultimate world federation—ranging from "minimal" to "maximal"—would shadow the federalists throughout their existence. Although a minority, a strong segment of the student membership agreed with the majority of adults that the contemporary "minimalist" formula presented in Asheville and slightly modified in St. Louis was the one most likely to resonate with majority of Americans.

In March, UWF staff commenced a new public relations project, soliciting articles and columns from its best known leaders and its best writers, including students, for free distribution to college and community newspapers. The most popular writers would be offered to mass circulation newspapers and magazines. The invitational letter claimed more than 350 UWF adult and student chapters as of March 8. At approximately the same time, a staff member wrote to Benedict that the headquarters could not yet provide an accurate membership figure. The previous month, the UWF Finance Committee junked its current fundraising appeals and recruited a group of high-level Madison Avenue specialists to produce a new appeal. In April, a brown paper envelope and package was sent to every member and some friends, inaugurating yet another new campaign, this one called the "Drive for Five." Its goal being the recruitment of five new members by each existing member, the creators quite possibly believed that the three-word rhyme made new content unnecessary. The goal was 100,000 new members. It did not succeed.

A week-long "training school" for 14 of the students who volunteered to perform field work for a semester took place in February at UWF headquarters. Heading the "faculty" were Columbia historian Carl Van Doren and New York University political scientist Clyde Eagleton. The students mapped out a schedule to organize in 15 states. The House of Representatives scheduled hearings on a resolution favoring a U.N. Charter revision conference to make the organization "capable of enacting, interpreting and enforcing world law to prevent war." Rep. Walter H. Judd was leading this fight in the House Foreign Affairs Committee.

The American Association of the U.N. went to court to challenge four private restrictive covenants that prevented Negroes from purchasing property, using Articles 55 and 56 of the U.N. Charter as the basis of their challenge. These articles require respect for human rights without regard to race. The A.A.U.N. brief reminded the U.S. Supreme Court that the Charter is a treaty approved by the U.S. Senate and therefore the supreme law of the land, superseding all local, state, and federal laws, including those permitting racial discrimination in the form of restrictive covenants.

*Student Division Field Worker Natalie Rogers (third from right) meets with a budding college chapter in 1948. Rogers was promoted to Student Director the following year.*

## Establishment Leaders Petition for United States Support of World Government

So imbued in the culture had the world government issue become that the 1948 SAT exam carried a question about it. In Cleveland, more than 200,000 citizens signed petitions pledging to bring about world government. The petition drive was sponsored by the three local newspapers, the governor and his predecessor, the mayor, the local police force, and trade unions, as well as leaders of the three major religious denominations. Close to 7,000 residents of Philadelphia's Main Line, a community of influence and wealth, signed a similar petition, specifically endorsing the federalist resolutions before both houses of Congress. The 1948 Republican Presidential candidate Harold E. Stassen urged his party to adopt a platform plank calling for a 1950 U.N. Charter revision conference, after taking a series of steps to strengthen the Western economies and armed forces, as well as to combat Soviet propaganda.

With Truman's proposal to renew the draft, federalists were divided between support for and opposition to both conscription and universal military training. In February, for the first time *The Student Federalist* newsletter published a complete and up-to-date list of the recognized and active student chapters. After deleting those that had become inactive or with memberships below 10, the list totalled 149 units in 31 states and the District of Columbia. Seventy-seven were college and university chapters and 68 secondary school units, of which 36 were in prep schools and 32 in high schools. Four were mixed. New York had the most chapters at 27 and Massachusetts was second with 16. By April the chapter total reached 201. (The official list of college and high school chapters comprising UWF's Student Division in November 1948, appears in Appendix 16.)

So optimistic were the leaders of the Student Division that they voted to increase membership dues to $1.50 from $1, to organize 3 secondary school institutes for the spring break and 7 full-fledged summer institutes, while releasing a new 13-page study guide and a 45-page bibliography. One-year-old Americans for Democratic Action, the new anti-Communist haven for the nation's liberals, voted in convention to endorse world federal government, but only *after* passage of the Marshall Plan (the European Recovery Plan) by Congress. Former Vice President Henry Wallace also supported creation of a world government, without any provision for a legislature, but only after the West makes fundamental compromises with the Soviets.

In March, a Princeton federalist delegation, including four students, visited President Truman with a petition calling for the immediate establishment of world government, with or without the Soviet Union. Truman rejected this proposal, stating it would exacerbate the current power struggle. Instead, he endorsed a strengthened United Nations, blaming the Soviets for obstructing such a move.

## Soviets Complete East Europe Takeover; Kremlin Rejects Federalist Proposals

Meanwhile, dark clouds were rapidly forming abroad. Four Soviet scientists denounced Albert Einstein for endorsing world federal government, characterizing it as a capitalist plot. Stalin rejected not only the Baruch Plan but also the American offer to include the Soviet Union among those nations that would receive economic assistance to revive their economies under the proposed Marshall Plan. The Communist parties of the states bordering the Soviet Union dispensed with any democratic pretense and, under the cover of Red Army tanks, seized control of their governments. Thomas Masaryk, son of the Czech nation's founder and the elected leader of that nation, was thrown through a window to his death in what came to known popularly as "defenestration," an old Czech practice, but a new tactic in the Kremlin's armory.

The headquarters of the World Federation of Democratic Youth (WFDY) was swept clean of youths from the democratic countries, all of whom were escorted to the Prague airport and expelled. After that, WFDY was unabashedly a front for the Kremlin. (WFDY had been the sponsor and organizer of the World Youth Congress in Prague the previous summer.) The Communist parties of France and Italy, financially and diplomatically backed by the Soviets, stepped up their drives to topple the governments of both nations, using a variety of methods, including general strikes, to destabilize them. The American response was to buttress the parties of the democratic center and left with material support.

In the spring of 1948, the Soviet military began to build up pressure on Berlin, an island of Western presence surrounded by Communist-controlled East Germany. The rail lines bringing supplies and food to the city were gradually squeezed. Beleaguered Berlin was fast becoming a symbol of the struggle between the Soviets and the West, between Communism and capitalist democracy. Then on June 2, when all the ground logistical lines of delivery were severed, the Americans began an historic airlift that over the remainder of the year kept Berlin's population from starving or freezing. The Cold War was underway.

These grim developments failed to deter UWF's zeal or activity. Cord Meyer, oil executive W.T. Holliday, and ex-State Department executive Thomas Finletter testified on May 11, 1948, before the House and Senate Committee hearings on world government proposals. Republican party conventions in North Carolina, Minnesota and Maine approved pro-world government resolutions. Presidential candidate Robert A. Taft, perhaps spurred by his rival Harold Stassen, endorsed world government.

Influenced by its European counterparts, UWF's Executive Council, with strong student support, welcomed the "exploration of American participation in the People's Constituent Assembly," and authorized its Executive Committee to elect UWF's 26 delegates to the second convention of the World Movement for World Government in early September in Luxembourg.

Preceding that meeting was the World Student Federalist Congress in Hastings, England, for which the Student Division authorized the election of its delegates. Seventeen student federalists signed up to make the journey by boat. The Student Division's own Joseph Wheeler, the key organizer of the Concord conference in 1946 and of the first student institutes, was elected President of World Student Federalists, a move that recognized not only Wheeler's leadership abilities but also that the UWF Student Division was the largest of the world's student federalist groups. Wheeler's election helped to cement further the students' international commitments and ties.

## Intensive Volunteer Organizing Almost Doubles Student Membership to 9,500

If there were any doubts about the intensive field work by the 15 volunteer organizers, coupled with the extensive programs conducted under Abe Bargman's direction, those doubts vanished at the second Student Division convention Nov. 12–14, 1948, in Minneapolis. Field Director Natalie Rogers reported to the student assemblage that between Jan. 1 and Nov. 12, membership had risen from about 5,500 to 9,500 members, and the number of chapter increased from 149 to 272 in 40 states and the District of Columbia. At this date, the Student Federalists were probably the largest secular student organization in the nation. (It may be argued that the new National Student Association *represented* far more students, on the basis of having four or five U.S.N.S.A. activists on a given campus and counting the entire student body as "members" of the national organization. In reality, the number of truly active individuals working on behalf of U.S.N.S.A. was often smaller than the chapter membership of the campus federalist group, which frequently comprised many, if not most, of the student activists in the federalists and related, or compatible, organizations.)

Among the collaborating student and youth groups during this period were the Student League for Industrial Democracy, the Youth Division of the NAACP, the United Student Christian Council, the Students for Democratic Action, the Collegiate Council for the United Nations, the YMCA, the YWCA, the B'nai B'rith Youth Organization, World Republic and United States National Students Association.

The 1948 convention delegates voted to increase the students' ties to the other student federalist groups, including increased financial support for the

World Student Federalists. They agreed to hold a mock United Nations Charter revision convention among students and to study its results as a guide to future conferences. Individual chapters were urged to stage their own mock charter revisions to enact and enforce world law. After endorsing greater political action, they accepted the adult decision that chapters refrain from endorsing or opposing political candidates. The most original idea was a proposal to invite representatives of other youth and student groups to join with the Student Division in organizing world government caravans.

*At the 1948 UWF Student Division convention in Minneapolis, Duke junior Ralph Fleming (left) was elected chairman and NYU's Murray Frank vice chairman. Fleming reads national editorial comments in support of House Concurrent Resolution 64 to transform the United Nations into a world federation. Both Fleming and Frank were war veterans (photo from World Government News).*

The convention delegates elected Duke University junior and two-year Navy veteran Ralph Fleming, Jr. as their new chairman. New York University's Murray Frank was elected Vice Chairman. Eight students were elected to the adult Executive Council—the veterans James Burns, Curt Farrar, Ralph Fleming, Larry Fuchs, Don McIntosh, Fritjof Thygeson, Harris Wofford, and the only new addition, Bernard Hennessy of Syracuse. All eight were also elected to the National Student Council, along with the newest crop of national leaders—Murray Frank, New York University; Russell Baldwin, Duke; Harlan Hockenberg, Iowa; Marie-Louise Cullum, Alabama; Ed Brenner, Carleton; Richard Goodman, Williams; William Holbrook, Minnesota; Jack Matlock, Duke; and Lee Williams, Princeton.

## Broad Coalition of National Membership Organizations Endorses World Federalism

A broad-based coalition of national organizations had endorsed world federal government. They included the American Veterans Committee, American Education Fellowship, Americans for Democratic Action, Association of American Colleges, Committee on Public Affairs, Council for Democracy, Catholic Association for International Peace, Emergency Committee of Atomic Scientists, Evangelical Church of the Brethren, Friends of Democracy, Fellowship of Reconciliation National Council, Methodist Church Commission on World Peace, Moravian Church (Southern Province), NAACP, National Education Association, Protestant Episcopal Church, Religious Society of Friends Peace Board, Southern Baptists, Synagogue Council of America, United States Junior Chamber of Commerce, and World Citizenship Movement. Granted most of these organizations were liberal to begin with; nevertheless, they represented a sizable grass-roots following.

## As Cold War Heats Up, UWF Student Membership Plummets

Notwithstanding all of the sanguine signs, the decline of the student membership had begun in the first month of 1949. By the end of January, the total had dropped from 9,500 in November to 7,600 and 221 chapters; by May, the membership had edged up to 7,800. On Dec. 3 Student Director Natalie Rogers reported to the Executive Committee in Providence that the number of 1949 paid memberships through the end of November had declined by 2,822 to a total of 4,560. Counting memberships paid the previous December, she stated, the total paid student membership came to 5,934. By January 1950, the membership had dropped even further to 5,562, despite a slight growth in the number of chapters to 231. Between September 1948, shortly before the membership had peaked, and January 1950—roughly 16 months—the Student Division had dropped 109 chapters! Student rumblings were emerging in chapters throughout the country. No doubt some of the decline was the product of Cold War disenchantment. But the decline in membership produced a decline in income, relegating the students to the position of "poor relative." The so-called adult executive staff numbered a total of 17 in March 1949, whereas the total number of student executives numbered 3—Field Director (Rogers), Project Director (Bargman), and Publicity Director (Dorothy Stout).

It was becoming apparent that the adults felt that if the students could not pay their own way, they would be obliged to cut back their staff and programs. In fact, some of the student staff salaries were being paid through the Student Volunteer Fund, consisting of contributions from the students themselves or from their friends. At the beginning of 1949, UWF adult membership approached 33,000 compared to about 7,500 student members. The adult fortunes, however, appeared to have moved in the opposite direction. On March 1, 1949, the total membership had reached 40,985, a doubling in 11 months, because the total membership the previous March 31 was reported to be 20,465. The number of chapters had soared during the same period from 379 to 652, and the 25 state branches were 6 more than the year before.

## Tensions Grow Within UWF Between Students and Adults

Student dues were much less than those of adults. Thus, it seemed fair to the adults that the students, with about 18.7 percent of the membership, should have only 15 percent of the staff as their own, especially because many of the adult staff members served the entire organization. Further, the students continued to press for policy initiatives not well received by the adults, including stands on interim foreign policy issues, a People's Constitutional Conference, a bias toward a greater maximalist world government, and so forth. The financial crunch compelled the students to cut back on summer institutes, literature, and other activities. At the June 21–23, 1949, convention and board meeting, one of the major topics of discussion was the growing student perception that UWF was distancing itself from the merger agreement that provided for a broad degree of chapter autonomy. In fact, later resolutions had affirmed the right of student chapters to issue policy statements that did not conflict with UWF's stated purposes or policies or with consensus statements made by the National Executive Board. There was also student pique at the failure of the Executive Council to elect Professor Frederick Schuman of Williams to the Advisory Board.

In the summer of 1949, Cord Meyer resigned as UWF President (officially, to complete a fellowship for graduate studies at Harvard before joining the CIA). He was replaced by another war veteran and writer, Alan Cranston of Los Altos, California, who was later to chair the state's Democrat party and then to serve four terms as U.S. Senator for California. The student leaders were frankly informed by the UWF's new executive director, Robert Walker, that the students could not anticipate an expanded program in the following year unless most of the funding for such an expansion resulted from student efforts. Because the students had accepted UWF's claim that it no longer possessed the resources to subsidize the students, the Student Executive Committee decided to launch its own fundraising drive for the fall with the insistence that the Executive Committee itself retain exclusive control over the spending of these funds.

On another level, the student council tried to resolve the contradiction between UWF's dictum that UWF bylaws bound the Student Division to UWF policy as opposed to the policy statements that could be issued by the World Student Federalists, to which the Student Division was affiliated and to which some degree of loyalty was owed. The Student Council thereupon asked UWF to give the Student Council the power to bind its chapters to World Student federalist policies. (Not only was Joseph Wheeler the World Student Federalist (WSF) President when the third congress of WSF convened in Amsterdam in August, 1949, but of the 15 members of the WSF Executive Committee, 5 were from the UWF Student Division. In addition to Wheeler, they were Steve Benedict, Fred Carney, Ralph Fleming, and Alastair Kyle. With Americans accounting for such a high proportion of the leadership, they assumed a substantial financial and policy burden in trying to expand American student support for the three-year-old WSF.)

All of these bones of contention were at work, eroding the papered-over unity achieved by the Asheville and the St. Louis conventions. Students had

Lord Boyd Orr (center), president of the World Movement for World Federal Government, addresses the Third Annual Conference of the World Student Federalists in Amsterdam, August 1949. On Boyd Orr's left is Norman J.Hart, WSF Organizing Secretary, and on his right is Joe Wheeler, WSF President and U.S. Student Federalist leader.

begun to ask what the "up side" had been of their having agreed to merge with the adults. It had been assumed, perhaps without any real inquiry, that the adults had substantially larger resources, real and potential, which they would agree to share with the students once unity was achieved. Clearly, very little of that expectation was to be fulfilled. It also ought to be remembered that a great many of these students were grown men who had served in the armed forces during the war, as well as young men and women of considerable maturity for their age, both at the high school and college levels.

Instead of a separate convention, the students organized an assembly on October 28–30 when they met as part of the UWF's 1949 convention in Cleveland. This effort to save money did not sit well with the students, whose executive committee met to urge planning for a separate convention the following year. The students at both meetings dealt with three recommendations to improve relations between student chapters and the adult chapters at the state

*The Student Division 1949 convention delegates elected Murray Frank, shown here at the podium, as national chairman. Seated at his left is national UWF leader Mildred Blake.*

level. They also adopted plans to make the student council more representative of and receptive to chapters in the field.

Murray Frank was elected National Chairman and Jonathan Fine, a Boston high schooler, Vice Chairman. The new student council reflected a blend of leadership from the previous three years with a new crop, including Joan Clark, Smith; Bill Fankhauser, California-Berkeley; Jonathan Fine (who became a medical doctor and founder of Physicians for Human Rights); Priscilla Johnson (later a Soviet specialist at MIT who translated a book by Stalin's daughter and wrote a book on Lee Harvey Oswald's life in the Soviet Union); John Kemeny (who became president of Dartmouth); Harry Lustig, University of Illinois (later a prominent physicist); Jersey City high schooler Peter Novick (today an historian at University of Chicago); Irwin Robinson, University of Michigan; Rheta Siegal; John Sutter, Harvard; Henry Thomson,

Syracuse; Immanuel Wallerstein, Columbia (later president of the International Sociological Association); Herb Weiss, New York University (subsequently a major expert in the affairs of the Congo, formerly Zaire); Ted Weiss, Syracuse (who later represented Manhattan's liberal West Side for six terms in the House of Representatives); and Anna Wright, University of Chicago.

Despite the decline in membership and income from dues, the special fundraising drives among the various leaders and their friends bore significant results. Not only were the students' key headquarters positions retained, but also the Student Division added two other paid positions. The National Chairman and the Student Director both occupied paid positions, as did the student, chapter, and student projects directors. Chairman Murray Frank, Student Director Natalie Rogers, Projects Director Bernard Hennessy, Chapter Secretary Bonnie Shaner, and Publicity Director Marie-Louise Cullum completed the staff of the student division. From the minutes of the student council meetings and the budgets, it appears that most received about $50 a week for their services.

## Federalists Victimized by Opponents of Free Speech; Students Seek Bar Against Racism Within UWF

At an Executive Committee meeting in early December 1949, the members voted to resist the decision of the Palo Alto high school principal to force the student federalist chapter to leave the school because of anti-world government pressure in California. The California state conference was asked to take public action against this development. A poll of the chapters expressed strong support for a separate student convention a day prior to the adult convention. The remainder of the meeting was taken up with the question of racial discrimination practiced by student federalist chapters. At the Cleveland assembly, the students passed a resolution calling for the revocation of charters of those chapters found by a National Student Council to be guilty of barring any person because of color, creed, or nationality. The same resolution urged the Executive Board to follow the same policy among adult branches.

Following up this resolution, the Student Executive Committee passed a specific resolution and presented it the next day to the Executive Board, calling for the revocation of the charter of any state council or local chapter found to refuse membership on the grounds of race. The Board deflected the recommendation, suggesting that all acts of discrimination be presented to the

National Executive Committee, which would "take the necessary steps to correct the situation."

Student Chairman Murray Frank, clearly troubled by the refusal of the National Executive Council to act, drew up a four-page paper, outlining the history, those bylaws provisions that barred discrimination as opposed to the "practice" of not enforcing the prohibition, and the political, social and moral pros and cons of actively expelling any chapters or state councils that prevented Negroes from joining UWF. He also presented the dilemma of seeking Third World leadership for world government from an organization that tolerated racial discrimination in its midst. He reported on his discussions with Walter White and other NAACP leaders who, although in agreement on the goal of world government, provided no meaningful support to UWF because of its "inadequate"—read nonexistent—stand on colonialism. Frank asked the question, "Would the NAACP support UWF if we actively opposed discrimination in our ranks?," and the important practical follow-up, "Do we need or want the support of the NAACP? Would we gain more than we lose in financial and membership support?"

Apparently, the UWF adult leaders never resolved this issue internally, believing they were taking the most pragmatic alternative in the pursuit of American support for world government. Most of the students, however, experienced in working in coalitions with NAACP youth and with student leaders abroad, came to an entirely different conclusion: The issue could not be side-stepped without harming the moral strength and ultimately damaging the political validity of the cause. How, it was asked, could students support a universal world government that would be three-fourths non-white, while countenancing racial discrimination in our midst? The question was not an idle one: Our student allies, especially the USNSA and SDA and, of course, the NAACP, were dealing with the race issue head on. Soon, the YMCA and the YWCA, as well as the religious youth and student organizations, would also face the same question.

Further, student division leaders were participating in the formation of the youth division of the National Social Welfare Council that was to become the American member of a new alternative to the Communist-dominated World Federation of Democratic Youth. That new global entity was called the World Assembly of Youth (WAY), officially founded in August, 1949 in Brussels. The student federalist leaders played a major role in the formation and operations of both the national and international entities. There was simply no place for racial discrimination in their home base. Thus, another major bone of contention had been raised between UWF and the students. At Stanford, which had never before admitted a Negro undergraduate, the Federalist and USNSA leaders organized the university's initial NAACP student chapter with the avowed goal of compelling the university to admit its first Negro student. After a visit from Roy Wilkins, then administrative assistant to Walter White, we demanded in late 1949 that the university remove the photograph from the admissions application. The university complied, much more swiftly than we could have imagined. By the spring of 1950, the university announced that the first black undergraduate student had been admitted for the fall of 1951. He was a Compton College transfer, a reputedly straight A student, and a four-letter athlete named Ed Tucker. After that, the bar rapidly disappeared.

## CROSS-COUNTRY CARAVAN BY STUDENT FEDERALISTS HIGHLIGHTS 1950

The major programmatic focus for the students in 1950 was the organization of the spring/summer world government caravan. Staff member Dee Frazer began the advance work in April, with a prolonged stay in California, after which she visited each of the planned stops along the way to Washington, D.C. The caravan actually began in Alaska when John and Virginia Meloney left Fairbanks along the Alcan Highway on April 9. After spending six weeks in Seattle working on a world government referendum, they joined the Western Caravan in San Francisco where, on June 15, six federalists in three autos departed from the War Memorial Opera House after a press conference. With a police escort, they crossed the Oakland Bay Bridge to Berkeley, where they were greeted and endorsed by the mayor. The next day, the Utah governor signed a federalist petition in Salt Lake City, where some of the federalists were interviewed on the radio. On June 17 Denver's Mayor Quig Newton greeted the caravaneers after a parade through the downtown area. Among the remaining stops in Colorado, the caravan was greeted by the President of the University of Colorado and the petition signed by the law school dean. Heavy rains and mechanical failures forced the caravan to skip Kansas City, Independence, and Columbia, Missouri, but it did make it to St. Louis for a five-day break to attend the National Student Council meeting beginning on June 24.

A second leg of the caravan, beginning in New York City, made stops in Iowa and Illinois before joining the Western leg in St. Louis for the NSC meeting. After a lengthy parade through St. Louis and numerous radio appearances, the caravan, now 6 cars long with 27 riders, left St. Louis for Indianapolis, where they were met by some public figures for photo opportunities. However, pressure from the local VFW resulted in the cancellation of appearances by the Governor and Mayor. Local law enforcement personnel stopped some of the caravaneers for "questioning" in both Ohio and Pennsylvania.

It was after a sizable and warm reception in Cincinnati that the participants learned of the North Korean invasion of the South the day before, resulting in a sharp drop in student morale. The remaining stops in Dayton, Columbus, Pittsburgh, and Harrisburg were cordial but not as enthusiastic as the earlier ones. Arriving in Washington on June 29, the caravaneers were greeted by UWF President Alan Cranston at the International House. The next day, they presented the petitions gathered along the transcontinental route to the Secretary of the Senate before the press and a stellar alignment of senators and representatives as well as spokespersons from veterans and farmer groups. Almost 40 student federalists participated at various stages of this publicity-generating trek. (A list of Student Division participants in the 1950 caravan appears in Appendix 23.)

(After the text of this book had been completed, we learned that the Student Division had organized a similar caravan in 1949 under the direction of Phyllis Barnhill, a Connecticut College graduate who was named Student Director the following year. The caravan had been proposed by Student Project Director Abe Bargman. It also started in San Francisco and made stops in Berkeley, St. Louis, and elsewhere before concluding in Washington D.C., where a bound petition was presented to Vice President Alben Barkley and to various members of Congress.)

The caravaneers' experience of being taken in custody by state police and local cops was a by-product of the growing hysteria produced by Cold War anti-Communism. Before Senator Joe McCarthy launched his own witch-hunt, the ground had been well prepared by a group of opportunistic political figures, mostly Republicans, and private self-appointed watchdogs. The House UnAmerican Activities Committee (HUAC), originally under J. Parnell Thomas of New Jersey, began its heavily publicized investigation into alleged Communist activities in the motion picture industry in 1946–7. Somehow, the Committee's mission began to legitimize parallel or related efforts and demonstrated to the most ambitious office seekers that a great deal of public attention and publicity could be generated from charges against celebrated persons or institutions.

*Student Federalist California chairman William Friedlander of California-Berkeley, spokesman for the UWF student caravan that crossed the nation by car in the summer of 1950, presents a book of signatures to petitions supporting world government to Secretary of the U.S. Senate Leslie Biffle (photo from World Government News).*

## STUDENT FEDERALISTS FIGHT BACK AGAINST RIGHT-WING EFFORTS TO SILENCE THEM

One of the earliest witch-hunters was California's State Senator Jack Tenney, whose only claim to fame was that he had written "Mexicali Rose." Spurred on by hate-mongers such as Gerald L.K. Smith and Wesley Swift, Tenney initially led a state legislative assault on alleged Communist infiltration among the unions in the state, including those in the movie business. When these efforts were eclipsed by the Congressional probes, he shifted his attack to other targets, including the world government movement. The California student federalists met with virulent opposition in town after town, including the cancellation of auditoriums for speeches and meetings, because the charges by Tenney and others had been swallowed hook, line, and sinker by the local and state Veterans of Foreign Wars posts and even by those of the American

Legion. It was just such pressure that impelled the Palo Alto High School principal to require the local federalist chapter to remove itself from the school.

Student federalist units in California, especially at Berkeley and Stanford, chose to fight back. On a few occasions, we were threatened with violence in smaller towns after showing up to conduct meetings at public halls that had withdrawn permission at the last minute. We undertook the research necessary to connect the attacks with Gerald Smith, Swift, and a dangerous crackpot of the right known as Father Riker. Some of this material was given to a young Los Angeles NBC newscaster by the name of Chet Huntley, himself affiliated with the California UWF. Drawing from the student federalists' research, Huntley attacked these critics of world government with some well-chosen editorial comments on the local NBC station. Smith and others sued Huntley and the student federalists for libel. The local NBC station handled the suit and the court upheld Huntley.

However, overzealous watchdogs sprang up everywhere in the nation. A nondescript "patriot" by the name of Myron C. Fagan had formed the Cinema Education Guild in Hollywood in 1947 and published a scurrilous pamphlet called "Red Treason in Hollywood," in which he smeared by association a great many industry workers, including stars, for attending meetings or signing petitions that also might have involved Communists. Scores of individuals, most of them non-Communists, lost their jobs as a result. When the anti-Communist gambit lost its appeal, Fagan switched his target to the United World Federalists, devoting two full issues of his newsletter to an imaginary Red conspiracy behind the world government campaign (even though the Stalinists had uniformly opposed the concept).

In a promotional flyer, Fagan wrote:

Up until April 1949, not a single true American in our entire land seemed to be aware of the frightening act of treason planned by the United World Federalists and similar groups in cahoots with them. In our July-August and September bulletins, we fully describe that conspiracy. They were headed for sure success until CEG [Cinema Education Guild] broke their stride!

The first bulletin, a 36-pager, claimed to "document" that "*known* Reds [had] organized that movement!" Basically, what Fagan had done was list those Hollywood figures whose reputations he had earlier besmirched as "Reds" for

*World citizen's identity card*

having associated with some petition or public protest meeting in which a few Communists also took part and match up their names with those appearing on world government and UWF letterheads and literature. This form of double guilt-by-association served the extremist elements who opposed world federalism, but more moderate individuals and groups, on the theory that were there's smoke, there's fire, suffered an acute loss of nerve in countless situations involving UWF and the student federalists.

    The Chairman of the California Student Division, William Friedlander of Berkeley, California, decided to challenge Fagan by writing him to ascertain the names of the 41 Communists that Fagan claimed at a public meeting on February 16, 1950, had organized UWF. Friedlander was careful to state he wanted the names of real Communists, not just "Reds," noting consistent Communist and Soviet opposition to world government. He also questioned why the FBI and HUAC had not responded to Fagan's charges of treason by investigating and exposing UWF. Fagan's handwritten reply was 1) he was drafting a 100-page expose on UWF, naming names and describing techniques, which would be published in April (it never was); and 2) similar charges had been made against his earlier claims about Reds in Hollywood, but finally HUAC took them seriously. He hoped they would do so with UWF as well. No serious Congressional committee investigation of UWF ever took place, but that did not deter the professional anti-Communists, including those on campus, from attacking the UWF and the student federalists as "Reds" instead of seriously debating the concepts themselves. A few months later, Wisconsin's Senator Joseph McCarthy made his infamous West Virginia speech, accusing the State Department of harboring a sizable number of Communists. Very few Americans in public life displayed the courage and reason to stand up against this escalation of witchhunting.

In the University of California at Berkeley, the administration, under pressure from an increasingly conservative legislature, inspired the Board of Regents to impose a Loyalty Oath on the faculty. In May 1950, I decided to run for the office of off-campus student government representative to the Stanford student council known as the Executive Committee. Because most of the off-campus students were veterans of World War II, we fashioned a "shocking" platform of four planks that totally disrupted Stanford's "pre-natal equilibirium." The first called for restoring Stanford's membership in the United States National Student Association. The second urged the Stanford student body to support the University of California professors who refused to sign the newly imposed Loyalty Oath. Third, we asked the Stanford students to send a delegate to the Rome Congress for World Government. Finally, we called for permission to debate political issues on campus.

In a four-way race, I won by less than two dozen (third-place) votes. The fraternity crowd was furious. Controlling the current student government, they held a "trial" and found me "guilty" of littering because dozens of my campaign flyers mysteriously landed on the mile-long Palm Drive entrance to Stanford. I was "sentenced" to 40 hours of manual labor at the community home for recuperating patients from the Stanford hospital. No other candidate was brought to trial on the littering count. What the frat leaders and their hacks failed to understand is that I had fashioned a ticket of sorts and that five of my colleagues had also been elected to the Ex Com, including Graduate Student Representative Elliot Schreier and Sophomore Representative Phil Saeta. Our first order of business the following September was to restore Stanford's ties with USNSA.

The Stanford federalists, together with the NAACP college chapter and the members of the off-campus Young Democrats, their memberships overlapping by more than 50 percent, endorsed my initiative as a member of the student government that resulted in the Stanford student body voting in a referendum to condemn the Loyalty Oath and to support those professors who refused to sign. (The Stanford Board of Trustees later repudiated this referendum, foolishly stating that the students had no authority to take such a vote. Thus, they gave us two news breaks instead of one, at the same time radicalizing the student body.)

It was becoming clear to student federalists (and student activists in general) across the nation that the protection of civil liberties at home was a *sine qua non* of any sane debate over the merits of the world federalist cause. To the alliance with the NAACP, we decided to add a collaboration with the American Civil Liberties Union (ACLU).

Recognizing the growing common cause among liberal and internationalist student, youth and adult movements, Student Chairman Murray Frank, Student Director Phyllis Barnhill, and Projects Director Bernard Hennessy devoted a considerable portion of the first six months of 1950 to building coalitions with these groups. Frank made a concerted effort to effect a collaboration with the rapidly growing Students for Democratic Action, through Executive Secretary Sy Reisin and Field Secretary Ralph Dummit. Although he reported on these meetings in less than enthusiastic terms to the National Executive Council in March, two months later SDA delegates at their own national convention approved a ringing resolution in support of world federal government.

Around the subject of a "peace force," Hennessy pursued coalitions with the American Friends Service Committee, the United Christian Youth Movement, the American Association for the United Nations, and the Congregationalist Service Committee. At the same meeting, Student Director Phyllis Barnhill emphasized the difficult financial situation faced by the student division, noting that the membership had dropped to 4,934 by the end of March, including a 300-member loss just from the previous month.

The June 23–25, 1950, meeting of the National Student Council in St. Louis, which concluded just as the General Assembly-endorsed Korean "police action" began, reported in detail the efforts by Frank and Hennessy to fashion close relationships with such groups as Collegiate Council for U.N., Students for Democratic Action, National Student Association, National Federation of Catholic College Students, Fellowship of Reconciliation, the Shawnee and Mount Holyoke Institutes, and the Experiment for International Living. The Council members were appraised of the continuing decline in membership; by June, it had dropped to 4,665 with 221 chapters of uneven strength and effectiveness. Frank's field report stressed that where good leadership existed, the units were strong and energetic.

## June 1950 Student Council Meeting Reveals Further Student-Adult Discord

Two reports from California discussed the experiment to merge the student and adult chapters that, in the view of field worker John Parker, was a disastrous failure. The distinction between student and adult chapters no longer existed there; although in some cases student chapters merged with adult units, in other cases chapters remained on campus with the same status as adult ones, but reporting directly to the state conference. Parker said that the strict policy rulings of the California state branch had produced tension and poor relationships between the students and adults. The adults, he said, displayed a "tendency to discount the students." The political fighting resulted in cancellation of the California segment of the national caravan. The merger, he predicted, would fail.

Bill Friedlander, California Student Chairman, observed that the right-wing opposition had reached a level where federalist chapters were being asked to leave campuses and had contributed to the state legislature's rescission of a world government resolution. He also reported that the students often experienced confusion over the correct interpretation of UWF policy and that the student expression of the need for an education program, which students felt the Ashville merger had provided, was deemed inconsistent with the UWF program as practiced in California. The student leaders, pointing to the success of the caravan, resolved that programs identified as student efforts separate from those of the adults were essential to their success in organizing.

Before hearing from six other field workers, the Council held a lengthy discussion about the organization of the Young Adult Council (YAC) as the American member of the World Assembly of Youth (WAY). (Initial organizing meetings of WAY had been taking place in Britain and Europe since late 1949 with American representation by YAC's predecessor. In the summer of 1950, WAY held a major council meeting in Ankara, Turkey, and several more in Europe subsequently.) Student Division Chairman Frank and several of his federalist Council colleagues were playing important roles in the initial organization of YAC, it was noted.

The Student Executive Council elected the following delegates to represent the student division at the World Student Federalist Congress in Folkstone, Britain, at the end of August: Larry Fuchs, Chairman, Paul Priest, Walter Lehman, Hildreth Strode, Bill Andrews, James Roberts, John Kemeny, with Priscilla Johnson and Natalie Rogers Fuchs as alternate delegates. Except for pledging a $1,000 contribution to WSF over the following year, they went uninstructed.

The remainder of the meeting time was devoted to further discussions of the relationship between the students and UWF, the shortcomings and requirements of the current structure and programs and the strategies for impacting on the UWF convention scheduled for October 1950 in Washington, D.C. Council members and chapter leaders had been corresponding for many months over the various options; meanwhile, the ties that had partially bound the adults and students deteriorated further. (Only when subject to external attack from the extremists, one leader had observed, do the students and adults forget their differences.)

# 5

# THE "REBELLION" OF THE STUDENTS

### Wallerstein's Critique of UWF Policies Calls for Support of World Revolutionary Forces

Into this simmering organizational stew, a pungent element had been introduced by a student who was at that time their most intellectually gifted leader. He was Immanuel Wallerstein, a Columbia undergraduate, and a member of UWF's National Executive Council. Since the latter part of 1949, Wallerstein had been engaged in a discussion by correspondence with UWF and student leaders over the future ideological direction of the organization. A sociology major who was multilingual, he formulated pointedly what so many of the students had sensed but were unable to articulate.

Wallerstein's premise was that the majority of the world's peoples, presently under colonial rule, were determined to become free not only by achieving political independence but also in order to determine their own economic future and cultural rebirth. To oppose this movement "is unwise, unjust, and dangerous," Wallerstein said, "and any national policy that does not foster this revolution for freedom is doomed to failure." Noting that the West no longer possessed supreme power, he warned that it must make a major adjustment to this revolution of rising expectations from the world's majority, who were non-white, non-Christian, and non-modern. His analysis acknowledged that the Soviet Union was exploiting the divisions between the Western colonial powers and the non-white majority currently under its rule but demanding freedom. As long as this condition existed within a framework of world anarchy, he went on, the solution of institutionalized law is more difficult to realize, even though it provides the only hope for peaceful change.

After his drafts produced many comments from friend and foe alike, Wallerstein made a number of revisions and, in what appears to be the final version in 1951, urged UWF leadership acceptance of the following statement:

"That the significance of the world revolution for freedom must be brought to the attention of the American youth community; and that we must place into perspective the power struggle between the United States and the Soviet Union; and that we must support the just struggle of two thirds of the people of the world to achieve freedom; and that we must depose from any leadership in this movement for freedom the Communists whose methods would destroy freedom; and that we must preserve and expand freedom at home, combatting tendencies to limit traditional liberties in times of crisis; and that we must support the United Nations and its specialized agencies and seek the development of the U.N. into a world federal government." (Full text of Wallerstein's proposed student credo appears in Appendix 25. An expansion of the premises contained in his credo appeared in an article Wallerstein wrote for the May 1951 issue of *Federalist Opinion*. Entitled "Revolution and Order," the article is reprinted in Appendix 26.)

Attached to an earlier version of this credo was a four-point action program, recommending that both the UWF and the student federalists work for "an expanded, multilateral program of technical assistance and world development; the elimination of racial and religious discrimination throughout the world; negotiating of differences between nations through the U.N., combining compromise with devotion to fundamental principles, while recognizing the limitations of negotiations in a lawless world; and a wider understanding of the need for a world federal government."

For most of the students, the Wallerstein proclamation placed the short, medium-, and long-term interests and concerns in a relatively seamless package—an umbrella of interests under which virtually all of the students would be able to work, even if the structural and programmatic problems with the adult state branches continued. A great many of the students had decided to enter upon graduate studies focussed on various parts of the Third World, especially Africa, but also the Indian subcontinent and China. Others were more focused on domestic inequities—economic, social, and racial. (Wallerstein wrote his credo four years before the Supreme Court decision on

*Mary Coleman.*

*Herb Weiss.*

*Don McIntosh.*  *Bill Friedlander.*

*Brown v. Board of Education.*) A smaller number devoted themselves to using medicine as a tool for social justice. Many sought public service, either through elective office or through diplomatic and/or economic aid postings. Virtually all were to become engaged, in the European sense, in the public life of their nation and the larger world.

Tragically, the men and women who led the UWF were unable to grasp this vision of the not-too-distant future in their zeal to convert the "average American" to the simplistic world government cause of preventing war. No doubt most agreed with the Wallerstein characterization of the future; however, they feared that support of such objectives as the "world revolution"—even for freedom—would turn away the vast majority of Americans. UWF's consensus vision was against war; it offered little to be in favor of. The growing national consensus was against Communism; it also offered little in the way of a positive ideology. What Wallerstein and the student federalists were seeking was an ideological alternative to Communism that would resonate both at home and among the majority of the world's peoples.

## October 1950 UWF Convention Further Reduces Student Authority

At the October 12–15, 1950, UWF convention in Washington, D.C., during which the students held a parallel convention while attending UWF's plenary sessions, the adults summarily dismissed the Wallerstein memorandum. A total of 530 delegates attended, and they went several steps beyond that ideological rejection by virtually wiping out the student division in all but name. The UWF delegates authorized adult state branches to charter and service student branches, which had been the responsibility of the student division. They eliminated the National Student Council and replaced it with a student affairs board comprised of ten students and three adults to govern student chapters. The finances of the student division were absorbed into the overall UWF finances. A Student Advisory Council of students and adults was also created and regional vice presidents were authorized.

More than 150 students, including 68 delegates, attended the 4-day convention in the segregated national capital. This was the first time most of the students had experienced America's system of Jim Crow first hand and the experience impacted heavily on most of them. Refusing to succumb to institutionalized segregation, the students held their convention at the interracial Friendship House, where they also slept and took most of their meals.

*World Government News,* which had become UWF's membership publication and had replaced *The Student Federalist* as the students' monthly newsletter in 1949, wrote that the new organizational structure had been "enthusiastically approved by UWF's General Assembly." The same could not be said by the majority of students who realistically concluded that their power was inadequate to block the changes. Perhaps out of duty, outgoing chairman Murray Frank wrote in the same house organ insert that the convention had been "successful, productive, and mature." The fact is that the adults held the financial trump cards as well as the delegates' votes, the student division was almost broke, and the membership continued to decline.

The students, in a close vote, elected another Navy veteran, 25-year-old Thomas "Duke" Robertson, a middle-of-the-road graduate student at the University of Colorado, as the Student Chairman over Immanuel Wallerstein. The convention delegates elected these students to the Executive Board: Ed Brenner, Nonie Clark, Murray Frank, Larry Fuchs, Thomas Robertson, Fritjof Thygeson, and Immanuel Wallerstein. Only 6 new members were elected out of 45 to the adult-dominated National Executive Board. From the students' viewpoint, the most important was Dr. Robert Redfield, chairman of the social science department of the University of Chicago, who became the students' inspiration and the Board's conscience. Cord Meyer, still at Harvard, became Honorary President and Chairman of the Executive Committee. Five regional vice chairmen were elected by the students for the first time: Steve Wiley of Princeton, Northeast; Robert Byrd, Southeast; Dale Hiller, Midwest;

Kirk Brady, Rocky Mountain; and myself, West. They were made ex-officio members of the Student Affairs Board.

Despite their deep disappointment with UWF's rejection of financing for the student's staff requests and for new projects, and despite the overwhelming decision of the convention delegates to eradicate any differentiation between student and adult chapters except the level of dues, the UWF's student leaders left Washington committed fully to making the new structure and emphases work. In Chicago on Dec. 8–9 the new Student Affairs Board met. The staff and volunteer reports covered a frenetic degree of field work, organizing new chapters and desperately trying to hold on to existing ones. (Between October and November, the number of student chapters dropped from 175 to 138, and Chapter Secretary Bonnie Shaner Palace observed that at least 36 other chapters failed to demonstrate membership of at least ten, the minimum for chartering.)

Chairman Murray Frank reported a new debate kit, emphasizing universalism, had been created by the staff for college distribution. The kit provided the arguments on behalf of the negative position of the topic: "Resolved that the non-communist nations should form a new international organization," an obvious response to the deepening Cold War and the Korean action.

## Student Leaders Become Major Force in U.S. Youth Delegation to World Assembly

The influence of the Wallerstein memorandum was felt in a number of ways: the post-convention student-prepared package mailed to 65 student and youth organizations; the decision to hold a leadership training institute to help build a core of federalists with more profound knowledge of federalists' principles and how major world issues relate to them; agreement to organize seminars throughout the country to expose student and youth leaders from other organizations to the federalist concept and its relationship to the burgeoning world revolution; approval of a resolution to spur the interchange of ideas between U.S. federalist units and federalist units abroad; and approval of a project by CARE to raise funds for books to be distributed in the Third World by UNESCO, a project in which USNSA leader Rob West served as College Director for CARE. West addressed a number of UWF chapters to gain support for the project.

Perhaps the most extensive manifestation of Wallerstein's memorandum was the major role taken by student federalists in the formation of the Young

Adult Council (YAC) in May 1950, about which Wallerstein spoke at length at this meeting. He described YAC's history and roots in the Soviet takeover of WFDY two years earlier and the function of YAC as a coordinating committee of representatives of internationalist and socially conscious youth and student groups and as the American member of the World Assembly of Youth (WAY). (In 1951, the YAC members were the American Red Cross (College Units); American Unitarian Youth; American Youth Hostels; Collegiate Council for the United Nations; NAACP Youth Division; National Board YWCA; National Council, YMCA; National Federation of Settlements; National Jewish Youth Conference; Student Division, United World Federalists; United Christian Youth Movement; Universalist Youth Fellowship; and Youth Department, National Catholic Welfare Conference. In future years, some of these groups would disappear, and YAC added the Association of International Relations Clubs and the Student League for Industrial Democracy.)

The initial YAC project scheduled conferences for study and action in five cities in early 1951 relating the role of American Youth to Point Four, the first important U.S. postwar technical assistance program that encompassed Third World nations. (The five cities chosen were Denver; Palo Alto, California; Madison, Wisconsin; Richmond, Virginia; and Boston. Each happened to be either a stronghold of the student federalists, NSA, or SDA or a combination thereof.)

The Council also learned that Murray Frank had been appointed chairman for these conferences and that Immanuel Wallerstein was named chairman of YAC's International Affairs Committee and Herb Weiss a member of YAC's Executive Committee. The UWF student delegation to YAC comprised Frank, Wallerstein, Weiss, and Duke Robertson. Now, the Student Affairs Board was called upon to ratify these "nominations" that demonstrated the key role being played by federalists in this newly born national agency representing the broadest spectrum of American students and youth. (In early 1951, Murray Frank and Gene Schwartz, who held posts with both USNSA and the student division, were employed full time by YAC to work on the planning and organization of the 1951 WAY Congress, along with YMCA leader and YAC Vice Chairman Ernest Howell and Donald Sullivan.)

Wallerstein reported further that the federalist influence did not end at U.S. shores. He and other federalists were also becoming involved in the shaping of the international federation WAY, which, he observed, would be holding its initial full Congress of non-Communist world youth in the USA in the summer of 1951 at Cornell University. As the American representative, the

YAC delegation, he noted, would be entitled to about 25 delegates and the federalists were doing everything possible to maximize the number of federalists and supporters of world government in that delegation.

Wallerstein also reported on confidential meetings held among representatives of NSA, UWF, and YAC leaders to evaluate the 1950 congresses held by the International Union of Students and the World Federation of Democratic Youth, as well as the meeting by WAY. The YAC and UWF leaders were prevailing upon USNSA to cooperate in the planning of the WAY Congress in 1951. Another consequence of the Wallerstein memo was the decision by the Board to name Abe Bargman, Curtis Farrar, and James Roberts, World Student Federalist Chairman, as delegates from the UWF Student Division to the World Congress for World Government in Rome in April 1951.

A further manifestation of the inspiration provided by the Wallerstein memorandum was the discussions underway among such student federalists, SDAers, and NSAers as Doug Kelley, Herb Eisenberg, Al Ettinger, Sandy Kravitz, Jean Alexander, Murray Frank, Bill Friedlander, Ken Kurtz, Gene Schwartz, Rob West, Harris Wofford, Peter Weiss, and Bernard Hennessy to organize an independent, private, non-profit agency to promote youth and student participation in technical assistance programs in the Third World—in short, a non-governmental Point Four program (which many later claimed to be the model and inspiration for President Kennedy's Peace Corps).

With the retirement of Phyllis Barnhill as Student Division Director, Elaine Klein was promoted by the Board to this post, and Bonnie Palace took Elaine's post as Field Secretary. One of Bonnie's last acts as chapter secretary was to notify the Board that the Dec. 1, 1950, bank statement showed a balance of under $1,200. She reported that UWF owed the Student Division two monthly payments of $510 through November, which, if paid in a timely fashion, left the Division with about $1,600 as of December 1.

These modest resources were a direct function of the continuing membership decline. Her unofficial membership figures showed a total of 3,870 on October 1 and 4,172 on December 1. Exacerbating this precarious position was the realization that 3,696 of the 4,172 memberships were due to expire on December 31. Clearly, the national headquarters of UWF had no intention of bailing out the students or of even providing some meaningful temporary relief. The received wisdom was that the adult leadership wanted to see the student movement down on its knees as a supplicant; absent such surrender, many adults would, it was felt, have been just as happy to see the students go away so that they would no longer be either a policy "embarrassment" or financial drain.

In January 1951, the official year-end figures were tallied by UWF. The student membership had declined to 4,377, roughly half of the total at the end of 1948. On the adult side, the membership had slightly increased to 35,612. The student proportion of UWF's membership since 1947 had been halved, declining from about 20 percent to under 11 percent. In less than three years, the single most successful component within the American world government movement had risen, peaked, and rapidly declined after merging with the four adult organizations and losing its independence as a student organization.

Whatever benefits were to have been bestowed on the Student Federalists for having merged with adults in a united movement had failed, in any appreciable way, to materialize. The adults, instead of subsidizing the students and allowing them sufficient latitude to learn while doing (as, for example, both the NAACP and Americans for Democratic Action practiced with their youth divisions), had almost immediately begun to impose limits and exercise restraints on the students' policy initiatives and on local student chapter autonomy, while refusing to apply their superior financial capacity to help the students to finance their efforts, their staff, and their publications. Unlike the students, the adults for the most part found it difficult to tolerate serious deviations from the adult party line, and it would also appear they "punished" such deviationism by withholding financial support. In short, they were behaving as if they were parents dealing with rebellious children. Nor did the adults perceive how their own narrow insistence on ideological purity mirrored the behavior of their sworn enemies—the Communists. The students not only appreciated the irony; they joked about it.

## Despite Student Objections, UWF Severs Relationship with *World Government News*

In a rather shameless demonstration of their demand for one unified "party line," UWF's leaders undertook another power move in early 1951 by deciding to sever their relationship with *World Government News*. The official line was once again the need for economizing because of the sharp drop-off in income. Critics of the move pointed out with merit that any effort to start up its own house organ would cost at least as much. UWF's leaders antipathy to

*World Government News* was rather simple; it published objective news and feature articles about the entire world government movement at home and abroad, devoting substantial space to new proposals such as the peoples' constituent assembly. Except for the students, ideologically it was the last important strand of maximalist persuasion within the United World Federalists, which strongly contradicted the views of the majority of the UWF officers and Board. UWF's leaders believed that their members should not be exposed to any notions not in accord with their own narrow consensus. However, they realized how popular the publication was among the rank-and-file, so they kept most of the organization in the dark that the matter would be dealt with at the National Executive Council Meeting in mid-February 1951.

By coincidence, the California state branch was holding its annual convention in Asilomar over the same weekend. Fritjof Thygeson phoned us from New York to reveal the UWF leadership's well-kept secret. As head of the Stanford delegation, I proposed a resolution with the opposite intent, which

*Fritjof Thygeson.*

*Immanuel Wallerstein.*

the state UWF leadership sought to quash and, when this was unsuccessful, to delay until the decision had taken place in New York. During the floor debate, it became clear that most of the members present regarded *World Government News* as the sole outstanding communication from the national office that was "must" reading. The final vote was virtually unanimous in favor of keeping *World Government News,* but the leadership's delaying tactics prevented the results of that vote from reaching the National Executive Council until *after* they had made their final decision to sever the relationship with this vitally important publication. (Needless to say, without the subscriptions automatically accorded every dues-paying UWF member, *World Government News*'s days were numbered.)

The methods employed by the adults in gaining this "victory" and others demonstrated to many students that the Communists were not the only cabal ready to justify any means by the ends. It was a lesson in how to thwart democracy, and it was not lost on many of the students.

## WALLERSTEIN RESIGNS FROM NATIONAL EXECUTIVE COUNCIL, CHARGING UWF WITH INEFFECTIVENESS

On February 23, in a letter to UWF board chairman C.M. Stanley, Immanuel Wallerstein resigned from the National Executive Council. (The text of Wallerstein's letter appears in Appendix 24.) Copying UWF President Alan Cranston and Student Chairman Duke Robertson, Wallerstein wrote that his resignation was not based on the "recent administrative and program decisions" nor on the "many policy issues that have split UWF." Instead, he was resigning because of his conviction that UWF, as presently constituted, is not doing "any effective work to achieve its goals." In his view, two main tasks confront federalists: The first, "which has been UWF's prime concern, is the immediate redirection of U.S. foreign policy along more constructive lines. . . . [in respect to which] UWF has impossibly limited its scope and will not succeed in what it is attempting to do." The second task, which "UWF seems . . . to have no serious inclination to undertake, [is] the long-range and more important one. This is the task of providing a new ideology that can rehabilitate a sick world, the task of proclaiming the doctrine of one world, which is manifest heresy today, and a readiness to accept the inevitable consequences and recriminations."

Wallerstein's letter, which was shared by many student leaders, had a major impact on the thinking of the student leadership. His concluding paragraph was quoted in several places because it began with the statement "I have lost faith in UWF because UWF has lost faith in itself and its idea." Describing UWF's activities as "ineffective," he accused it of a "serious error of omission" by avoiding the struggles for freedom and justice rending the global fabric, and added that, in any event, the accomplishment of the two tasks would require that the structure, premises, and membership be "radically altered."

The next form of pressure by the adults came in the form of a warning from United World Federalist management that, unless the students generated significantly more income from dues and other sources, their staff and headquarters activity would be drastically cut back.

The students response was to undertake an intensive membership drive. Chairman Duke Robertson embarked on a nationwide speaking tour, including appearances before scores of schools and colleges throughout the Mid-Atlantic and upper South. Bonnie Palace concentrated on Pennsylvania and New Jersey. Elaine Klein covered New England, Nonie Clark upper New York state, and Dorothy Weichel parts of New Jersey. Dorothy Weichel, Dee Fraser, and Bernie Hennesey, with help from other federalists, organized the Young Adult Council "Point Four" conferences in Denver, Boston, and Madison. Herb Weiss, having graduated from New York University, undertook a cross-country speaking tour by hitchhiking from the New Jersey exit of the Holland Tunnel, where he was deposited by Elaine Klein and Bill Friedlander, to the Midwest and then to the Pacific states. As the new organizational liaison director, Friedlander extended the division's outreach to scores of national and regional organizations.

In early April 1951, under the direction of Nonie Clark, a three-day foreign policy conference was organized by the students, mostly those from the Princeton chapter. The federalists and their views gained considerable prominence among the 235 students attending from 69 different schools. Among the speakers were Stringfellow Barr, Cord Meyer, Jr., and *Washington Post* editorial writer and advocate of unfettered speech, Alan Barth. A major fundraiser was being prepared for May geared to the parents and friends of student federalists at the home of Princeton student Richard Pierson's parents in Manhattan. Heading the speakers' list was Oscar Hammerstein II.

## STANFORD STUDENT BODY VOTES TO SEND DELEGATE TO 1951 ROME CONGRESS ON WORLD GOVERNMENT

A number of student chapters had been attracting attention by focussing on the April (1951) Congress of the World Movement for World Government in Rome. The University of Chicago chapter was stimulating debate over the structure of a world federal government. At Stanford, I started a small war by proposing, as a member of the student government, that Stanford send its own delegate to Rome. Meanwhile, UWF authorized me to serve as one of their official delegates. Almost immediately after my Stanford proposal was aired, the far right responded, including one student who described world government supporter Albert Einstein as an "alleged" scientist. Even my conservative fellow members of the student government, including the daughters of J.C. Penney and A.M. Gianini, were able to ascertain Einstein's legitimate credentials. Another Congress sponsor, Eleanor Roosevelt, was attacked as a fellow traveler.

Slowly, these excesses helped us to form a bloc within the student government that, with the support of the campus NAACP, Political Forum (almost a euphemism for the ACLU), USNSA, and the off-campus Young Democrats, produced a majority in favor of both the proposal and the funding for it (about $700).

As the prime mover, I was told in no uncertain terms to remove myself from consideration. A subcommittee of the student council then selected a moderate, well-spoken individual who led our campus manifestation of the

*Shane Riorden.*   *Gil Jonas.*

Institute of International Relations to serve as Stanford's delegate. Derek Bok (later president of Harvard) agreed to attend the congress during our spring break. In the event of any illness, Bok was to inform the alternate choice to attend in his stead. The university administration was in an uproar over this unexpected development (as was the Board of Trustees). Dean Laurence Kimpton, later chancellor of the University of Chicago, and grad student Mark Hatfield, the future governor and senator from Oregon, and the university's bird-dog for the politically correct, had a long talk with Bok. When we returned from spring break, we learned he had never used the ticket (claiming illness) or phoned the alternate to take his place. Nevertheless, we had won the fight for the minds of the students—at least temporarily.

Not a single Stanford professor whom we asked had agreed to serve as our faculty advisor. In fact, the faculty as a whole took cover from the increasing right-wing attacks that were now commonplace in California. To remedy this situation and gain a hearing among the faculty, we arranged for Professor Robert Redfield, one of the world's leading social scientists, to be invited to speak at our prestigious Tuesday Night Series. We undertook to raise $500 to fly him from the Yucatan, where he was engaged in a dig, to San Francisco and thence to Chicago. His speech, "A Social Scientist Looks at World Government," was seminal.

After the speech, the appropriate faculty hosted a reception for him (to which none of the student federalists were invited). When he returned that night to my apartment, I asked him anxiously what the faculty response to his speech had been. With characteristic understatement, he looked at me for a moment and said: "None whatsoever. It was as if I had committed a great indiscretion and no one present was going to embarrass me by bringing it up."

Despite intensive student activity, the April 21 meeting in St. Louis of the Student Affairs Board, attended by only five members, heard the dreadful news: The current paid student membership had plummeted from almost 4,400 on January 1 to 1,758 as of April 16. Nor was this decline confined to the Student Division: Since January 1, the adult paid membership had declined by almost 17,000 to 23,060. After transmitting the sum pledged to the World Student Federalists, only $535 remained in the Student Volunteer Fund.

The next message from the adults might as well have been telegraphed. The Board members present, with the help of Student Director Elaine Klein, formulated a worst-case scenario for the student division's forthcoming fifth national convention in June. Key committees were established with a view to exploring the alternatives in policy, program, and projects, with a steering committee representing all views, composed of Dale Hiller, Iowa State, as the chair, and Harry Lustig of Illinois, Wallerstein of Columbia, Nonie Clark, now a volunteer, and me, Jonas of Stanford. The committees were to report back to the convention on the following points:

What should UWF policy be?
What should the program of the student division be?
What should the structure of the student division be?

It was fully understood by the chapter chairmen, as well as the committee members, that the answers to these question could well produce an unmendable schism between the UWF leadership and the students. Within a month, the UWF management notified the student staff that all but one employee would be dismissed by June 30 as a result of the financial vise gripping them. At this juncture, Student Liaison Director Bill Friedlander, no doubt with the knowledge and encouragement of student leaders and staff, began to explore the possibility of merging the student division with still independent and well-financed World Republic, largely a product of Northwestern University in Evanston, Illinois, where Friedlander came from and to which he had belonged as a high school student. He also prepared a concise paper for chapter chairmen, outlining the various options before the rapidly expiring student division.

Short of fighting at the convention to reverse the tide (a most unrealistic option considering the predominance of adults), the options boiled down to accepting the total elimination of any distinctions between adults and students within UWF and remaining within the organization to fight to change its policies and priorities; forming a new student organization together with leaders from other groups to fight both for world government and the issues students regarded as related to the goal, while also retaining UWF membership; or working out an arrangement for a student program with the tax-exempt, non-membership Association for Education in World Government, while retaining membership in UWF. This memorandum was distributed by mail on June 1, exactly three weeks prior to the June 21, 1951, convention of the student division, which followed by one day the scheduled Student Affairs Board meeting to hear the subcommittee reports.

## Showdown at Des Moines in 1951: Adults Reject Student Pleas, and Students Bolt

For most of the students attending this crucial series of meetings in 1951, including the UWF convention beginning on June 22, simply getting to Des Moines in 1951 was in itself a wearing experience. The West Coast members drove for three days, whereas East Coast delegates either drove or took a chartered bus for the better part of two days. There followed at least 72 hours of nonstop debate and in-fighting, during which we dropped off to nap for 15 minutes before resuming the battle. (The student delegates were offered "A Guide to Des Moines" by the editors of *Federalist Opinion*, May 1951. This editorial appears in Appendix 31. The publication's editor-in-chief was Harry Lustig.)

Almost from the outset, it became clear that the UWF leadership could not find its way clear to making any significant concessions. UWF Chairman Norman Cousins, for whom the students had the greatest regard and whose own personal views were close to ours, pleaded with us not to make a final break with the organization. Some of the students sided with him, but the great majority, perhaps tired from too many years of sacrifice, came to the inescapable conclusion that UWF no longer, if it ever did, offered the environment in which they could feel comfortable ideologically. The events developing outside UWF in the student and youth areas offered a great chance for achieving the goals that students seemed to share on the issues we most took to heart, such as economic development, defeat of colonialism, opposition to racism, and support for civil liberties. We wanted a serious campaign to offer compromises with the Soviets that did not dilute Western security and a universal world organization that could be strengthened both to prevent war and to offer some glimmer of the ultimate attainment of economic justice for the world's have-nots.

After it became obvious from negotiations and joint committee meetings in Des Moines that further discussion with UWF would prove fruitless, the students voted overwhelmingly (more than 4 to 1) to adopt an 11-part resolution effectively breaking off with UWF. In the preamble, the students declared that "the present status of the Student Division within UWF, Inc., cannot be continued at this time because of fundamental differences in program and approach between the two groups and the unwillingness of UWF, Inc., to continue adequate financial support of the Student Division," in addition to which UWF's General Assembly "has felt it was unable to meet the minimum

*The crucial third "all-nighter" in Des Moines in June 1951, when the leadership of the UWF Student Division, after having their "demands" rejected by the UWF Board, voted to separate from the United World Federalists and form their own independent student organization. Seated, from left to right, Gil Jonas, UWF Board member and negotiator Jerry Voorhis, Student Field Director Bonnie Palace, Neil Parsons, Herb Weiss, Student Division chairman Duke Robertson, Immanuel Wallerstein, Student Executive Director Elaine Klein, and, with their backs to the camera, Nonie Clark and Virginia Riorden.*

requirements stated by the students in convention assembled for the continuation of a separate Student Division with UWF, Inc."

Based on these reasons, the SD "considers its structural relationship with UWF, Inc. effectively terminated as of December 31, 1951," to be replaced "by a separate U.S. federalist youth organization . . . responsible for its own policies, program, and finances." Expressing the hope that "attempts be made to part from the UWF, Inc., on friendly terms," the resolution pointedly added "that it is especially desirable that there not be a Student Division . . . within UWF, Inc., after the establishment of the new federalist youth organization."

## Students Form Interim Committee to Chart New Course

The resolution thereupon formed the Interim Committee of American Federalist Youth (ICAFY), composed of 21 students representative of the regional and ideological diversity of the student division. Most of these leaders had chapter constituencies. The ICAFY consisted of Dick Pierson, Princeton; Ed Brenner, Yale; Richard Boeke, Yale; Nonie Clark, Smith; Murray Frank; Jack Fraser, Palo Alto High School; Bill Friedlander; Larry Fuchs, Harvard; Dale Hiller, Iowa State; myself, Columbia; Harry Lustig, University of Illinois; Charles Melchior; Virginia Riorden; Thomas "Duke" Robertson, University of Colorado; Fritjof Thygeson, Stanford; Al Upin, University of Minnesota; Immanuel Wallerstein, Columbia; Herbert Weiss; Ted Weiss, Syracuse; Steve Wiley, Princeton, and Elaine Klein (ex-officio). Richard Pierson, an ideological moderate with views closer to those of the UWF adult majority, was elected chairman.

The same resolution charged the interim committee with drafting detailed proposals for policy, program, structure, and finances, to be presented to a founding convention between September 1, 1951, and January 10, 1952. Interested groups of federalists would be invited to discuss the problems that a new organization faced. Delegates to be invited to the founding convention were primarily chapter representatives of the Student Division and "such persons as will be accredited by the interim committee." The resolution called for continuing the present officers, governing bodies, and representatives of the SD in office until December 31, 1951. (Presumably this would retain the same persons representing the Student Division as Young Adult Council representatives as well.)

The rank-and-file membership were to be informed of the decisions taken by the student convention in Des Moines both by returning delegates informing their chapters and by cooperative efforts of the interim committee members with the officers and staff of the present SD. (Elaine Klein, an integral member of the seceding group of students, the one remaining student staff member at that moment in time, sent a complete package and report to every student chapter, student officer, national officer and council member, national staffer, and state branch.)

Most importantly, the umbrella resolution directed the interim committee be guided by Wallerstein's credo statement, which the ten-member Student Relations Committee, seven of them students, of the National Executive

Council had considered on June 22 in an effort to find a way out of the deadlock. (The adult members of the committee were Mrs. Ronald McLaughlin, Chair; Harrison B.W. Hoffman and Oliver Quayle, III. The student members were Ed Brenner, Joan Clark, John C. Holt, II, myself, Neil Parsons, Duke Robertson, and Immanuel Wallerstein.)

That committee had unanimously agreed that the UWF General Assembly was faced with two alternatives: First, grant the Student Division the right to "issue a supplementary credo that it may expand upon but does not conflict with the policy of UWF, Inc.," or second, recognizing both the students' determination to pursue such a credo as well as to act upon world problems if such a right were granted to the students, then "UWF is urged to give its warmest encouragement to those students who feel it incumbent on them to form a separate student organization."

The credo, which so dramatically broadened the federalist ideology, was clearly a major stumbling block in any rapprochement. It was not the only one, however. The steadily dwindling resources of the overall movement, especially those of the students, meant that radical triage needed to be applied to staff, programs, and priorities. The majority of the adults and a small number of students believed that political action, mostly lobbying in Congress and among state legislators for world government resolutions, was the fastest and most likely way to effect a significant reversal of American foreign policy. (The latter would then take the lead in promoting a major charter revision of the United Nations that would restrict its changes to peace-keeping alternatives.) Murray Frank recalls that UWF's retained Washington lobbyist, Ted Waller, was highly influential among UWF's National Board members. At this juncture in 1951, many of the students, however, strongly objected to Waller's narrow description of UWF's goals to members of Congress in order to win their support.

These views were deeply and sincerely held by the UWF leadership, and few among the rank-and-file, except the students, challenged the basic assumptions of this position. Now that funds were increasingly scarce, it logically followed that those programs that did not directly and immediately contribute to UWF's political agenda must be excised so that the political strategy remained sufficiently funded.

Except for a handful among them, these premises were rejected by the students, who more than before wanted the major priorities of UWF to be long-term education and field work to organize chapters and state branches, to which much of the education would be targeted. The students for the most part held no illusions that successful lobbying would produce serious change in the United Nations's powers. Meanwhile, other forces had been unleashed around the globe which, the students believed with equal sincerity and conviction, needed to be dealt with *now* if an informed following was to be mobilized for the long-term goal of world federal government.

It needs also to be admitted that the adults wanted no part of an outspoken policy on racial discrimination and were almost equally reluctant to cope with the pressing issue of colonialism. Admittedly, both complicated the political acceptability of world government for many Americans; the students believed that it was better to face those complications now rather than sweep them under the rug so that they could explode later when more support for world government had been generated. Students also had fewer reservations about linking their movement to a growing global revolution because students more than adults still remembered that the American uprising in 1776 was itself a revolution. Nor were students quite as timid as the adults in combatting the anti-Communist witch-hunt, while placing themselves squarely against the anti-democratic and expansionist policies of the Kremlin. Neither the invocation of J. Edgar Hoover or Joseph Stalin frightened them to the same degree that the adults seemed to be intimidated.

Thirteen students who voted against the decision to separate, led by David M. Stanley of Iowa, perhaps the most conservative individual student in the movement, sought to sabotage the secession by reconstituting the student convention, ignoring the lack of a quorum, and passing a series of "resolutions" according themselves the power originally in the hands of the elected leadership by electing themselves as the officers and Student Affairs Council. Perhaps fittingly, the only Southerner ever to hold the chairmanship of the student federalist movement, Ralph Fleming, formerly of Duke, was elected again as "chairman" by these 13 students. Throughout his tenure, the issue of race had never been raised. The other members of the "student board" were Bob Byrd, also from Duke, David Hanson, Bob Jackman, Ben Reukberg, and Stanley. They later added Dale Hiller and sought to have Elaine Klein fired and replaced by Neil Parsons.

As they appeared before the UWF General Assembly still meeting in Des Moines, each of their efforts to be recognized as the legitimate student leadership in place of those who had voted to secede by the year's end was rejected by the adult delegates. Clearly, the vast majority of the adult delegates in Des Moines still hoped they could find a way to retain the bulk of the student membership. For the time being, Dave Stanley's heavy-handed and colorless efforts to achieve the same goal with the Executive Council were also stymied. The UWF General Assembly decided to leave all of the unresolved student issues to its Executive Council.

## LAST-DITCH NEGOTIATIONS FAIL TO PRODUCE ACCORD

Richard Pierson continued to hope, in his secret heart, that with the correct wording, a modus vivendi could be negotiated that would restore the seceding students to the UWF. The Executive Council appointed six of its members, under the chairmanship of Louis B. Dailey, to meet with Pierson and other ICAFY members throughout July in an attempt to breach the divisions with its own recommendations. On that committee were several liberals whom the students regarded as sympathetic to their cause. The members were Norman Cousins, George Holt, John Kemeny (former SF leader), Mrs. Milton Lapidus, and Courtland Hastings. They fiddled with the board and council proposals, returning in the end to a student council elected by students and a committee of the adult council on student affairs consisting of six adults and four students.

They reaffirmed that there could be no exceptions to the rule that all UWF members and units are bound by UWF's policy. They recommended that UWF pay the difference between the total income from student dues and the actual cost for two salaried staff members; that the students set up their own special fund for contributions over which they would have complete jurisdiction; and that UWF pay the costs of sending every student member a copy of their new house publication, *The Federalist*. For the most part, the ICAFY members had little with which to disagree over these recommendations.

As usual, it was over the subject of substantive policy that the two parted. The committee attempted to rewrite the student credo so that it would be acceptable to the UWF Executive Council at their September meeting. Try as they might—and they took several cracks at it—they were unable to abandon the Cold War mentality that infused their own proclamations. Thus, they characterized the "world revolution for freedom and justice" as underlying the split between the Soviets and the United States and asserted that this split "is in danger of deteriorating into a mere power struggle."

To the students, the U.S.-Soviet schism had already become a major power struggle in which American policy shared some of the culpability. The world revolution, in the minds of the students, stood apart from the struggle but was also being cynically exploited by the Soviets, whereas American policy too often supported the wrong side or the wrong forces, such as Chiang Kai Shek, Syngman Rhee, the racist regime in South Africa, Latin and Central American despots, Spain's Franco, and Portugal's Salazar. The list went on.

The adult committee's rewrite ended with this sentence: "The claim of the Communists to be the only true advocate of freedom must be exposed as false." The student proposal was 180 degrees in the other direction: It called for American foreign policy changes to ally our foreign policy with the world revolution for freedom and justice and to support the aspirations of those peoples fighting for their freedom.

When it finally became apparent to the entire ICAFY membership that no ideological bridge was possible, Pierson drafted a letter from ICAFY to all of the UWF's Executive Council members, anticipating that the student convention would reject the proposal by the Dailey committee. In that event, Pierson proposed a "fraternal" relationship between the new student organization and UWF, in which each member of the former would receive a copy of *The Federalist*, that there be a regular exchange of information and ideas between the two, that members of either organization could attend the other's convention as an observer, and that the Council decline to elect officers for the Student Division after December 31 and integrate into its overall structure any remaining student chapters.

Finally, in what must be regarded as an exercise in futility, Pierson asked the Council to state to the founding convention of the new organization that "it looks with favor on possible affiliation with ICAFY" or its successor.

In September, the UWF Executive Council met in Columbus. Pierson, Ed Brenner, and Charles Melchior pleaded the ICAFY case. The Council, however, by a strong majority rejected a proposal to retain the status quo. David Stanley then amended the report to restore the old structure, which passed handily, after which the entire Dailey committee report was adopted. The Council by a large majority rejected ICAFY's Alternative Proposal, but Stanley's effort to discuss the seating of three ICAFY Council members was ruled out of order by his father, Max Stanley, Council Chair.

## ICAFY Issues Call to Student Activists for New Organization

Over the summer, including an August meeting in Cornell where so many ICAFY members had been involved with the WAY Congress, the ICAFY members met frequently to produce a call for a founding convention of new world

*The World Assembly of Youth (WAY) plenary sessions met daily at Bailey Hall on the campus of Cornell University.*

*Inside Cornell's Bailey Hall, the WAY delegates met in a format resembling that of the United Nations General Assembly.*

government organization appealing to both students and youth under 30 that would have "a broader policy than any American world government organization to date; a program emphasizing education, field work, and the training of leaders; greater chapter autonomy (than that granted by UWF); and a magazine that would "help to build in the United States strong, creative public opinion in favor of measures necessary to create a free, just and prosperous world community." (The full text of the ICAFY call to students and youth to form a new organization appears in Appendix 32.)

*Hanging over the WAY proceedings and the student federalist deliberations in 1951 was the global threat of nuclear annihilation, as depicted by this cartoon from the St. Louis Post-Dispatch that appeared in a federalist publication. (Reprinted with permission of the St. Louis Post Dispatch, copyright 1950.)*

The call revealed that, for the most part, voting representation at the convention would be by invited individuals who pledged to work within the organization, with a maximum of 10 from any single school, college, or community, except that delegates traveling 1,000 miles would receive two votes and those traveling 2,000 miles, three votes. The audience invited were both present and former youth members of the student federalist movement and selected student and youth leaders who shared the overall philosophy of the convention callers. Those most encouraged to attend were leaders from SDA, USNSA, SLID, YPSYL, NAACP Youth, USNSA, the Quakers, and some other religious groups.

The call and subsequent discussions made it clear that the founders were not looking for large numbers but, somewhat patterned after Britain's Fabian Society, able and effective leaders and communicators. The committee chairs were Wallerstein, Policy; Frank, Program; Nonie Clark, Finance; Pierson, Structure; and Virginia Riorden, Convention. Three weeks before the founding convention, Wallerstein was drafted into the U.S. Army.

## American Students Federalists a Major Force in First World Assembly of Youth, August 1951

As already noted, many of the ICAFY leaders had devoted August 1951 to the World Assembly of Youth Congress at Cornell University, Ithaca, New York. Immanuel Wallerstein cochaired the U.S. delegation while serving as president of the Young Adult Council. In addition to Wallerstein, among the 25 elected American delegates were student federalists Mary Coleman (University of Chicago), and Herb Weiss, as well as such friends as Al Lowenstein, USNSA; Ruth Schacter, CCUN; Toby Osos, YWCA; Ernie Howell, YMCA; Walter Carrington and Eleanor Landy, NAACP Youth Council; and later Ted Weiss, of the student federalists. Federalists Elaine Klein and Bill Friedlander were among the 20 alternates, as well as the NAACP Youth Director, Herb Wright; Jeanne Alexander of United Christian Youth Movement; Lacy Thornburg of USNSA; and Fran Potter of YWCA. Federalists Murray Frank, Bill Friedlander, and I worked on the Congress staff, with Gene Schwartz handling some of its publicity chores.

The 400 delegates and observers attending the WAY Congress from more than 50 nations met in plenaries, workshops, caucuses, and hearings to fashion both policy and programs appropriate to a global non-Communist youth

*Four of the student federalist leaders who served as either delegates or alternates on the U.S. delegation at the initial congress of the World Assembly of Youth in 1951: Herb Weiss, Duke Robertson, Immanuel Wallerstein, and Elaine Klein.*

organization. With a few exceptions, the American delegation consisted of students and youth under 30. (The two exceptions were Bernice Bridges, Executive Director of the National Social Welfare Assembly, official sponsor of YAC, and David Davis, who listed his affiliation as the American Association for the United Nations but who was, to the knowledge of all of us, a government figure that most of us believed to be connected with the State Department. All YAC and WAY staff reported to Bridges, who was counseled by Davis.)

We were also aware that government funds were paying for all or most of the congress, including the staff, the lodging, and the food. As the congress progressed, we learned from a number of delegations that their travel had also been paid by an American source, presumably the U.S. government. Two decades later, when the media broke the story that the CIA had funded many of these liberal and socialist non-governmental activities, there was a good deal of conjecture about the role of Cord Meyer, Jr., in the CIA's covert programs of support for anti-Communist democratic organizations, national and international. In respect to the 1951 WAY Congress in Ithaca, however, research indicates that Meyer had not joined the CIA until many months after the 1951 WAY Congress had concluded. He later directed the program that covertly subsidized such democratic organizations. However, insofar as the 1951 WAY Congress and earlier meetings are concerned, the State Department transmitted the funding while "encouraging" some private sources of funding as well.

According to his biography, Cord Meyer, Jr. graduated with his Ph.D. from Harvard in June 1951 and did not begin his CIA career until October 1951, when he took a position under Frank Wisner to implement Directive Number

NSC 10/5 dated October 21, 1951, which assigned to the CIA "the responsibilty for mounting an expanded covert action program," (Meyer, Cord, *Facing Reality,* New York, 1980, pp. 64–6.) He could not have played any role in the original support for YAC or WAY, although he certainly became a significant force within the CIA for clandestine support of liberal, democratic socialist and Christian democratic student, youth, religious, political, and trade union forces as a counterweight to Communist appeals. The Soviet Union, of course, was covertly financing similar pro-Communist or Communist organizations across the globe during the Cold War. The overriding question in respect to covert U.S. financing of democratic forces ought to be: "Was the cause of freedom better served because of this covert support?" A secondary question also arises: "If the covert American support had not been forthcoming, who would have supported these anti-Communist democratic institutions, organizations, and individuals?"

The British, French, Belgian and Dutch delegations, on the other hand, regarded the WAY Congress with a degree of gravity not shared by the Americans. As a result, much older men and women, many of them government bureaucrats or operatives, in the 40 to 50-year-old age group, were seen directing and leading these delegations. It was widely rumored that M. Jousselin of the French delegation was himself a high-ranking officer of the Deuxieme Bureau. As the younger and more idealistic Americans reached out to establish relationships with delegates from colonial areas ruled by the West Europeans, the reaction of the latter's elder delegation leaders became quite apparent. Their job was, in large measure, to hold the colonial delegates, mostly hand-picked, from bolting the colonialist discipline, in the same way they were being "protected" from Communist subversion. As we gradually encouraged delegates from such remote places as Upper Volta, Chad, Ubangi Chari, and Dahomey to take some tentative steps toward independence from their colonial rulers, the colonialists began to play hard ball, taking their toll on the families of the delegates back in the colonies and making the delegates aware of the price. The Americans clearly had much to learn.

From WAY's early days, the American member's position was that each colony would be regarded as a nation-state with the same voting privileges of any other state. Thus, even Puerto Rico was accorded "independent" status in WAY, and when her delegates rose up to demand national independence from the United States, the American delegation also rose to its feet in enthusiastic, vociferous support.

*WAY delegates followed the proceedings with earphones that carried the simultaneous translations in four languages: English, French, German, and Spanish.*

On the other hand, articulate delegates such as Wallerstein, Lowenstein, the two Weisses, Howell, and Schachter were pretty much the match of any of the delegates, regardless of age. The Congress also proved a propitious place for the members of ICAFY to discuss the merits of a new student/youth organization with global interests and to encourage attendance at the founding meeting in October.

Following the conclusion of the Congress, Friedlander and I, among others, led tours of delegates throughout the Midwest, Northeast, and Washington, D.C., during which "liberal" Europeans tested the racial attitudes of the Americans as far west as Detroit and Minneapolis and most especially in the capital of the nation, where blacks could eat with whites only at one governmental cafeteria. (Several WAY delegate tours visited Minneapolis in order to attend the 1951 United States National Student Association convention.)

The heady experiences with WAY through the Young Adult Council proved to be an irresistible lure to a number of the student federalist leaders by the end of the year. Even more costly to the leadership of the student movement was the call of the military draft. Virtually all of the young men who had been too young for World War II were drafted between 1951 and 1954 into the armed services. Among the first was Wallerstein, who later managed to persuade the U.S. Army to grant him leave to attend the WAY Council in Dakar in 1953 from his base in Panama. At the same time, many of the World War II veterans were now reaching 30, getting married, and settling down to careers and family.

# 6

# AS THE COLD WAR HEATS UP, THE FEDERALIST CAUSE COOLS OFF

## EAST-WEST CONFLICTS INCREASE IN 1951 AND 1952

In retrospect, 1951 and 1952 did not benefit from the most auspicious astrological signs: Forces were converging that mitigated against the kind of student movement represented by the federalists. The "dirty" war in Korea did not help. Now the French were facing more violence in North Africa and Indochina; the Communists had seized control of China and were about to intervene in Korea; the Dutch were still hoping to retain control over what was to become Indonesia; the Afrikaners were devising a new form of tyranny over their black and colored subjects that would ultimately be called *apartheid*; Peronism still clung to power in Argentina and through all of Latin American, not a flicker of democracy could be seen. In Eastern Europe, the Soviets were consolidating their hegemony with a heavy hand over the once independent nations of the region, while pursuing a paranoid witchhunt of their own against non-Russian nationalities and political deviationists. Only the Atlee government in Britain was systematically (and peacefully) liquidating its colonial holdings on the Indian subcontinent and in West Africa.

Domestically, the McCarthy era was reaching it peak; progress to eliminate racism appeared stalled in the courts, except for Truman's no-nonsense executive order desegregating the armed services. The U.S. Army in Korea was attempting to carry out that order amidst the fighting. With the rise of the postwar birth rate and the rapidly expanding economic prosperity, fed by federal subsidies to veterans and a massive new national highway program, the prospect of a class conflict within the United States diminished to an historic low.

## AMERICAN STUDENT LEADERS CONVENE IN PHILADELPHIA TO FORM WORLD

Within this context, 80 delegates met at the Chestnut Street YWCA in Philadelphia, October 19–21, 1951, to answer ICAFY's call to form a new federalist youth organization. Ideologically, the participants ranged from Fair Deal Democrats to socialists and pacifists and largely but not exclusively adherents of world federalism. They included several USNSA leaders, including outgoing president Allard Lowenstein, and leaders from SDA, NAACP, SLID, YPSYL, IDPA, World Republic, and several religious youth groups. To the disappointment of some, perhaps many, little new in the way of policy or program ideas emerged from the lengthy debates. By now, the students well understood each other's positions and one's response to those positions. As the convention chairman, I can attest to the fact that the same basic views which had dominated student federalist and allied discussions over the past five or so years were often repeated during this founding convention.

Thus, although the final policy statement might have appeared to be fashioned arbitrarily, with no apparent organizing relationship between and among the major planks, the students present for the most part understood the connections between atomic disarmament; Third World economic development; the eradication of racial bigotry; the need to stand up to censorship, loyalty oaths, and witchhunters; the liberation of nations from Western colonialism and Soviet imperialism; the establishment of world law and enforcement and interpretative institutions as well as a world legislative mechanism; a universal world organization (of independent nations that can freely delegate their sovereignty to a strengthened United Nations or a world government in its place); and a system of representation that does not negate totally the one-man, one-vote ideal. These principles were embodied within the policy statement of the new organization, relating the objective—world government—to the gradually enlarging world revolution for freedom and justice and to the formation of a world community to which world citizens could entrust their loyalties and their lives. (The text of the policy statement and of programmatic material, both of which appeared in the WORLD organizing brochure, is reprinted in Appendix 33.)

The most difficult debate was over the name: The compromise was an acronynm spelling WORLD—World Order Realized through Law and Democracy—not exactly elegant but workable. (One delegate urged us to find an acronym that is easily recognizable, giving as an example IBM. It had not yet been understood by the general culture that such acronyms were valuable only because of millions of repetitions.) That nobody was happy with this compromise suggests that it might have been a good one.

To demonstrate that the student federalists were determined to share with sister youth and student groups power over policy and program, they persuaded USNSA leader Ken Kurtz, a follower of Lowenstein who had a few weeks earlier lost the vote for the president of USNSA by a tiny margin, to accept the paid chairmanship of WORLD and to work in New York City, where he was to attend Columbia's graduate school. The federalist leaders tried as well to persuade representatives from other student and youth groups to accept board positions with WORLD. Only two agreed: Doug Kelley of SDA and IDPA and Dick Carter of World Republic.

### New Student Organization Gains Financial Subsidy

Discussions with Dick Carter had reached a most fruitful point. After attending the Philadelphia convention and reading the policy and program statements, and holding discussions with Harry Lustig on behalf of the WORLD Board, he enthusiastically recommended to his own board that the grant from Mrs. Anita McCormick Blaine of $1,000 a month "until world government is achieved" be transferred from World Republic to WORLD. The recommendation was approved in December, effective January 1, 1952. In addition to this annual sum of $12,000, the new dues schedule called for $5 for regular members, $2 from high school members, $5 from associate members, and $7.50 from couple memberships, each of whom would receive one copy of the projected quarterly publication, the keystone of an educational program that would also hold annual national policy institutes on foreign policy.

The new organization was committed to promoting social and technical assistance programs, including support for Point Four, as well urging individuals to serve with the International Development Placement Association in developmental projects abroad. WORLD promised to help create a closer world community by encouraging American communities to adopt counterparts in the Third World to receive material aid and to exchange correspondence and individuals, as well by persuading Americans to register as world citizens. Finally, WORLD pledged to fight all forms of discrimination and to support academic freedom and student rights, as well as the freedoms of speech, thought, conscience, and association, and to extend these principles to the Universal Declaration of Human Rights.

On the final day of the Philadelphia convention, nine members of the new Board met to adopt formally the name WORLD that had been left in a form of limbo by the delegates, to agree on a salary for the new chairman, to authorize setting up a bank account, and to establish the New York Board members as a temporary executive committee. With Kurtz presiding two days later, the executive committee appointed a styles committee to work over the documents approved at the convention, assigned Kurtz and Frank to investigate closer collaboration with other youth and student groups, divided responsibilities for creating a new office, and instructed Kurtz to see UWF and Alan Cranston. The financial report by Virginia Riorden and Frank was almost bullish with a total of $2,577 in cash and pledges for the two months remaining in the year. (The World Republic commitment had not yet been made.)

An Executive Committee meeting on December 5 revealed that UWF had chosen to ignore the Student Division's decision in Des Moines to abolish itself by seeking to revive the student division and by hiring a new director. Clearly, the plea of poverty three months earlier had been cast aside. The UWF leadership felt so uneasy about another world government organization in the field, after so much energy had been invested in the merger, that they ignored their previous decisions. Now, the adults were determined to pay a price, perhaps not the full price, but a price nevertheless to thwart any possible competition with the new student and youth organization.

Ken Kurtz immediately met with the UWF executive staff to provide them with a complete picture of WORLD's plans, including urging individuals to retain their UWF memberships. WORLD hurried into the mail a recruitment package to all old student federalist members and to those who had shown an interest in the formation of WORLD in Philadelphia and thereafter. World Student Federalists complicated UWF's initiative by recognizing WORLD for membership. Even more complicated was the fact that the American member of WAY—the Young Adult Council—recognized UWF's Student Division as one of its members.

WORLD's Executive Committee recommended the following approach to UWF in subsequent recruitment discussions: Emphasis should be placed on the policy differences between the two groups, as well as on the fact that

WORLD grants its local units far greater autonomy. Second, WORLD's pursuit of former student division members was to generate its own memberships, not to detract from UWF. Third, cooperation with UWF and its chapters was urged by WORLD on every appropriate occasion, including shared mailings with WORLD. Finally, WORLD urged its members to retain their UWF memberships as well.

## First WORLD Board Meeting Organizes New Entity in December 1951

On December 27–8, 1951, 15 of 20 National Board members met at the McBurney YMCA in Manhattan to learn that an office had been leased, more than 70 paid memberships had been recorded, as well as three chapter applications processed, with four in the works and three more expected soon. Stationery and newsletter forms had been printed, membership cards were expected imminently, and a basic organizing piece was expected in January. Pledges of $342 had also been received since the founding convention. WORLD had initiated talks with UWF seeking cooperation; three WORLD members had been placed on the IDPA Board.

Harry Lustig announced that World Republic's Board had met recently and approved passing on their monthly grant of $1,000 to WORLD for one year with no strings attached. After the year has passed, the World Republic Board promised to evaluate WORLD's activities to decide whether to continue the grant. The Board formally approved the bylaws that had been provisionally approved at the founding convention. The Board elected a six-member executive committee composed of Murray Frank, John Holt, Tom Levy, Shane Riorden, Virginia Riorden, and me. After a long discussion, the Board approved a plan to publish a quarterly journal of thought and opinion with an annual budget of $1,400, not including payment to the managing editor.

Programmatically, the Board unanimously approved a proposal by Ted Weiss for WORLD to arrange for the adoption of a town or village in the Third World by an American community with which WORLD would work to provide resources. The Board decided to organize a national advisory committee of prominent people and to employ another staff member, in addition to Ken Kurtz, now that the World Republic grant had been approved. Virginia Riorden filled that post.

## Student Federalists Play Key Role in First Private Overseas Technical Assistance Agency

The Board also decided to work more closely with IDPA. As the first nonsectarian, private, student technical assistance program, the IDPA was founded in 1952 with leadership from Harris Wofford and Stringfellow Barr, the founders of the Foundation for World Government, another entity blessed with the largesse of Mrs. Anita McCormick Blaine. IDPA forged a close relationship with WORLD, which had three members on IDPA's board. Two Foundation employees, Peter Weiss and Clifford Dancer, served as IDPA Executive Director and Chairman. The other officers were Herbert Eisenberg, Vice Chairman (former international vice president of USNSA); Al Ettinger, Secretary (former Executive Director of SDA); and Gene Schwartz, Treasurer (a leader in USNSA, SF, and YAC).

The IDPA Board included former St. John's College President Stringfellow Barr (who in June had made the keynote address to the annual ADA convention, after which the delegates voted for a resolution supporting world government); James Farmer, soon to become program officer of NAACP and later president of CORE; and ADA founder and developmental expert Robert R. Nathan, one of President Roosevelt's noted braintrusters. Among the student leaders were Jean Alexander, Murray Frank, Bill Friedlander, SDA leader Doug Kelley, Sandy Kravitz, WORLD President Ken Kurtz, Frank Parker, Arthur Pratt and USNSA founder Rob West. The advisory board included such giants as ACLU founder Roger Baldwin, philosopher Scott Buchanan, Unitarian leader Rev. Donald Harrington, Howard University President Mordechai Johnson, theologian Reinhold Niebuhr, Quaker leader Clarence Pickett, social scientist Robert Redfield, former Congressman and cooperative leader Jerry Voorhis, and Haverford College president Gilbert White.

At that time, Barr was speaking as President of the Foundation for World Government, which had received its initial $1 million "endowment," when in 1948 Harris Wofford waltzed an elderly Anita McCormick Blaine around a dance floor while seeking her financial support. She is reputed to have "formalized" the grant by writing it on a brown paper bag. In 1949, Wofford transferred his energies to the Foundation, which managed to make a small number of modest grants to world government groups, before deciding to expend its resources on a summer-long visit by its delegation to "study" the kibbutz in Israel as a potential model for Third World development. Among those comprising the delegation were Wofford and his wife, Clare, IDPA's Chair Cliff

Dancer and Executive Director Peter Weiss, Tom Hughes, and Helen Ball. Perhaps the Foundation's most important contribution was the publication of Barr's essay, "Let's Join the Human Race," in pamphlet form.

IDPA's mission was to promote the idea of service to developing nations by Americans with specialized skills who could provide technical assistance and know-how abroad, while living at local wage levels as employees of governmental or nonprofit agencies engaged in development in Africa, Asia, or Latin America. (The text of one of IDPA's most effective recruiting brochures, "Train These Hands," is reprinted in Appendix 39.) IDPA worked with potential employers abroad, who spelled out their developmental needs and technical assistance requirements. IDPA then proceeded to recruit individuals possessing these appropriate skills, temperament, and commitment, providing counseling and training, while guiding the candidates through practical work experiences in social and economic development for a minimum assignment of one year. Thereafter, IDPA made their work experience available through educational programs to the American people.

In its initial year, IDPA provided a highly qualified physicist to the faculty of the University of Indonesia; a group of social workers, as well as a nurse and farmer, to the Ghandi-founded basic education center at Sevagram, India, to assist with village developmental programs; a graduate of a leading school of technology to Nigeria to initiate a science program for a secondary school; and enrollment of two Americans, a Jamaican, and a Canadian in six-month courses on the administration of cooperatives in Nova Scotia, after which each would be assigned abroad.

The highest level of skilled experts were placed by such agencies as the U.N. Technical Assistance Board and the U.S. Point Four program. IDPA's niche focused on the middle-level skills of teachers, farmers, medical providers, social workers, and others willing to engage in the daily routine of village or town life in these desperately poor nations. IDPA's example inspired such major political figures as Senator Hubert H. Humphrey, who called for a government-sponsored program in the 1960 presidential race, and John F. Kennedy, who coopted the idea and actually brought it into being as the Peace Corps in 1961.

It was no coincidence that, during the 1960 presidential races, Tom Hughes, who earlier served as Humphrey's administrative assistant, and Harris Wofford had become Presidential candidate John F. Kennedy's first liberal advisor and supporter. Both Wofford and Hughes had, along with Weiss and Dancer, been

*Helen Dale, upper left, the WAY Secretary General, chairs a WAY steering committee meeting in Berlin. The American committee member is Gil Jonas, extreme right, a student federalist.*

early architects of IDPA through the Foundation for World Government and had participated in the Foundation's study team, which spent the summer of 1950 on an Israeli kibbutz. The Woffords had earlier visited India, including Gandhi's Sevagram center. The entire IDPA budget was funded by the Foundation for World Government.

The IRS compelled IDPA to terminate its existence in 1955 when two right-wing bureaucrats in the IRS tax-exempt section ruled that IDPA was, in the words of Peter Weiss, "an employment agency," not a charity or educational institution, and therefore "not entitled to tax exemption."

Among the many student activists who served in the Peace Corps as program executives were Harris Wofford, Murray Frank, Larry Fuchs, George Carter, Walter Carrington, Gloria Gaston, Bill Haddad, Bill Delano and me.

At WORLD's first Executive Committee meeting of 1952 (Feb. 25), a member reported that UWF had established a policy in which it regarded as unacceptable the membership of any of its national, state, or chapter officers on the Board or as an officer of a group "with conflicting views." The resolution was clearly aimed at WORLD. After the members completed a long but inconclusive discussion on technical assistance and U.S. foreign policy, I reported having been invited earlier as WORLD representative to a far-left (Trotksyite) anti-war meeting directed by Bogdan Denitch and Michael Harrington, which surprisingly sought to woo WORLD's support. Kurtz reported that WORLD had been invited to sponsor a fundraising meeting to protest the death of NAACP field worker Harry Moore in Chicago. The meeting was reported to be disappointing. A vote in favor of contributing to the meeting's expenses was defeated. Jonas's motion to contribute $25 was also defeated, and the staff was instructed to investigate the matter further. However, the committee voted to contribute $10 to YAC's Harry Moore Fund for a program of regional human relations in the South.

The Executive Committee voted to apply to YAC for formal membership. (Meanwhile, YAC "resolved" the immediate problem by having WORLD and UWF's Student Division share the representation.) Motions by Kurtz to lower the membership dues and by me for WORLD to spur the 1952 campaign for president of Justice William O. Douglas were defeated. The Committee named an education committee and voted to explore the hiring of a field worker.

On March 23, an emergency meeting of the Executive Committee was held to reveal that WORLD had been notified that the World Republic grant would be terminated as a result of a communication from the lawyer representing Mrs. Anita McCormick Blaine's niece and heir, Nancy. On March 29, the scheduled Board meeting, for lack of a quorum, became an Executive Committee meeting, during which the Committee made immediate plans to cut back its expenses, including giving notice to Virginia Riorden. Meanwhile, the members agreed to take on a wide range of fundraising initiatives to bail out the new organization. Ken Kurtz agreed to scale back his monthly salary to expenses only.

Because of the anticipated crunch, the meeting tabled a half dozen important matters, although it elected the following to the advisory board: William O. Douglas, Luther Youngdahl, James Warburg, Stringfellow Barr, Walter Reuther, Mark Van Doren, Robert Redfield, Roger Baldwin, Robert Hutchins, Albert Einstein, Edmond Taylor, Frederick L. Schuman, Mordecai Johnson, and Bishop Bernard Sheil. Also unanimously passed was a resolution to recommend to all chapters that they support April 6 demonstrations against South

Africa's racial policies. From this point forward, the organization was operating on an ever-diminishing shoestring: The appeal to Nancy Blaine, who had recently married veterans leader Gil Harrison, proved fruitless. Indicating that she was following her husband's advice, she firmly rejected the appeal to restore the World Republic grant to WORLD.

Gil Harrison, an AVC colleague of Cord Meyer, phoned me during this period to demand that the WORLD Board accept the decision to halt the grant without resorting to legal action. Implying that Mrs. McCormick Blaine was not really "responsible" for her previous actions, Harrison threatened to have her declared mentally incompetent if we challenged his decision. Further, he said that we student federalists would then be responsible for Mrs. Blaine's humiliation. Harrison, on his wife's behalf, managed to "restore" tens of millions of dollars, mostly from recipients of Mrs. Blaine's generosity. With this fortune, he bought a controlling interest in *The New Republic* from Michael Straight, who had exhausted his own fortune trying to sustain the liberal periodical. Harrison then proceeded to force Straight from the picture by terminating his employment. With a sizable share of the remainder, Harrison formed the New World Foundation as a vehicle for funding his pet causes, mostly liberal, under Vernon Eagle's direction. Years later, it was seriously suggested that Harrison, who was friendly with many of UWF's leaders, had been persuaded by them to withdraw the WORLD subsidy without notice, even though the original agreement with World Republic called for two months of notice. The motive for this UWF initiative would have been quite simple: their leaders correctly predicted that WORLD could not survive for long without the subsidy. It is interesting that Harrison either was unable or unwilling to pressure Harris Wofford to "return" another million dollar gift from Mrs. Blaine, which at the time constituted the principal asset of the Foundation for World Government.

## New Federalist Quarterly "World Frontiers" Launched

Shoestring or no, the organization possessed the talent to produce the first issue of a thought quarterly entitled *World Frontiers* under Shane Riorden's direction as editor. The issue was well received both among academics and leaders of sister youth and student groups. The initial issue touched almost all of the bases that had clouded the water with UWF: "Third Force in Asia"

(Wofford); "Where We Stand" on U.N. charter revision (McIntosh); "The Wiggins Case" about academic freedom (Al Upin and Maurice Copeland); another civil liberties case, a Supreme Court decision by Justice Douglas; "As Europe Sees Us" (Frank); "Vishinsky's Laugh" on relations with the Soviets (John Holt), and "Point Four—Another American Tragedy?" (Jonas). (The Friends Service Committee subsequently reprinted the last article in connection with its campaign in favor of Point Four.) Edmund Taylor's "Richer by Asia" was also reviewed. Three of these articles appear in the appendixes: "Where We Stand," Appendix 34; "The Wiggins Case," Appendix 37; and "Point Four," Appendix 38.

In the fall issue, Herb Weiss presented a long analysis of the Middle East crises; Elliot Berg wrote about poverty as Africa's foremost problem; and Don McIntosh explored Marxism and Russian Nationalism as they related to federalist strategy. This issue included a poem by Mark Van Doren, "Let There Be Law." The book reviews covered Alan Barth's *The Loyalty of Free Men* and Hans Morganthau's *In Defense of the National Interest.*

John Holt, who was then NY State Executive Director of UWF and later became one of the nation's foremost advocates of teaching progressive methods of reading and writing to children, faced "The Problem of Russia" in the third issue. The lead editorial dealt with "The Meaning of Revolution," which was followed by George Houser's "Civil Disobedience in South Africa," and John Logue's "Ambassador Kennan and Professor Mitrany," an attack on Kennan's containment views. The most controversial piece was Robert Redfield's scathing "Internal Security in America." Professor Redfield's eloquent article on the threat to civil liberties is published in Appendix 36. The *World Frontiers* editorial, "The Meaning of Revolution," appears in Appendix 27.

The fourth and final issue of the first volume opened with McIntosh's "The Vanishing American Dream." Virtually all of the remainder was devoted to Third World issues, starting with my argument that nationalism was both the temporary force obstructing world federalism but also the necessary ingredient to propel colonial nations into independence, after which they could freely determine whether to join a federal government. Rom Landau wrote about the role of Morocco "Between East and West," and Bruce Cutler reported on events in Salvador; Peter Weiss reviewed deCastro's *Geography of Hunger,* Bill Friedlander wrote of George Houser's *Non-violent Revolution in South Africa,* Virginia de Coningh wrote of Justice Douglas's exploration of

*A social gathering between meetings of a WAY Congress in Berlin includes two student federalists, Immanuel Wallerstein (extreme left) and Gil Jonas (second from right). Seated next to Jonas is Gerrit Kreveld, the leader of Belgium's Socialist youth and later Assistant Secretary General of the Belgian Socialist Party.*

the Himalyas, and Ann Miller introduced us to Ralph Ellison's masterpiece on race in America, *The Invisible Man*.

Thus, in one year of publication, the WORLD leadership and friends had produced a body of thought exceeding that of the adults in five times that duration. Alas, the fourth issue coincided with the realization that alone the organization could not function much longer. After its publication, Shane Riorden resigned as editor and Virginia Riorden as executive director in order for Virginia to accept the post of Secretary General of the World Student Federalists in Amsterdam, accompanied by Shane.

The remainder of the school year and well into the summer were plagued with financial problems. Membership failed to grow in any significant manner; monthly income and expenditures averaged between $200 and $300 for each category. In the late spring, a small policy institute was held in Chicago with modest results. On a policy level, the group struggled to catch up with its dues commitment to the World Student Federalists (WSF) while urging that body to adopt a global viewpoint instead of a European one. The tenacious manner in which the Europeans clung to their colonial empires had become a major preoccupation for the student leadership in WORLD. Wallerstein, Weiss, Frank, and their YAC associates had been expanding their anti-colonial initiatives within the World Assembly of Youth.

Now the American member of the World Student Federalists was telling the British, French, Belgians, and Dutch that they too needed to adopt a world view: "We are world citizens first," the proposed policy statement from WORLD said to the other student federalists. "WSF should do everything in its power," the statement read, "to aid in the elimination of colonialism. WSF should assert the right of every area to realize its potential through development programs, land reform, and reclamation projects made possible by the aid of more fortunate peoples. WSF should support the right of colonial peoples, such as the Tunisians, to a hearing before the U.N. . . . and should condemn racial discrimination, whether it be found in South Africa, the United States, colonial areas, or elsewhere. WSF should equally condemn the mass enslavement found in totalitarian countries." The anti-colonial commitment proved to be a hard sell in Europe, even among federalists.

As the Executive Committee prepared for WORLD's second annual convention, they voted to reduce their overhead by moving from their New York headquarters in July 1952. Harry Lustig was appointed to make the convention arrangements at the University of Illinois in Urbana, where he was a graduate student. In August, the Executive Committee voted to incorporate. Because of diminished enthusiasm, the number of delegates expected at the convention was in doubt. However, $1,500 in contributions swelled the coffers as of mid-August to $1,933.

Held between September 18 and 21, 1952, the convention attracted 21 delegates and less than a dozen observers. It focused mostly on program direction, with one school advocating intensive education targeted to small groups of adherents and the other seeking a greater priority in field work and membership/chapter expansion. Because of the difficulty in attracting quorums for the national board meetings, the new bylaws adopted in Urbana assigned the policy, program, and financial decisions between conventions to a National Executive Committee composed of nine elected members, including the Chairman. I was elected chair of both the board and executive committee. Virginia deConingh (a recent Smith graduate), Don McIntosh, Virginia Riorden and Shane Riorden were elected to the Executive Committee. They then coopted Murray Frank but, under the new rules, were required to leave the selection of the remaining three members to the board. Virginia Riorden was named Executive Director and the national office was officially located at her home in Manumit, Pennsylvania. Wellesley graduate and WORLD member Lucy Law was elected chair of the "reconstituted" Student Division of UWF at about the same time in 1952 and, after graduating, sought to bring the Student Division and WORLD back together. She administered the World Student Federalist office in Amsterdam before the Riordens arrived to take over in 1953. In 1954, she attended the World Assembly of Youth Congress in Singapore.

I was taking Chinese studies at Columbia's East Asian Institute and School of International Affairs, was authorized to receive $20 a week toward living expenses, plus travel costs for field work. I arranged my class schedule with Columbia so that I was finished every Thursday evening and commenced again on the following Tuesday morning. This permitted field trips by car throughout New England and the mid-Atlantic states. McIntosh announced formation of a chapter at Columbia. In October, I traveled to Yale, where a small reunion took place with Wofford, Dick Boeke, Jesse Margolin, and Dick Kelton, with whom I had worked at Stanford. All agreed to undertake speaking assignments and organize a Yale Law School chapter.

## WORLD Launches American Campaign to Free Morocco from French Colonial Rule

I organized a meeting at Columbia in November 1952 at which Professor Rom Landau, a spokesman for Moroccan independence, recounted the history of and arguments for Moroccan independence. The reception was so strong that I wrote scores of student groups, including WORLD chapters, at colleges throughout the nation to sponsor Landau at public meetings. (As Landau later wrote in his book *Among the Americans,* this initiative accounted for most of his public efforts to influence American policy in support of Moroccan independence.)

For the most part, the American press had observed a blackout of news from Morocco during this period, when the United Nations was considering the Moroccan appeal. Anti-French riots were not reported, even in the *New*

*Lucy Law (Webster) departing from New York harbor in 1953 to work in World Student Federalist office in Amsterdam. Lucy was UWF Student Division Chair in 1952.*

*York Times,* a strong supporter of the French, until *after* the U.N. had voted on the issue.

I prepared a brief supporting the Moroccans that was sent to each chapter and to allied student and youth groups. The exercise provided the student federalists as an organization with their first concrete struggle against functioning colonialism. It also opened the door to support for the Tunisians and later the Algerians.

During the same time frame I personally served as voluntary public relations staff for the *Istaquil* [Independence] party of Morocco (headed by Messrs. El Fassi and Balafrej), who were struggling to make their case known at the U.N. without any real resources. Fighting for Morocco's independence, they also supported the ascension of Sultan Mohammed V to the throne as king of Morocco. Until his death in 1999, his son Hassan had ruled Morocco for more than three decades. The full text of WORLD's Moroccan memorandum and the WORLD Board resolution supporting Moroccan independence appear in Appendixes 29 and 30.

I also organized a meeting at Columbia for Professor Z.K. Matthews, the first member of the African National Congress permitted to go abroad. He was teaching at the Union Theological Seminary when he spoke at Columbia to almost 80 students and a young black actor who had just completed his first movie role in "Cry the Beloved Country," Sidney Poitier.

WORLD's National Board on Dec. 20 also adopted resolutions demanding repeal of the McCarran-Walter Immigration Act and the McCarran Internal Security Act, both of which were extensions of the McCarthy hysteria against "Reds." The same Board voted overwhelmingly to call for the end of Senate Standing Rule 22, which required a two-thirds vote to limit debate (i.e., cloture). This rule had enabled Southern bigots to filibuster any civil rights measure until it died. WORLD proposed that a simple majority vote replace the two-thirds rule. The Board voted against urging President Truman to commute the death sentences of the Rosenbergs, who were convicted of handing atomic secrets to the Soviets, and against overhauling the Electoral College.

This Board meeting, the first since I had replaced Kurtz, delved in depth into the declining state of the organizations. I lamented to the Board the lack of involvement or support from most of the past student federalist leadership. With only 9 functioning chapters and a membership hovering around 190, I said, there was simply not enough of an underpinning to sustain a national organization. After having spoken to or written every WORLD member in the northeast plus leaders in other regions, I had concluded that there was an overwhelming lack of interest and initiative. I expressed doubt whether it benefitted WORLD sufficiently to pay me for field work when there was no follow-up to organize chapters or generate memberships.

The Board members split into several viewpoints in the subsequent discussion. McIntosh expressed the view that the older student federalists were suffering from battle fatigue. Lustig defended the present approach, asking only "for more of the same." Others argued that, given the atmosphere of recession and oppression, most youth and student groups were dormant or losing ground rapidly. Murray Frank thought WORLD should not aim for a sizable membership, but the remainder expressed support for continuing and, in effect, hoping "for the best."

Shortly after that meeting, I initiated a series of meetings with SDA National Chairman Sandy Levin (now a long-term Representative in Congress from Detroit) about the possibility of merging WORLD with SDA. Both of us felt that the other's strengths would complement that of our own group; SDA's forte was domestic issues, and the WORLD's expertise was foreign affairs. SDA in 1951 had endorsed world federal government at its convention. ADA, the parent group, had taken the same stand in 1952. The WORLD constituency had the same positions on civil liberties and race relations as did SDA. There was, it seemed, a good deal of overlapping that worked toward consolidation.

## Merger of WORLD and Students for Democratic Action Fails

Then, in mid-March I notified my draft board that I no longer sought conscientious objector status. Within days, the board ordered my immediate conscription. Over the next five weeks, I also lost my two permissible appeals (in record time). I thereupon notified the WORLD board and executive committee of my impending conscription. Harry Lustig was appointed Acting Chairman. In early June, Lustig and Sandy Levin met in Urbana to discuss possible merger, followed by another meeting between Levin and Murray Frank with Ginna deConingh. As a result, Levin came to the June 14 WORLD Board meeting in Chicago to argue for merger. He described the SDA relationship with the adult ADA, which not only subsidized the student group but accorded it a broad degree of policy latitude to take stands on any student matter and any other subject as long as the stand does not contradict ADA policy, almost precisely the terms that the student division had sought from the UWF board. On foreign policy, SDA was generally in line with the positions taken by Justice William O. Douglas. Levin acknowledged that the SDA resolution supporting world government was really an expression of a "long-range goal, although they [SDA] have never devoted much time to specific discussion or action."

The WORLD Board defeated, by 5 to 4, a motion to abandon the merger proposal. It voted, 5 to 3 with one abstention to send two representatives to the SDA board meeting on June 20 to present the merger proposal; if SDA were to respond affirmatively, the joint boards would be established to explore policy, program, and constitutional questions and draft joint reports. Should sufficient consensus arise, the two groups would hold a joint convention in Philadelphia. These motions were then submitted to the Board for approval by mail.

## WORLD—AND STUDENT FEDERALISTS—QUIETLY FADE AWAY

On September 12, 1953, in Pennsylvania, the majority sentiment of the remaining WORLD members was to carry on with what remained of the WORLD membership and not to merge with SDA. What was left of the student federalist legacy were a few dozen diehards, many of them long-term veterans, who were still convinced in the face of overwhelming evidence to the contrary that the American people, especially the youth, could be persuaded in the face of so many obstacles to rally around the world government banner. Most of them had never been enamored of the student majority's insistence on taking strong stands on a variety of interim foreign policy issues, and even fewer felt compelled to declare themselves on either race or civil liberties. Ultimately, their views were not very different from that of the same UWF from which they had parted two years earlier. Eventually, those that remained active rejoined the UWF and its successor, allowing WORLD to expire in 1954 quietly and alone, without any fanfare.

Many of the student federalists remained thoroughly committed to the same values and principles for which they had fought from 1943 to 1953. Placing the quest for freedom and justice over that for peace, more than a dozen segued into the world youth movement through the Young Adult Council, with lasting impact both on their fellow American youth leaders and on those who attended the WAY meetings (many of whom would become leading political figures in their own nations). They participated in American political life either as candidates themselves or on behalf of candidates who at each time and place represented the same commitment—internationalist, anti-colonial, anti-racist, pro-economic development and to those measures that would reduce the danger of nuclear holocaust. They continued to support U.N. charter revision and multilateral approaches to aid and peace. A sizable number became authoritative academics, either with regional expertise or with specialization in international organization and institutions. Several were themselves executives administering aid in the Third World.

Their likes among activist students were never to be seen again in this century. Their combination of intelligence, commitment, idealism, and pragmatism would have been impossible to replicate, because so much of it stemmed from the experiences of the Great Depression, the Second World War, the explosion of the first atomic bomb, and the founding of the United Nations Organization, only to be subverted by the Cold War and the rise of anti-Communist hysteria, against the long historical backdrop of both colonialism and racism here and abroad. The simplistic anti-war protests of the 1960s hardly compared to the complexities encountered by the student federalists in an earlier and less sophisticated age. They proved too powerful to overcome, but not for want of trying.

# *Appendix 1*

## Program Distributed at the Student Federalist Convention

*Affiliate of Federal Union, Inc., Columbia University, New York,*

*New York, March 31st to April 2nd, 1944.*

We Federal Unionists believe that if a free society is to exist anywhere in the world, the United Nations must win a complete victory over the Axis dictators and militarists and establish a just and durable peace.

We believe that an international organization to include all the peoples of the world is essential to peace, to international law and order, and to the economic progress and spiritual development of international organization.

But this is not enough. The ultimate condition for just a lasting peace is a Federal Union of mankind. As the first step toward this end and as the best way to win the war and extend those basic freedoms for which we are fighting, we believe that we, the people of the United States, should lead in forming now a nuclear Federal Union of all those peoples willing and able to accept an international federal constitution, assume and perform its responsibilities, and enforce its bill of rights. We call upon our fellow citizens to join with us in the prompt realization of these aims.

*Federal Union Policy Statement adopted at Peoria Convention November 13, 1943.*

*Appendix 2*

# PETITION—TO THE VOTING PEOPLE OF OUR COUNTRY

We, the young men of America of pre-ballot but early draft age, wish to register our firm belief in the following basic principles for which we will give our lives if need be.

We want complete victory. Mankind cannot exist half slave, half free. In this, the greatest of all struggles for civilization, the United Nations, the forces of freedom, must emerge victorious. We are willing to fight and die so that this victory can be gained.

We want world government. The world today is interdependent; it is a unit and, like any other political unit, requires government. As long as there is anarchy in international relations, ever-recurring disputes will always lead to war. Therefore, we believe the first step toward a better world is the establishment of international government.

We want a democratic world government. World government is not enough. The Nazis demand this too, but theirs is instituted and maintained by force—a world in chains, economic, political, and social. We today must resist this barbaric idea with an even stronger idea: democratic world government, securing decency and freedom for all peoples.

We want a federal world government. A government with power to control only those problems which are international, guaranteeing self-government for national affairs. A government whose laws are made by elected representatives for the people themselves—this is a federal government.

The federal form is the only form which holds power democratically, the only form that can unite the differences in race, language, and nationality that exist in the world. It is a form of government tested and proved under widely different conditions. We believe it is the only form of world government which when established will lead to real peace and security.

These are the principles we believe in and will fight for. But we'll have fought in vain if the American people do not hold these principles in common with us and fail to do their part to put them into action. We must not be unprepared for peace as we were for war. We must win this war for good and all, therefore:

- One, we urge that the American public discuss and determine the form of our future world.
- Two, we ask Americans to press for action in the forming of a federal world government.
- Three, we petition the President and the representatives of the American people in Congress to call at the earliest practicable moment a convention of representatives of all free peoples to frame a federal constitution under which they may unite in a democratic world government.

| Name | Address | Age |
| --- | --- | --- |
|  |  |  |
|  |  |  |
|  |  |  |

*Petition circulated by the Student Federalists during the 1944 election.*

*Appendix 3*

## Vote for Federalists in the Election of 1944
*Election Statement #1 Issued August 20, 1943*

In 1944, America will face the most vital election in its history. On November 4, 1944, the citizens of the United States will vote themselves either a part of the human race or a world apart; either into isolation or into a federal union; either a partner in "man's vast future" or a partner in the other possibility, World War Three.

At that time, the chance for effectively organizing the peoples of the world will be at its highest ebb. Not only will victory for the United Nations probably be well in sight, but everyone will still feel the hardships of war, and perhaps most important of all, the United Nations will still be united. On the other hand, the problems of peace will still be unfaced, and the onrushing picture of a possible epidemic of normalcy and isolationism will darken the horizon.

The political situation will only be described as confusing. Both parties will be split over the issue of world policy. As Senator Ball says, "The real issue is whether we organize the world effectively or not." This issue will split into two parts, isolation or participation in world organization and federation or league. As Representative Will Rogers, Jr. put it, "The first battle to get the United States to participate to the fullest extent in international affairs is just about won. Why, even Ham Fish favors the Fulbright Resolution. The isolationists are backed up against a wall on that question."

The great fight will come on whether we organize the world *federally* or not. On this question, the irate isolationists, the new nationalists, and the loose leaguists are peculiarly united. But so must be the federalists! Federalists must unite and work and study and vote as never before. They must choose and elect the right candidates, or they and the world won't have another chance till the Third World War knocks sense into us.

To achieve federal union from this war, we must elect a federalist president in 1944. If we fail in this, we have failed in everything, and we have failed not only ourselves but the rest of the people of the world.

It looks at this time as if Franklin Roosevelt will be the Democratic candidate. Mr. Roosevelt is not an isolationist, nor a leaguist, nor, unfortunately, a federalist. We believe he is an internationalist, working for a United Nations bureaucracy with no government to tie it together. Mr. Roosevelt's actions agree with his wife when she says that the United Nations should have more and more world conferences, tackling specific economic problems and breaking down economic barriers. This is a far cry from a federal union. This plan is better than mere anarchy, but it is far short of necessary and is playing with dangerous dynamite that will explode in the worst war the world has yet seen.

There are several other democratic possibilities. Henry Wallace, who believes in federation but has shown no plan to achieve it, might possibly receive the nomination. This would be the best choice for Democratic federalists to push on their side. The enemies for federalists to fight among the Democrats are numerous and evident. Wheeler, Gillette, and Farley are the most dangerous and powerful.

The Republican side of the 1944 political fence is both brighter and gloomier with possibilities. There is a large, loud group of world-minded Republicans who are filled with enthusiasm and determination. There are three outstanding Republican statesmen who believe in federal union, who have a plan to achieve it, and who are determined in their program. These are ex–Governor, Lt. Commander Harold Stassen of Minnesota and the Atlantic Ocean, Supreme Court Justice Owen J. Roberts, and U.S Senator Joseph H. Ball. These are three "white hopes" of the whole world. Federalists must see that one of these three men is elected president. Wendell Wilkie believes in world unity but not in world union. He, at present, has produced no plan to achieve "one world." Until he does present a real plan for federation, he does not deserve our support.

Our enemies among the Republicans are widespread and powerful. We all know them: Bricker, Taft, Vandenburg, Nye, Lindburgh, and perhaps Dewey and McArthur.

As students, our position may be confused. We can't vote, but we can influence that vote. This fight for federalism will be so close that any extra help may be the deciding factor. Federalist candidates must receive our complete and active support. These are the statesmen that will count. If it is a choice between an internationalist and an isolationist, we know where our choice must lie, but our real strength must be behind federalists.

In concluding this picture of 1944, let us realize the job before us. As Paul Kern, ex-Civil Service Commissioner, wrote recently: "Just as 1864 ended the efforts of this nation to survive half slave and half free, so 1944 may end the half slave world. And as 1864 preserved a federal union of states, so 1944 may establish a federal union of free nations, based upon the political and military strength of the United Nations and powerful enough to prevent future wars. The candidate who promises this can win. The candidate who, when elected, can achieve it, will be the first president of the world."

Let us see this picture clearly. Let us join the ranks of real federalists and win this election for federal union. This election will decide whether our future is that of fighting another "war to end wars" or of being loyal citizens of our state, our country, and our United Nations government. And so now the responsibility lies with us, the responsibility for our own future. We students face a time of great danger and opportunity. Let us win our future in the election of 1944.

*Vote for Federalists Committee, 9 Heathcote Rd., Scarsdale, New York, drafted by Harris Wofford and colleagues, Autumn 1943. After FDR and Dewey were nominated, most Student Federalists including all of the principal leaders, supported Roosevelt.*

# *Appendix 4*

# THE STUDENT FEDERALIST CONCORD CHARTER

We must make world citizenship a political fact.

Existing governments have demonstrated that they are incapable of preserving peace and protecting human rights in an interdependent world. The atomic bomb blasts forever the illusion that power politics give us peace.

Only a new world sovereignty based on the principles of federalism can destroy the irresponsibility of nationalism while preserving national identity.

The United Nations Organization is not a federal government. It has no authority over individuals; it can only make recommendations to or negotiate treaties with member nations; and it cannot prevent the secession of any nation. It will not be adequate unless it is capable of making, interpreting, and enforcing the law.

Therefore, a federal government must be created, either by calling a convention under Article 109 of the United Nations charter or by international action.

We recognize frankly that the United States and the Soviet Union are the two chief obstacles to such action. Either is powerful enough to take the lead.

To awaken America, Student Federalists will 1) stimulate thinking on the urgent need for federal world government; 2) educate our generation in the principles of federalism; 3) find, train, and organize the necessary leaders; and 4) support all steps which lead to a federal world government.

*Unanimously adopted on February 1946 at Concord, Massachusetts*

# *Appendix 5*

## TO AMERICA'S PUBLIC LEADERS

*Student Federalists, Inc. (letterhead), 299 Madison Avenue, New York 17, NY Telephone: Murray Hill 2-8836, Campaigning for Federal World Government in Our Time.*

| Executive Committee | Standing Committees |
|---|---|
| Clare Lindgren (Univ. Minn), President | Maxine Bublitz (Wellesley), Public Education |
| Dorothy Nessler (Wellesley), College Chairman | Jane Fisk, Public Relations |
| Wilder Crane (Wisconsin), High School Chairman | Charles Nelson (St. John's), Study Courses |
| Stephen Chadwick (Yale), Veterans Chairman | Cushing Niles (Wash. D.C.), Graduate Service |
| Foster Parmelee (Okla. A & M), Treasurer | J. Warren O'Reilly (CCNY), Finance |
| | Mary Ellen Purdy (Scarsdale), International |
| | Joseph Wheeler (Bowdoin), Camps & Institutes |

On the inside pages of this folder are printed nine questions on foreign policy and world government. These are the questions we are studying and debating. These are the questions we believe will prove to be the most crucial ones facing our generation. We hope you will take the time to answer the poll and return it to us.

Read what Justice Owen J. Roberts says about us:

"Student Federalists is the most significant, effective developer of sound public opinion of our time. If it can persuade the majority of American youth to join in discussing and forming sound opinion respecting the obligation of everyone toward the people of the world and toward world order, it will have done a work unparalleled in history."

We believe the issues raised here will become the great popular issues in this country. This poll gives American leaders in government and in the fields of public opinion an opportunity to clarify their positions and to place them before the public.

---

*For Public Information on the Opinion of America's Public Leaders*
## QUESTIONS ON FOREIGN POLICY AND WORLD GOVERNMENT

1. Do you believe the United Nations as now constituted is capable of establishing lasting peace?
2. What do you advocate for peaceful world control and development of atomic energy?
3. Do you support the goal of a federal world government? If not, in what objective do you place your hope for world peace?
4. What do you consider the chief obstacles to achievement of world government?
5. Do you believe the United States should make the goal of world peace the central core of our foreign policy? If not, what should be the chief purpose of America's world policy?
6. What points do you advocate for our present foreign policy?
7. If you want world government, what steps do you advocate toward its achievement? (Please check one or more.)

( ) Supporting and gradually strengthening the United Nations.
( ) Working to call a New World Constitutional Convention under Article 109 of the United Nations charter.
( ) Calling a separate World Constitutional Convention outside of the machinery of the United Nations.
( ) Others: Please list.

What steps will you take in supporting or initiating measures directed to the establishment of world government?

Do you support the Student Federalist program as outlined in our policy statement printed on page 4 of this folder? [Ed. note: See Appendix 4]

Do you have any further comments or suggestions?

*This document was distributed in 1946.*

# Appendix 6
# Marxism and Federalism

by Thomas L. Hughes*

*This article was originally written as a lecture, delivered at the Student Federalist Institute in Chicago in the fall of 1946. We are very grateful to the Institute and to Mr. Hughes for allowing us to print the lecture.*
*The Editors,* Yale Political Journal, *1947*

Why am I particularly interested in the relationship between Marxism and Federalism? I am a federalist precisely because I am primarily concerned about economic and social problems. I have come to believe that no long-range steps may be taken toward a better economic and social life so long as the political relations between nations remain unregulated. Federalism for me is the only rational political system which has a chance of harnessing the extravagances of nationalism and absurdities of absolute sovereignty.

Economic and social problems will be ultimate factors in determining the survival value of a world government once it is achieved. But the solutions to these problems cannot be realistically attempted until we have better political forms through which we may operate. Federalism as a political form is crucial at the present point in history because it alone can act as a catalytic agent which will halt the cut–throat competition of nationalism in favor of a rational approach to world affairs. We are very much in danger of stumbling into suicide under the sponsorship of atomic bombs, and only a political readjustment which spells some measure of physical security from the atomic threat can stave it off.

*Abridged by Virginia Riorden in 1999 for this book.

## Traditional Marxist Doctrine
*Dialectical Materialism*

Doctrinaire Marxism, if there is such a thing, depends—as do most doctrines—on what its individual or collective adherents want to make of it. "Marxists" are inordinately jealous of the right to interpret their master as they see fit. You remember the story of Harold Laski's lecture at the New School for Social Research in New York, when he found himself heckled by communists. When the non-communists in the audience started to hiss the hecklers, the professor from England retorted: "Leave them alone. After all, we are all followers of Marx—they in their way, I in his."

Marxism, in any case, was a philosophy of history and a critique of capitalist industrialism and 19th century political economy, rather than a prophecy of future socialist policy. Marx was far more concerned with the struggle than with the goals toward which it tends. [He did not] attempt to forecast in detail the nature of a future socialist community.... A new productive system was bound to involve new institutions, which no one could anticipate. Marx was emphatic that the future must settle itself.

The great attempt of his life, however, was to proclaim the broad outlines of the forces and trends which would produce that future. Closely knit to Marx's analysis of capitalism as an economic system, and integrating that criticism as a philosophy of a history and life, was the Marxian dialectic....

It was the concept of a dialectical materialism that distinguished Marx from his "Utopian" socialist predecessors, Fourier, Proudhon, Owen, et al., and that gave Marxist doctrine its cherished slogan, Scientific Socialism....

Marx borrowed the outline of his philosophy of history from Hegel's triadic law as the basis of all-historical growth and progress: thesis, antithesis, and synthesis. Historically, Marx says, economic phenomena predominately determine all historical facts and make it possible to explain them. The "class struggle" is the motive power which underlies the historical process, and it is to the impulses which are at work in the satisfaction of economic demand that significant changes are to be traced. The economic class which controls the "forces of production" in a given economic era—no matter whether it be Asiatic, Classical, Feudal, or Capitalist—calls forth its antithesis, and as the "forces of production" advance to new stages, a portion of the former "underdog" class rises to unseat the oppressors, and a new class society (synthesis) appears. The crowning feature of the present capitalist era, however, is that class conflicts have been simplified; only two hostile classes remain face to face, the bourgeoisie and the proletariat. By his analysis of capitalism, Marx concluded that the inherent trend of the economic forces in capitalist society contained "contradictions" which would set the stage for socialism. He anticipated a concentration of capital into fewer and fewer hands, a consequent growth in the size and poverty of the proletariat, and then with a constantly increasing cycle of capitalist wars and industrial oppression, the class struggle would break into the open, the proletariat would throw off its masters, and since no other class element—no antithesis—would any longer be present, a "classless society" would ipso facto have been established.

For Marx, the economic foundation thus determined legal and political institutions, literature, religion, and art. This was all "superstructure," dependent in the main on the economic substructure ("Unterbau"). Political conflicts are only the superficial evidence of the class conflicts that have existed at every epoch of history. Superior individuals have been able to play prominent roles, but for the most part they have been only unconscious marionettes acting out a drama of whose real significance they were ignorant.

Immediately, however, we arrive at the dilemma, or the apparent dilemma, which has vexed followers of Marx from his time to ours. The crux of the controversy has always been: How can a system, which relies on historical inevitability, leave any room for ethical aims? Marx both *wanted* socialism and tried to demonstrate that it was *inevitable*. But is there any virtue in desiring and working for the inevitable? How can socialists demonstrate the superiority of one ideology over another?...

A socialist idea is not firmly grounded, [critics say], if it does not accept at the very beginning the possibility of non–realization of its goals. The only characteristic of socialism which can make it my duty to work for it is its goodness or its betterness to any alternative, not its "wave-of-the-future" type of dialectical inevitability.

There is no escaping the fact that both Marx and Engels deliberately tried to overemphasize the economic and systematic approach to history and deliberately overlook "opportunities" to do justice to other factors. Why did two men whose minds were certainly not simple deliberately weight their arguments so that their proletarian audience would very probably accept dialectical materialism as a simple dogma of faith? The answer itself is to be found in the historical setting in which Marx and Engels worked.

The mundane and practical motives, so frequently overlooked, are referred to in Otto Ruhle's biography of Marx.

Marx wrote at a time in history when:

> ... nothing but an act which would bring encouragement would save the imperiled cause of the proletariat. A treatment that would overcome the sense of inferiority, a method of education that would re-establish self-confidence and revive self-esteem, was essential. The proletariat needed a miraculous energy that could only be inspired by a great conviction. Then came Marx and supplied the inspiration. He made the class struggle a law of historical evolution and depicted socialism as the necessary and logical outcome of that struggle. By placing his doctrine at the disposal of the proletariat, he provided this class with the means for compensating its social sense of inferiority through the practical application of the knowledge thus gained.

For Marx's purposes, his deliberate choice of emphasis was admirable: His brilliant economic analysis and the scope of the dialectic were monumental contributions to economic and social thinking. On another level, a more simple faith in the historic necessity of their task gave new life and mass drive to the workers of the world, upon whom Marx counted to carry his ideals to fruition. He knew, however, that his real problem was not what values to uphold, but how to make them fruitful in history. The doctrine of dialectic materialism then was not only a new and spectacular analysis of history which Marxists still consider to be valid, but also a campaign tactic for world revolution. Both considerations are of tremendous importance still in socialist thinking, and an understanding of both is essential for a federalist approach to Marxism.

*Marxist View of War*
[The Marxist] attitude toward war is of course directly significant for federalists, as well. According to the dialectic, the state reflects the class struggle and is therefore merely a convenient tool of the dominant economic group. Since it is dependent upon class control for its usefulness, the state "withers away," in Engels' phrase, once the classless society has been firmly established....

Nationalism is therefore the prerogative of the bourgeoisie. *The Communist Manifesto* proclaims without hedging: "The workingmen have no country. We cannot take from them what they have not got." War, as an instrument of state policy, is therefore by definition an instrument of capitalist policy. It is remarkable, however, that the theory of war in Marxist literature stops at this dialectical definition. Lenin's later additions on imperialism as the "last stage" of moribund capitalism add little theory to the simple Marxian assumption that war is an instrument of capitalist competition. One is struck by the superficiality of Marx's ideas about war. "However, the war may end," he wrote during the Franco- Prussian War, "it has given the French proletariat practice in arms, and that is the best guarantee of the future." The proletariat has by now had plenty of such practice; our problem is how to get less of it!

Engels, likewise, after a remarkably accurate prediction of the nature and even the lineup of World War I, added:

> . . . only one result is absolutely certain: general exhaustion and the establishment of the conditions for the ultimate victory of the working class. The war may perhaps temporarily push us into the background, but when you set free forces which you will be unable to control, things may go as they will: At the end of the tragedy, you will be ruined and the victory of the proletariat will either be already achieved or at any rate inevitable.

Yet now after two world wars, the victory Engels expected appears to be all too *evitable.* Capitalists may have "set free forces" which they are "unable to control," but the socialists are equally unable to control them. The "general exhaustion" which Engels mentions is exactly that—general, including the proletariat. Such mechanistic reasoning sounds fairly fantastic a half century after it was written.

A similar Marxian illusion is that the victory of one or the other side in a modern war may advance the cause of socialism. See, for example, the extraordinary letters Engels wrote to Bebel in 1891 on the proper line to take in the war he saw materializing between Germany and France–Russia. He reasoned that because German Social Democrats "have the almost absolute certainty of coming to power within ten years," a German victory was essential:

> The German victory is therefore the victory of the revolution, and if it comes to war, we must not only desire victory but further it by every means. We must demand the general arming of people.

How may such, almost frivolous attitudes be excused? Only when we consider again the historical period in which Marx and Engel wrote. Marxism has never had a well-developed theory of war precisely because its founders were not pressed by circumstances to view war as a major problem. In the century after Waterloo (1815–1914), there was only one war in Europe between first–class powers—the Franco-Prussian War. Since the chronic world warfare of our day was utterly unknown to them, the theoreticians of socialism devoted their attention mainly to the internal class struggle and failed completely to work out a theory of the political significance of war. The gap remains to be filled.

Writing in the atmosphere of Victorian optimism and Darwinian evolution, Marx and Engels were inbred with the twin theories of their day—the perfectibility of man and the inevitability of progress. Far from being challenged by the Marxists, the idea of Progress was taken over by them, being used, in fact, as a psychological prop for Historical Materialism.

Leaving, now, the theoretical aspects of Marxism which have the greatest bearing on the issue of world government—the dialectic and the concept of war—let us review the practical efforts to achieve Marxism in this century.

## Practical Application Of Marxism
*International Socialism before 1914*
Before World War I, the point could be made that nationalism was the great "vertical" force that tended to level down and unify social and economic groups within a country (as it surely does even now), while collectivism, including all the schools of Marxism, was in theory a horizontal force cutting across boundary lines and national allegiances. The theories of Marx and Engels accepted as a fundamental proposition an international unity of the masses, particularly of the industrial workers. The Marx-Engels Manifesto, inviting the workers of the world to unite, encouraged capital to unite also as Marx had predicted it would. And as predicted, capitalists generally established their lines of defense on national grounds. The reasons were obvious. It assured them control of the army and armaments. It enabled them to appeal to the middle classes who are always the most rooted element of the population and the most anxious for protection against any outside danger, real or imaginary. Finally, nationalism was the chief apology for a close tie-up between industry and government. At the turn of the century, Marx and Engels could have concluded with reason that the "class struggle" was pivoting in great measure on

the fundamental opposition of nationalism, identified with the interests of the privileged groups, and internationalism identified with the aspirations of the workers.

The great test of international doctrinaire socialism came with the war of 1914. There was no real assurance up to that time that the evolution of the class struggle, as defined by Marx, wasn't taking shape according to prophecies. Socialism was the only doctrine that seemed prepared to launch a frontal attack on the growing peril of extreme nationalism and to offer an international solution as an alternative. The possibility of a socialist strike against war was not to be discounted in the first decade of the century when socialists were rapidly increasing in numbers and political prestige everywhere. But German Socialists, the most powerful of all, goose-stepped off to war for the fatherland as soon as the Kaiser proclaimed from the balcony of his Berlin palace, "I know no parties; I know only Germans!" Socialists in all the warring countries rallied to nationalist banners, and the Second International collapsed. Nothing like it has ever been revived.

For three decades before the war of 1914, the Second International had been split apart on tactical grounds. The Continental and British socialist movements generally followed the policy of the German leader Bernstein, called "Revisionism," believing that the class struggle could be resolved through liberal, parliamentary practices, the organization of mass socialist parties, and election to office of socialist candidates. Vehemently opposed to the Revisionists, and advocating what he claimed to be the true Marxian doctrine of violent revolution, was Lenin, who with his determined group of kindred spirits carried on a sensational literary and propagandizing campaign from various European havens, notably Switzerland.

*The USSR*

When in 1917 Lenin performed one of the great tactical successes of all time and astutely engineered the Bolshevik revolution, Russia assumed the position of advance–guard of the world revolution. Lenin saw the function of the new communist state to be an active interference in Europe on behalf of revolutionary parties which he believed to be on the brink of success in Germany and Hungary. He stated his position frankly:

> We live not only in a state but in a system of states. It is inconceivable that the Soviet Republic should continue to exist interminably

side by side with imperialist states. Ultimately, one or the other must conquer. Pending this development, a number of terrible clashes between the Soviet Republic and the bourgeois states must inevitably occur.

As other revolutions abroad gradually failed to materialize, and civil war and economic pressures at home forced a retreat in strategy, Lenin was compelled by events to retract the announced ambitions of both his economic and foreign programs. Admitting the dictates of expediency and opportunities which made him the great tactician that he was, Lenin in 1921 spoke of his policy retrogressions as "one step backward in order to take a leap forward."

Under Lenin's successor, Stalin, however, the step backward was frozen at least for the short-run future, and the leap forward internationally was indefinitely postponed. Under the watchword of "Socialism in a single country," Stalin in 1926 objectively sought to revive the militant tradition of Russian nationalism as a bulwark of state policy toward dissident peasant and personal–political elements in the USSR. The direction and control of the Kremlin over the Comintern, or Third International, continued, but it was maintained more as a springboard for future action than a cardinal effort to return to Lenin's active attempts to foment world revolution.

The conclusion is almost inescapable that circumstances dictated Stalin's course. At any rate, the combination which resulted—*Russian Communism,* with the double implication of that phrase—uniting, as it did, the two most explosive forces in world politics, nationalism and collectivism, has become a uniquely dynamic force in world affairs. One could have predicted decades ago that whoever conducted Russia out of its backwardness would have influence on a world scale. But what could scarcely have been surmised was that the revolution would place at the helm of this potentially powerful national state men who were committed to the most starkly realistic doctrine of internationalism that modern times have conceived. For whatever reasons and for whatever ends, it is clear that two such dynamic forces, once merged by circumstances, would inevitably be merged for matters of international policy.

Thus today, Russian foreign policy is conducted under the most happy and convenient theoretical conditions imaginable: a nationalist-expansionist program objectively identical with the interests pure Russian nationalism would have under the Czars or any bourgeois exploiters, coupled with the unique advantage of comradely support from enthusiastic proletarians the world over, who have been convinced that the Stalinist line is true, that Russian and Marxian interests coincide.

To some of us, international communism seems to be the tool of Russian nationalism, but the very phenomena that support this view convince the faithful that Russian nationalism is the instrument of world communism. When Stalin refers in the same speech to "Capitalist encirclement" and our "our motherland," one can conclude that for his intentions, whatever they may be, the Marxist ideology and the ambitions of the czars are harmoniously blended.

But the two facets of Soviet strength are not an unqualified success. Because the USSR's nationalist success has outweighed its practical achievement of communism, a growing number of liberal critics abroad, delving deep into the ranks of the proletariat, are becoming increasingly hesitant about supporting a nation whose economic experiment, alone, they would have applauded. And what we have just now said is already the beginning of an evaluation of Marxism's current significance in reference to major world problems.

### Marxism's Current World Significance
*"Right Versus Left" in 1947*
The awkward thing, from a Marxist standpoint, is that if we look at the world in the terms Marxists think are decisive—that of shifts in class power and economic institutions—the outlook is promising. All over Europe, in Britain, and Asia, the bourgeoisie is on the run. From the viewpoint of the significant factors that Marxism stresses, the world should be closer to socialism today than ever before. On the contrary, however, the course of Marx's historical dialectic seems to be leading us *away* from socialism as Marx conceived it. Reforms are being made but often go hand in hand with a moral barbarism and threats of world annihilation.

As Dwight Macdonald, who calls himself a socialist, wrote in *Politics* recently:

> We are off balance. The process on which Marx banked so heavily is being brought about from the top, not the bottom, and is directed toward nationalism and war. The result is not the liberation of the masses but their even more complete enslavement.

For one thing, we need a new political vocabulary. "Right versus Left" has become meaningless. A force has arisen to blur the distinction and make most political antagonisms academic. Recall some recent headlines:

A putsch by fascist-minded Army officers overthrew the former conservative regime in Bolivia, backed by native big business and the U.S. State Department. The revolutionaries were anti-U.S.A., anti-capitalist, and anti-semitic. When they took power, they shot one of the "big-three" tin magnates, passed Bolivia's first laws favoring the exploited Indian miners, and strengthened the Army. Currently in Argentina, we see the pro-Nazi, dictatorial Army boss, Peron, leading a working-class movement against the bourgeoisie, decreeing enormous wage advances, trampling on property rights, and getting himself overwhelmingly elected president in the first honest election in years. The opposing candidate, Tamborini, was backed by Argentine big business, the U.S. State Department, and the *Nation* magazine!

It is revealing to compare Left-Right attitudes in the two world wars. In World War I, these attitudes were fairly consistent in themselves and cleanly opposed to each other. The Right was chauvinist and favored the war for the most straight-forward economic motives. The bulk of the Left, generally pacifist and anti-imperialist, submitted to the "necessity" of war in 1914 and 1917, since it was unwilling to take a revolutionary anti-war stand. After that war, the Right pressed for a Carthaginian peace and emphasized the collective responsibility of the German people, while the Left tried to lighten reparations and to limit war guilt to the German ruling classes.

The situation in World War II was much more complex because in the interim two phenomena had arisen which cut across the old alignments: Hitlerism and Stalinism. The Franco-Anglo-American bourgeoisie had seen the Kaiser's Germany as simply an imperialistic competitor, but towards Hitler, they had an ambivalent attitude. Insofar as he was a powerful competitor, they opposed him, but they supported him insofar as he had created an "orderly" society by liquidating his own Left and insofar as he seemed to be preparing war against the U.S.S.R. They put up with his aggressions, therefore, and failed to arm against him. On the other hand, they didn't trust him enough to join him in a war against Russia, as the Marxists (and evidently, Hitler, too) had supposed they would. They correctly saw that Nazism was something new and dangerous to them, not just an extreme form of monopoly capitalism. So they were unable to act at all.

The Left was also paralyzed by the cross-currents set up by events of the 20s and 30s which didn't fit into the old Left-Right pattern. On the one hand, the Left opposed Hitler for the same reasons the Right favored him and demanded "collective security" and a firm stand against Nazi aggression. At the same time, the disillusionment with World War I was still enough to make its general feeling about war negative; its whole tradition was anti-war. When war came, however, it was the traditionally war-hating Left which was enthusiastic, while the traditionally bellicose Right went into the fray with much the same reluctance the Left had shown in World War I and for many of the same reasons: They could see no way to avoid it, and yet they felt that their class interests would not be advanced by it.

The same reversal may be observed in postwar policies in the United States. The so-called Right favors a relatively "soft-peace," partly because it never believed in the war as an anti-fascist crusade and partly because it hopes to make Germany a barrier to Russian advances; the Left insists on the collective responsibility of the German people and presses for vengeance.

[Thus the] distinction between "Right" and "Left" becomes more and more blurred. There are antagonisms between Right and Left, it is true, sharp and sporadic battles. But these clashes are on secondary issues; they do not affect the trend towards war and national regimentation.

*Nationalism and War: A Marxist Dilemma*
Marx spent most of his life investigating the "laws of motion" of capitalism. This investment was justified by his assumption that if he could show, as he did in his dialectic, that these laws were working to destroy capitalism, he had also demonstrated the "iron necessity" of socialism. Yet (1) the working class has "come of age" without advancing us toward socialist goals, per se; (2) a great shift away from capitalism is taking place without advancing us any further toward those socialist goals; (3) modern war, far from offering "revolutionary opportunities" for socialism, is creating new conditions which make the struggle for socialism even more difficult.

Marxism regards war as a means to an end, a method of advancing class interests. Now, however, war has become almost an end in itself. Instead of advancing certain interests at the expense of others, war tends more and more to make the situation of the victors indistinguishable from that of the defeated, as in Europe today. More than one powerful war-making apparatus, with economies and social institutions deformed to support them, and the quite justified fears of every nation of attack from every other—these factors are the key to the problem, rather than the expansive needs of capitalist imperialism or the "contradictions" between Soviet collectivism and American free enterprise.

Furthermore, in recent years, the capitalist, motivated by rationalistic profit and loss considerations, fears the risk of war much more than the military man, the government official, or even the idealistic liberal. The critical corollary for Marxism is that modern warfare is so insanely destructive that the seeds of a new order are wiped out along with the old.

Nationalism now bends the class struggle to its own ends. Under the war system, socialists should not be the last ones in the world to recognize that their ideological enemies, the "ruling class," can monopolize more and more the will of the masses—not just in time of hostilities, but continually. They may use the appeal for unity against outside attack, and the more portentous the threat, the greater the appeal. This weapon is powerful psychologically because it plays on very deep fears and loyalties. It is powerful too in rational terms because it is perfectly true that national defeat is catastrophic for *all* classes.

It is true that Mussolini was demagogic when he transposed the "class struggle" theme by speaking of "proletarian nations" like Italy whose hope lay in rebellion against "bourgeois nations" like England, stifling at the same time his own Italian working-class movement the better to fight what might be demagogically called the "international class struggle." But he was not *just* being demagogic. Nor was Hitler when he joined those hitherto warring concepts "national" and "socialism." Everywhere, the class struggle *inside* nations is yielding to struggle between nations so that the main conflict now is between peoples and not between exploiters and exploited. You remember Emery Reves' pithy analysis in *The Anatomy of Peace:*

> England and Germany were both capitalist when they went to war. Nor was the United States Communist when it was attacked by Japan. The one major cause of the development of the Soviet Union into a powerful centralized state and not into a 'withering away' of that state, is that there were *other* sovereign power units in existence outside the U.S.S.R. and that as long as there are *several* sovereign power units, several national sovereignties, they are bound to conflict, no matter what their internal economic or social system.

The truth is that neither capitalism nor socialism can work comfortably within the nation-state structure. Even the ranks of the Communist International are not immune. For example, the Italian Communist Pietro Togliatti, like most Italians, has opposed the claims of Communist Marshal Tito of Yugoslavia for Trieste and Venezia Giulia. The French Communist stalwart, Jacques Duclos, has supported, like General de Gaulle, France's demand for international control of the Ruhr, which is opposed by German Communists. The more responsiblity and influence the Communists have gained in Europe, the less they have tended to present a united front in world affairs.

The nation-state system constantly works against the tendency toward rationally planned economics within communities. It is good Stalinist doctrine that the growth of socialism in Russia has been frustrated and stymied by threats from abroad. The hope that a perpetuation of economic and political chaos in the world might eventually set the stage for proletarian revolutions elsewhere, which would thus reduce the dangers Russia fears from abroad, had proved to be a risky, if not forlorn, hope. Can Russia herself afford the risk involved in delaying world controls over potential instruments of world destruction, particularly when other nations, harried by the same threats and suspicious of Soviet motives, may seek other than peaceful means for settlement as well? Indeed, the reverse aspect should give the Soviets equal pause: Let them remember that the so-called "Communist menace" bore a very direct influence on the rise of fascism in Germany and Italy, and the rise of fascism can hardly be twisted to the advantage of the proletariat anywhere.

We are living in an age of sub-rationalism. If I were a Marxist, I would have been convinced long ago that economic and social questions called for *rational solutions*. Marxism, though it inspires fervor and devotion, is formulated on *rational* precepts and must rely on them for enduring validity. Marxism today is caught, just as the world is caught, among the *irrational* forces of conflicting nationalism. Everything we have in the way of trends gives warning that Marxism, no matter where, cannot work for its Marxist goals so long as nationalism remains as an unbridled force that threatens to subvert our economic and social futures or destroy these futures entirely by physical annihilation. If I were a Marxist, in the interest of my creed I would want to clear the international field for an economic approach to economic problems. This is impossible as long as economists must clear their plans through war departments.

**Marxists and Federalists: What Common Ground?**
*Marxism—Reactionary?*
By endeavoring to cling to the absolute superficialities of a 19th century attitude toward war, Marxists are defeating the best in their heritage of critical

thinking. They are committing an error which Marx, Engels, and Lenin never would have duplicated: They blind themselves to changed conditions and critical contemporary problems. Marxists today are in danger of becoming reactionaries. The dialectic left no room for a force strong enough to kill historical materialism or turn it into new channels. Yet nationalism has done precisely that. It has turned the dialectic back upon itself and is steering proletariat and bourgeoisie alike off to destruction. Between federalists and Marxists there ought to be a reconcilable mutual faith in a resounding call for a new society.

*Practicality of a Federalist Proposal*
1) Ideological Hindrances
Ideological hindrances to an offer of federalism from the west to Russia, while I believe they are mostly psychological, nevertheless raise the problem of a difficult strategic retreat in the minds of Russian Marxists. Superficially, it might seem to them to be the easiest thing in the world for the United States and Britain, for instance, to make a world government proposal. Their logic would go as follows: In making such an offer, the Western "Allies" have nothing to lose. They ask us for approval of an international readjustment which means burying permanently much that has been the most dynamic and effective of Marxist propaganda. If the fatherland of the proletariat bends its knee to bourgeois proposals, we lose the faith—all over the world—of those for whom we fight.

A proposal for world government coming from the west to Russia must surely not be couched in terms of hidden significance; this seems to me to be one of the major defects in the psychological implications of the Baruch proposals, for instance. A real world government offer must, I think, go out of its way to appeal to the Marxian tradition.

In accepting an offer of world government, Marxists would be acknowledging the truth expressed by Mortimer Adler: "To think that there will be no need for government when no exploiters are left is to forget that though exploiters try to use government for their purposes, nothing but government can protect a just economy, once established, from the rise of a new exploiting class."—if Stalin has not already convinced his fellows of this truism!

A final ideological hindrance to a friendly Soviet response to a world government offer lies in the economic sphere. Although an offer of federation might at first be limited to the control of atomic energy and other instruments of war, it could not long postpone consideration of pressing international economic and social problems. The Russians would again be faced with an unresolved Marxist dilemma.

The Kremlin would undoubtedly criticise a purely political federation, with no duties but armament control and no obligation but to preserve the status quo, for its failure to deal with the economic and social frictions between and within nations. For example, though the U.S.S.R. *has* joined the United Nations for purposes of "peace and security," she has not yet joined the International Monetary Fund and the Bank for Reconstruction and Development; nor the United Nations Food and Agricultural Organization; nor the Provisional International Civil Aviation Organization; nor the United Nations Educational, Scientific, and Cultural Organization; nor the Emergency Economic Committee for Europe; nor the European Coal Organization.

Current international functional organizations may have been spurned by the Soviet Union on the grounds that such moves tend to mollify the class struggle, whereas the struggle should be aggravated in order to conform with the demands of the dialectic. Unfortunately, this is another point of theology which must be left to the Marxists themselves to solve.

2) Grounds for Hope

What indications, if any, give us grounds for hope that a world government proposal might not be rejected abruptly by Moscow?

First, the fervor for world revolution among the Russians is not at fever pitch. Harrison Salisbury, former chief of the United Press Bureau in Russia, says in his recent book:

> Certainly among the ordinary Russian people there could hardly be less interest in communism as an article for export. While the Russian press analyzes foreign events from the Marxist viewpoint, it never suggests that 'come the revolution' all this will be changed.

Second, all Soviet diplomatic moves seem to be marked by an effort to calculate chances. This was the hope that John Foster Dulles raised in his articles in *Life* last June:

> Soviet representatives have sometimes taken extreme positions, but Stalin has pulled back and relieved the tension when unexpected opposition was encountered. That indicates that Soviet policy is

subject to change if it can be made clear to Soviet leaders that that policy will not promote the safety of the Soviet Union.

It should be added that as long as we unilaterally try to force the Kremlin to change its policy, the prospects are dubious. We should make a proposal for world government which would involve identical changes of policy for all governments concerned.

Raymond Swing invites action when he says:

> What it would do to Soviet policy if the United States and the British, by full popular consent, pledged themselves to the abolition of war through world government, no one can say. If it were convincingly done, it would end Russian fear. What Russian policy would be with fear removed, no one can say. But no one is entitled to say now that Russia without fear would refuse to establish a world of law above nations.

*Decisions for America*
I am not optimistic. There are times when reality makes optimism ridiculous. I am not optimistic because I am convinced that ultimate responsibility for world government rests with America, and I am conscious of the job we have ahead of *us*.

We cannot abdicate our world responsibilities and hope to escape catastrophe. And by world responsibilities, I mean more than sending aircraft carriers into the Mediterranean. I mean taking the lead diplomatically to break the vise of nationalist rivalry while we still have time.

Meanwhile, to my Marxist friends, I would issue what seems to be a reasonable challenge, as well as an invitation. I would ask them as rational beings to recognize that progress is no longer assured. Progress and destruction are pushing ahead on parallel lines under the same bracket of scientific achievement. The Marxist concept of the future, so powerful an element in traditional socialist thought, has temporarily lost its validity. We now confront the actual, scientific possibility of The End being written to human affairs. World government alone has a chance of diminishing the terrors that nationalism presents. World government would for the first time in history clear the field for a rational, world-wide approach to the economic and social problems which Marxism rightly insists are basic in human relations. The Communist movement itself could grow on its rational merits or lose on its rational defects, without needing to sacrifice its principles for the sake of military security or protective expansion.

The ideal of a world under law is a generality that still glitters. Only when we have it can we hold out hope for that kind of future which Mr. Churchill saw in one of his better moments—when "all will be well and proud in our island" and men everywhere will break into "broader lands and better days."

*Appendix 7*

## Opinion from Moscow

*Mary Ellen Purdy and Steve Benedict, Student Federalist Board members, have translated a "cable from Moscow—special for El Nacional, "which appeared in that leading newspaper of Mexico City on January 3, 1946.*

"In the world profoundly disturbed by the great and devasting war," it begins, "there is no problem more important and more grave than the establishment of a firm and lasting peace. The peoples of the world need this peace to heal the deep wounds caused by the atrocious actions of the aggressors and to advance the life of society in all lands."

Then after general statements on the problems of the peace we find these comments on world federation:

"Recently, owing to the imminent functioning of the UNO, there have appeared in the international arena various projects and proposals, which according to their claims assure the stablest possible peace, but which in reality have very little in common with this objective. Although the UNO has not yet begun to function, certain impatient politicians are already elaborating plans for its radical re-organization, asserting in particular that peace will be guaranteed provided the UNO be transformed into a kind of World Federation in which the independent countries today would find themselves more or less in the same situation as the states of North America.

"Naturally, a splendid thing is the ideal of the future union of humanity, ultimately free from present social antagonism, but quite another thing is the verbiage expended on World Federation to which British conservatives and North American isolationists of yesterday are devoted. Because these new proponents of a World State do not even intend to put an end to the social and national oppression in the world today, the value of such high-sounding projects is null.

"At the same time, one must consider that the label World Federation often serves only to conceal the inane aspirations of several great powers to a role of domination over the entire world. It is significant that exhortations to perfect the United Nations Charter may be reduced basically to the demand for annulling the principle, established in the Charter, of the unanimity of the great powers, permanent members of the Security Council. Once again this principle of unanimity, called by its opponents the Right of Veto, is being attacked.

"However, there is a difference between the attacks of yesterday and those of today. Formerly, the defense of the small nations against the Dictation of the Great Powers was alleged. Now, the attack is carried on in an open way, and the atomic bomb is used as the principal argument."

After several paragraphs covering "cooperation between the great peaceful powers" and a number of statements regarding the cause of the failure of the League of Nations, this article closes with these words:

"Soviet public opinion firmly maintains a position favorable to strong cooperation of the great powers which have the major responsibility for peace in the entire world. That is what constitutes the primary condition and principal guarantee of success for the International Security Organization."

The Student Federalist *Jan-Feb, 1946, page 3*

## *Appendix 8*

## Delegates and Signers of the Concord Charter

The following students attended the conference as delegates and are signers of the Concord Charter:

Mary Ellen Avery, Wheaton
Helen Ball, Wheaton
Sheila Barshay, Mt. Holyoke
David Baumann, Scarsdale HS (N.Y.)
Virginia Beech, Wellesley, (San Marino, Calif.)
Steve Benedict, St. John's College (Annapolis)
George C. Bryan, Harvard
Maxine Bublitz, Wheaton (Miami Beach, Fla.)
Cecily Cannan, Radcliffe
Stephen F. Chadwick, Jr., Yale (Seattle)
Betty Cobey, Wellesley
Gilles Corcos, Lafayette College (France)
Veniette Caswell, Jackson College
Joseph Cosetti, Youngstown HS (Ohio)
Wilder Crane, Chippewa Falls HS (Wisc.)
Allan Davis, Yale
Ina de Leng, Bronxville HS (Holland)
Roger J. Dieudonne, Georgetown
Jane Driscoll, Radcliffe
Ruth Elmhirst, Sarah Lawrence
Susan Ervin, Vassar, (Minneapolis)
John Curtis Farrar, Yale
Jane Fiske, Vassar
Jacqueline L. Freeman, Boston University

L.D. Garinger, University of Tennessee
Neil Gillam, University of Minnesota
David Hollister, Norwalk HS (Conn.)
William S. Howe, Brown and Nichols Prep
Thomas Hughes, Carleton College, (Minn.)
Ernest Johnston, Selma HS (Ala.)
Lucia Johnson, Pine Manor
Patricia Kimball, Pomona College (Calif.)
Lester Kurth, Yale (Wisc.)
Alicemarilyn Langmaid, Boston University (N.H.)
Virginia Lastayo, University of Alabama
Clare Lindgren, University of Minnesota
Leo Linehan, Boston College
Mary Louise Louchheim, Sarah Lawrence
William R. Lynch, Phillips Exeter
Laura McIntosh, Arts Students League
Neal McNabb, Batavia HS (N.Y.)
Hobart McPherson, Batavia HS, (N.Y.)
Herbert Margulies, Fieldstone HS (N.Y.)
Robert H. Marshall, Somerville HS (Mass.)
Mary Ann Morris, Youngstown HS (Ohio)
Daniel Patrick Moynihan, Tufts
Dorothy Nessler, Wellesley
Charles Nelson, St. John's College, (Annapolis)

Charles Norris, Van Nuys HS (Calif.)
Cushing Niles, Washington, D.C.
Kenneth G. Olson, University of Minnesota
F. Warren O'Reilly, New York City College (Texas)
Alfred Parmelee, Chicago HS (Ill.)
Foster Parmelee, Jr., Oklahoma A & M College
Girvan Peck, Yale
Arthur L. Peterson, Yale (Calif.)
Colgate Prentice, Williamsburg, Va.
Mary Ellen Purdy, Scarsdale, N.Y.
Edith Reynolds, Washington, D.C.
Anne Rogers, Scarsdale HS (N.Y.)
Taft Russell, Perth Amboy, N.J.
Peggy Ruth, Smith (Cincinnati)
Lillian Sagik, Simmons
William C. Sawyer, Cambridge, Mass.
Fay Scheinfein, Simmons
Stephen Schwebel, James Madison HS (Brooklyn)
Marjorie Semonian, University of Colorado
Richard E. Shapiro, Yale (Calif.)
John Simon, Fieldston HS (N.Y.)
Sybil Smart, Mt. Holyoke (Mich.)
Hester D. Spencer, Wellesley (Pa.)
Emil Starr, Tufts
Mary Swingle, Radcliffe
Lois Van Arsdel, Smith
Joseph Wheeler, Bowdoin
Andrew Witwer, Jr., St. John's College (Annapolis)
Harris Wofford, Jr., Scarsdale, N.Y.
Ellen Yonneff, N.J. College for Women

The Student Federalist *Feb-Mar, 1946*

# *Appendix 9*

## Revised Concord Charter

We must make world citizenship in a world community a political fact.

Existing governments have demonstrated that they are incapable of preserving peace and protecting human rights in an interdependent world. The atomic bomb makes even more disastrous the illusion that power politics can give us peace.

Only a new world sovereignty based on the principles of federalism can destroy the irresponsibilites of nationalism and effectually attack the economic and social problems whose solution is essential to the creation of a world community.

We support the United Nations as the primary existing international organization attempting to achieve some of these aims of a world government. However, the United Nations is not a federal government. It has no authority over individuals; it can only make recommendations to or negotiate treaties with member nations, and it cannot prevent the secession of any nation. It will not be adequate until it is capable of making, interpreting, and enforcing world law.

Therefore, a federal world government must be created either by calling a revisional convention under Article 109 of the United Nations Charter, by strengthening the United Nations through fundamental amendments under Article 108, or by utilizing other international action.

To this end, Student Federalists will:

- Stimulate thinking on the urgent need for federal world government.
- Educate our generation in the principles of federalism.
- Find, train, and organize the necessary leaders.
- Support all proposals which embody the minimum essentials of federal world government.

We realize that to lay the foundations for world government the people of the world must awaken to their responsibility as citizens of the world community. To make world citizenship a political fact, we must work to create a world government dedicated to human rights and justice under law.

We Student Federalists, under this charter, are united in our determination to achieve federal world government in our time.

*Revision mimeographed and distributed to the Student Federalist membership.*

*Appendix 10*

# Soviets Reject World Federation

The UNO, said a Soviet spokesman named Lemin in a Moscow broadcast to Greece, was not "a prelude to anthing" but was an existing organization designed to work at once for peace. The "so-called world parliament," he said, was "Utopian and at the same time harmful and reactionary" and "directly in line with the idea of world federation and other stupid plans."

*From the* New York Times, *January 14, 1946*

*Appendix 11*

## Prospects for Concord
by Thomas L. Hughes, Carleton College

Depending on what we're willing to put into it, the Concord Conference may be either a spectacular bit of futility or a health-infusing stimulus to federalist action everywhere. Patently, if we're worth anything, we must envision something more comprehensive and certainly less innocuous than sending resolutions to cabinets and Congressmen, not to speak of state governors. The publicity attempt may or may not be unique—these people are forever getting resolutions—but surely some of us have been around enough to know that we will never get federation through a White House ukase!

**Unequivocal Decisions**
The electricity of idealism is important only as an outlet for enthusiasm firmly grounded in some sincere and determined thinking. Some lasting and unequivocal decisions on policy must be Concord's first objective; some meaty plans for coordinated action are an equally important second.

Let's face a few delicate indisputables which refuse to be glossed over superficially. In one sense, at least, San Francisco built on bed rock. It recognized the only nucleus which is available—the great powers with their veto guarantees. The only "nucleus" which lives up to its name is a necessity at the outset a *power nucleus*. This is incontrovertibly true. It means the Big Three, regardless of common political doctrine or lack of it, constitute the sole nucleus for world order now. Anything else is a coalition, not a nucleus; any alternative grouping of major powers is disruptive and dedicated to power politics.

**The Base Has Changed**
Union Now met with a terrific popular response in 1939 because it fit into the 1939 power politics picture and gave an emotional, logical, common-sense appeal to complement the power politics. Events conspired to give a power basis to the Union Now argument. If the plan had been adopted, it would have been an expression of the best method of organizing the anti-Fascist power community, with the added good fortune of a common political base on which to run the organization. Today, the latter is gone. The base constituency has changed, and it is futile to wish us back to 1940. We no longer have the convenient coincidence of monopoly power plus the Western concept of individual liberty.

So the decision is no longer whether to risk peace or freedom; these two are forever and indissolubly linked. Lacking peace, our freedom cannot endure. What is more, as Russell Davenport told the Pittsburgh Federal Union Convention, freedom itself to have any meaning now must be a synthesis of political and economic democracy. Consolidating the political freedom of the west by a separate federal union is not a nuclear world state except in the minds of its philosophers.

Nor is "freedom" or "individual liberty" a meaningful concept against the realities of crucial world issues in 1946. Rare is the person who knows what his neighbor's understanding of such terms really is. "Democracy" needs qualifications. For whom? Uganda? China? Isn't it hopeless to argue that outside nations would gravitate toward a "democratic" nucleus out of admiration for principles? And if they were led to it by economic desires, would a cooked-up democracy be acceptable?

**The Critical Question Now**
This is a relentlessly critical question now. There was no common recognition of what democracy meant at the unfortunate London Conference last fall. Byrnes wanted democracy, by which he meant the token right of Bulgarians to go to the polls and exercise the voting privileges which are granted only to a minority of South Carolinians. Molotov wanted democracy, by which he meant a redistribution of landed estates to peasants held in bondage for centuries. Which is more important, "democratically" speaking?

It's hardly that simple. In the Balkans today, more accurate alternatives would be Red or White? Class alternatives. Can you decide for "democracy" in situations where democracy as we know it is out of the question? We must talk in terms applicable to conditions.

World government proponents must emphasise the peace through which we can keep our freedom. They must stress federalism as a principle—the concrete, the definitely understandable, the universally applicable. Certain democratic concepts are inherent in federalism; an autocracy which has delegated certain functions to an international authority is necessarily limited to power. Student Federalists, continue your stress on democracy, but proclaim it as a goal, not a prequesite. Campaigning for parliamentary democracy as an international standard now is crushingly unproductive.

If we are serious about avoiding the disaster of war and doing everything humanly possible to stave it off, the "nuclear" proponents are doing a disservice to peace. If ever we expect to convince a world to turn from the byways of intrigue into the highway of unity, we had better profitably remind ourselves that the application of this suggestion is hardly limited to international relations. These policy difficulties should not be insuperable. I'm convinced that nothing less than a consolidation of federalist forces in the United States is required. Concord gives students the chance to begin!

The Student Federalist, *February–March, 1946*

*Appendix 12*

# Student Federalist Chapter List, January 1947

\# denotes a high school or secondary school chapter, and
\* denotes a college chapter.

Parrish High School Chapter#
Ernest Johnston, Selma, Alabama

University of Alabama Chapter*
Doris Strobel, Tuscaloosa, Alabama

Beverly Hills Chapter#
Mr. Quand, Beverly Hills, California

Deep Springs School Chapter*
Reed Holt, Deep Springs, California

Palo Alto Chapter #
Paul Watson, Palo Alto, California

Pasadena (Caltech) Chapter*
David Baron, Pasadena, California

Sequoia Chapter #
Fritjof Thygeson, Menlo Park, California

Pomona College Chapter*
Keith Kearney, Claremont, California

San Francisco Bay Area Chapter#
Frederick Harvey, Jr., San Francisco, California

Stanford Chapter *
Virginia Keerl, Stanford University, California

UCLA Chapter*
Alfred Ross Kraig, Los Angeles, California

Van Nuys Chapter#
Charles Norris, Van Nuys, California

Humboldt Chapter*
Jacqueline Anderson, Arcate, California

University of California (Berkeley) Chapter*
Betsy Jean Christian, Berkeley, California

Western Regional Headquarters
Robert Bennett, Stanford University, California

Yale Chapter*
Arthur Hostage, New Haven, Connecticut

Dayscroft School Chapter#
Warren Mackenzie, Stamford, Connecticut

Miss Porter's School Chapter#
Caroline Husted, Farmington, Connecticut

Connecticut College Chapter*
Gladys Stevens, New London, Connecticut

Loomis School Chapter#
Arnold Tovell, Windsor, Connecticut

West Haven (Nutmeg) Chapter*
Cleaveland J. Rice, Jr., New Haven, Connecticut

Pierre S. Dupont High School Chapter#
Harry F. Themal, Wilmington, Delaware

TRAWG Chapter*#
James Parreco, Washington, D.C.

Bethesda-Chevy Chase Chapter#
Sally Walter, Washington, D.C.

Washington Area Chapters
Eleanor Schneider, Washington, D.C.

Clearwater Chapter#
Ralph Van Fleet, Clearwater, Florida

Ft. Pierce Chapter#
O.K. Sheffield, Ft. Pierce, Florida

South Side Chapter#
Charles Wells, Jr., Jacksonsville, Florida

Springfield Chapter#
Jackie Price, Jacksonville, Florida

Riverside Chapter#
Mary Cooke, Jacksonville, Florida

Jacksonville Beach Chapter#
Thomas Morgan, Jacksonville Beach, Florida

Jacksonville City Council
Mary Cooke, Jacksonville, Florida

Winter Park Chapter#
George Saute, Jr., Winter Park, Florida

Plant High School Chapter#
Sam Keutzman, Tampa, Florida

Bradley College Chapter*
Thomas Cartwright, Dunlap, Illinois

University of Chicago Chapter*
Thomas Farr, Chicago, Illinois

Lemont High School Chapter#
Marella Kieft, Lemont, Illinois

Principis College Chapter*
Scott Putnam, Elsah, Illinois

Culver Chapter#
Charles Leavitt, Culver, Indiana

Ball State Teachers College Chapter*
Marilou Conners, Muncie, Indiana

Humboldt Chapter#
Dick Frederickson, Humboldt, Iowa

University of Dubuque Chapter*
William Nowak, Dubuque, Iowa

University of Iowa Chapter*
David Stanley, Iowa City, Iowa

Pine Manor Junior College Chapter*
Natalie Quigg, Wellesley, Massachusetts

Smith College Chapter*
Mary O. Stevens, Northampton, Massachusetts

Wheaton College Chapter*
Mary Ellen Avery, Norton, Massachusetts

Wellesley College Chapter*
Ruth Ferguson, Wellesley, Massachusetts

Williston Academy Chapter#
Norman Minty, Easthampton, Massachusetts

Dana Hall Chapter*
Anne Wofford, Wellesley, Massachusetts

Harvard College (Affiliated with Student Federalists)
Steve Minot, Boston, Massachusetts

Mt. Holyoke College Chapter*
Marie Corbin, Bridgman Hall, South Hadley, Massachusetts

Tufts College Chapter*
Percy Shuberth, Medford, Massachusetts

Winsor School Chapter#
Lucy Lowell, Westwood, Massachusetts

University of Minnesota Chapter*
Clare Lindgren, Minneapolis, Minnesota

*Appendix 12* 173

Carleton College Chapter*
Wilder Crane, Northfield, Minnesota

University of Missouri Chapter*
Bert Hurn, Columbia, Missouri

Mary Institute Chapter#
Mary Louise Bander, Clayton, Missouri

John Burroughs School Chapter*
Myrna Lazio, Richmond Heights, Missouri

St. Louis Area Chapters
Jerry Tucker, Webster Groves, Missouri

North High School Chapter#
Anna B. Jensen, Omaha, Nebraska

University of Nebraska Chapter*
Eugene Berman, Lincoln, Nebraska

Exeter Academy Chapter#
William Lynch, Exeter, New Hampshire

Blair Academy Chapter#
Lewis Berger, Blairstown, New Jersey

Perth Amboy Chapter#
Taft Russell, Perth Amboy, New Jersey

Pingry School Chapter#
Paul Priest, Summit, New Jersey

Brothers College Chapter*
Sheldon Walter, Madison, New Jersey

Madison High School Chapter#
Amabel Walter, Madison, New Jersey

Princeton University Chapter*
Herbert Blumberg, Princeton, New Jersey

New York Military Academy Chapter#
Jay M. Schwamm, Cornwall, New York

Bronx High School Area Chapter#
Edward Ryder, Bronx, New York

Brearley School Chapter#
Diane Duke, New York, New York

South Side High School Chapter#
Harvey Ottenstein, Rockville Centre, New York

Scarsdale Chapter#
David Baumann, Scarsdale, New York

Scarborough School Chapter#
Brett Boocock, Scarborough, New York

Curtis High School Chapter#
Arthur Kahn, Staten Island, New York

New Paltz State Teachers College Chapter*
Juanita Will, New Paltz, New York

New Rochelle High School Chapter#
Trudi Levy, New Rochelle, New York

University Heights Chapter (New York University)*
Larry Fuchs, Bronx, New York

Bronxville High School Chapter#
Eleanor Johnson, Bronxville, New York

Garden City Chapter#
John Donne, Garden City, New York

Wells College Chapter*
Jean Smith, Aurora, New York

Clyde School Chapter#
Carol Dennis, Clyde, New York

City College of New York Chapter*
David Kirk, New York, New York

Vassar College Chapter*
Eleanor Little, Poughkeepsie, New York

Columbia-Barnard Chapter*
Donald Mcintosh, Scarsdale, New York

Cleveland Heights Chapter#
Harold Miller, Cleveland Heights, Ohio

Youngstown-East Chapter#
John Vassil, Youngstown, Ohio

Youngstown-South Chapter#
Raymond Walla, Jr., Youngstown, Ohio

Oklahoma A&M Chapter*
Harold T. Hazelright, Stillwater, Oklahoma

Portland Chapter*
Emily Jones, Portland, Oregon

Lawrence County Chapter#
Donald Levine, New Castle, Pennsylvania

Haverford College Chapter*
W.D. Chapman, Haverford, Pennsylvania

Bryn Mawr College Chapter*
Pamela Wahl, Bryn Mawr, Pennsylvania

Swarthmore College Chapter*
John D. McCutcheon, Swarthmore, Pennsylvania

Brown University Chapter*
William Barton, Providence, Rhode Island

University of Texas Chapter*
Ruth Lognaro, Austin, Texas

St. Mary's Chapter#
Student Federalists, San Antonio, Texas

Texas College of Mines Chapter*
Mary Hart, El Paso, Texas

University of Utah Chapter*
Mark Cannon, Salt Lake City, Utah

College of William & Mary Chapter*
Wesley R. Cofer, Jr., Williamsburg, Virginia

Mary Washington College Chapter*
Betty Rice, Fredericksburg, Virginia

Norwich University Chapter*
Robert Rosselot, Northfield, Vermont

Rutland Chapter#
Donald Sherburne, Rutland, Vermont

Pan-Pacific Chapter*
Stephen Chadwick, Seattle, Washington

Mundunido Chapter#
Ralph Judd, Yakima, Washington

Chippewa Falls Chapter#
William Bollman, Chippewa Falls, Wisconsin

University of Wisconsin Chapter*
David Brill, Madison, Wisconsin

*Distributed by Student Federalists headquarters, Winter, 1947*

# *Appendix 13*

# WHAT HAPPENED AT ASHEVILLE

The major world government organizations in the U.S. are now one: United World Federalists. They will work from now on as a single group, with a unified policy and program and under the national direction of one executive council.

That was the important accomplishment of the national congress of World Government Groups, which met in Asheville, N.C., over the weekend of Washington's birthday, 1947.

The organizations which joined were five: Americans United for World Government, Student Federalists, Massachusetts Committee for World Federation, World Citizens of Georgia and World Federalists, U.S.A.

Dues-paying members of the five automatically became members of the new merged group. Active adherents, obtained through the efforts of more than 200 chapters, topped the 100,000 mark.

**Convention at Work**

The union accomplished at Asheville was not an easy one to bring about. Behind it lay long months of discussion and planning—much hard work by determined federalists who were willing to sacrifice personal predilections for common action.

The meeting was called by a liaison committee of federalist groups known as Movement for World Federal Government, U.S. Council, which had been set up in November. Convention sessions brought together representatives from 30 organizations (some of which have world government as only a subsidiary aim and hence were not eligible for merger). Participants came from Maine, Florida, California and 30 other states between. Those elected as delegates could represent and vote only for members in their home states, thereby assuring a convention which accurately reflected the views of all who are working for world government.

**Action Ahead**
When the delegates left Asheville they could look back on a job well done.

1. They had a bigger, stronger organization to push world government than had ever existed before.

2. It had a name that won almost unanimous approval:

United World Federalists—for World Government with Limited Powers Adequate to Prevent War. (The subtitle was adopted with the understanding that it accompany the name in small type.)

3. The policy statement (subject to revision only by national conventions) was brief, broad, and hopeful of results through development of the United Nations.

"Statement of beliefs: We believe that peace is not merely the absence of war, but the presence of justice, of law, of order—in short, of government and the institutions of government; that world peace can created and maintained only under world law, universal and strong enough to prevent armed conflict between nations.

"Statement of purposes: Therefore, while endorsing the efforts of the United Nations to bring about a world community favorable to peace, we will work primarily to strengthen the united nations into a world government of limited powers adequate to prevent war and having direct jurisdiction over the individual in those matters within its competence."

4. The constitution was broadly democratic, encouraged grassroots organization, and left room for local autonomy.

5. The executive council (30 members were elected at the convention from a slate of 79; 8 more have been added) is a representative group of able, ardent, and experienced workers for world government.

The world-minded public generally has received the results of Asheville with deep thankfulness that so important a movement has at last been able to achieve so high a degree of unity. However, as union has increased the potential of our accomplishment, so it has also increased the responsibility of every member to put his best effort into the task.

Other nations will have atomic bombs in a very few years. It is becoming increasingly obvious that only a United Nations strengthened into a capable and responsible world government can prevent a conflict in which probably half of the people of the united states would be killed. The time is short; but the General Assembly that meets in the fall of 1947 can call a review conference to revise the U.N. Charter.

**You Can Help**
Let us know that you're interested. Tell us you'd like to work for world government—the only effective way to keep peace. We can use you a hundred ways. If you're a student, join the Student Federalist group on your campus (there are more than 140 over the country) or start one with the help of national headquarters.

Tell us about the problems of organizing UWF in your community; maybe we can help with speakers, literature, ideas, and the name of neighbors we know are interested, too.

Circulate our literature; write to newspapers; tell your Congressman you want world government. Suggest a resolution favoring world government in your church, civic or social group, business association, labor union, or woman's club. Above all, talk about the idea to everyone you can.

Join United World Federalists!

**National Executive Council**
*(the Representative Body of Active Workers)*

R. Mayne Albright, North Carolina
Lawrence S. Apsey, Massachusetts
Helen Ball, New York
Mildred R. Blake, New York
Henry B. Cabot, Massachusetts
Cass Canfield, New York
Fred Carney, Illinois
Mrs. Raymond Clapper, Washington, D.C.
Norman Cousins, New York

Thomas K. Finletter, New York
Alan Green, Connecticut
Thomas O. Griessmer, New York
Mrs. J. Borden Harriman, Washington, D.C.
W.T. Holliday, Ohio
George Holt, Connecticut
Robert Lee Humber, North Carolina
Virginia Lastayo, New York
Samuel R. Levering, Virginia

John Levinson, Illinois
Clare Lindgren, Minnesota
Ralph G. Lindstrom, California
Thomas H. Mahoney, Massachusetts
Cord Meyer, Jr., Massachusetts
Edgar Ansel Mowrer, Washington, D.C.
Vernon Nash, Connecticut
Stewart M. Ogilvy, New York
Colgate Prentice, Virginia
A.J.G. Priest, New Jersey
Phillips Ruopp, Illinois
Duncan Spencer, *Treasurer,* New York
Raymond Swing, Washington, D.C.
Paul Thatcher, Utah

Carl Van Doren, New York
Mark Van Doren, Connecticut
F.R. Von Windegger, Missouri
Robert Wheelwright, Delaware
Abraham Wilson, New York
Harris Wofford, Illinois
*Vice Presidents*
Grenville Clark
W. T. Holliday
Norman Cousins
Robert Lee Humber
Thomas K. Finletter
Raymond Swing
Carl Van Doren
Other Officers to Be Elected

*Condensed from* World Government News, *March 1947*

# Appendix 14

## STUDENT FEDERALISTS: LIST OF DELEGATES AND OBSERVERS TO THE ASHEVILLE CONVENTION

*Voting Delegates
Virginia Anderson, Iowa City, Iowa

Michael G. Bache, Fort Belvoir, Virginia
*Helen Ball, New York, New York
*Abe Bargman, Box 60, New York
*David P. Barus, Montclair, New Jersey
Blandy Boocock, Providence, Rhode Island
*A. Dane Bowen, Jr., Austin, Texas
Ann H. Burroughs, Pittiford, Vermont
Edward Cammack, Chicago, Illinois
Glen O. Camp, Jr., Chevy Chase, Maryland
Dave Campbell, Iowa City, Iowa
Hardy A. Carroll, North Carolina
*Stephen P. Chadwick, Jr., New Haven, Connecticut
*Louise I. Chamberlin, Chicago, Illinois
*James R. Compton, Chicago, Illinois
Signey N. Cone, III, Greensboro, North Carolina
George W. Crouse, III, Akron, Ohio
*John Shelton Davis, Kilgore, Texas
Joynew Deming, New Haven, Connecticut
Dorothy Dick, New York, New York
Diane Duke, New York, New York
Virginia L. Fair, Berkeley, California
Thomas Farr, Chicago, Illinois
John Curtis Farrar, New Haven, Connecticut
Paul R. & Mrs. Farris, Tilton, New Mexico
Leland E. Ferer, Chicago, Illinois

*Katherine Fox, New York, New York
*Lawrence Fuchs, Bronx, New York
Louis B. Garinger, Knoxville, Tennessee
Alan Hamilton, North Carolina
*Arthur Hostage, New Haven, Connecticut
John W. Helfrich, Williamsburg, Virginia
Sheila Hines, Los Angeles, California
*Harlan Hockenberg, Iowa City, Iowa
G. John Honig, Madison, New Jersey
*Melvin B. Jaschke, Austin, Texas
*Phil Jaynes, Chicago, Illinois
Marona Allen Johns, Norton, Massachusetts
Willie H. Jones, Austin, Texas
Thomas John Kelley, St. Paul, Minnesota
Patricia Kimball, Claremont, California
William Kratt, New Jersey
*Alastair Boyd Kyle, New York, New York
Robert Clement Landwehr, Chicago, Illinois
Virginia Lastayo, New York, New York
*Donnew Levine, Castle, Pennsylvania
Elizabeth Levy, Illinois
Clare Lindgren, St. Paul, Minnesota
*Howard B. Lord, Chevy Chase, Maryland
*Donald S. Mcintosh, Scarsdale, New York
Laura Mcintosh, Scarsdale, New York

Mary Rose Margaretten, Perth Amboy, New Jersey
Richard Miller, Perth Amboy, New Jersey
*Stephen Minot, Cambridge, Massachusetts
Sherwin Montell, Ladue, Missouri
Howard Morgan, Tuckahoe, New York
John F. Mulcahy, Jr., Arlington, Massachusetts
*Foster Parmelee, Jr., Princeton, New Jersey
*James J. Parreco, Washington, D.C.
*Alexander M. Pope, Illinois
*Colgate S. Prentice, Williamsburg, Virginia
*Paul Priest, Summit, New Jersey
Edith M. Reynolds, Mt. Rainier, Maryland
William W. Rhoades, Asheville, North Carolina
*Robert E. Rossclot, Northfield, Vermont
*Kirk Sattley, Chicago, Illinois
Richard E. Sawyer, Chicago, Illinois

Eleanor Schneider, Washington, D.C.
Al Sellers, Haverford, Pennsylvania
Richard E. Shapiro, New Haven, Connecticut
*David N. Stanley, Iowa City, Iowa
Jerry Tucker, Webster Groves, Missouri
Norman Turk, Lincoln, Nebraska
Pamela Wahl, Bryn Mawr, Pennsylvania
*Sheldon E. Walter, Madison, New Jersey
William D. Walters, Minneapolis, Minnesota
Sally K. Walther, Washington, D.C.
Alma Weisberg, Wellesley, Massachusetts
*Joseph G. Whealey, Brunswick, Maine
Juanita Will, New Paltz, New York
*Harris Wofford, ,Chicago, Illinois
Dorothy Wynne, Chevy Chase, Maryland

*Extract from mimeographed list of delegates and observers to Asheville Convention, February, 1947.*

*Appendix 15*

# UNITED WORLD FEDERALISTS, INC.
*for World Government with Limited Powers Adequate to Prevent War*

Statement of beliefs: We believe that peace is not merely the absence of war, but the presence of justice, of law, of order— in short, of government and the institutions of government; that world peace can be created and maintained only under world law, universal and strong enough to prevent armed conflict between nations.

Statement of purposes: Therefore, while endorsing the efforts of the United Nations to bring about a world community favorable to peace, we will work primarily to strengthen the United Nations into a world government of limited powers adequate to prevent war and having direct jurisdiction over the individual in those matters within its competence.

**Unity and Diversity**
Any individual, in becoming a member of United World Federalists, commits himself only to the above short affirmation of belief and to the equally brief declaration of purpose adopted at Asheville. Wide liberty of interpretation is accepted and welcomed under these broad general statements.

In general, popular mass movements have been built upon agreement around a central broad principle without any attempt to secure adherence to a detailed blueprint. United World Federalists is acting accordingly. In consequence, without further authorization, no such clarifying statement as the attached may be publicly presented, either from the platform or in the press, as the "official position" of our organization. It is, at most, simply a general consensus of its Executive Council.

**Principles**
1) Membership: Participation in the world federal government should be open at all times to all nations without the right of secession.

2) Reservation of powers: All powers not delegated to the world federal government should be reserved to the nations and their peoples in order to guarantee to each nation its right to maintain its own domestic, political, economic, social, and religious institutions.

3) Enforcement of world law: World law should be enforceable directly upon individuals.

4) Balanced representation: Representation in the legislative body should be determined upon a just formula recognizing population, economic development, educational level, and other relevant factors—each representative to vote as an individual.

5) Bill of rights: The world constitution should include a bill of rights assuring equal and adequate protection to persons affected by the constitution and laws of the world federal government.

6) Revenue: The world federal government should have authority to raise dependable revenue under a carefully defined and limited taxing power independent of national taxation.

7) Amendment: Reasonable provision should be made for amendment of the constitution.

**Powers**
Such legislative, executive, and judicial powers as may be found necessary to the preservation of peace should be delegated to the world federal government. These should certainly include at least the following provisions, which should be incorporated in the world constitution itself:

1) Provisions prohibiting the possession by any nation of armaments and forces beyond an approval level required for internal policing.

2) Provisions requiring control by the world federal government of the dangerous aspects of atomic energy developments and of other scientific developments easily diverted to mass destruction.

3) Provisions requiring such world inspection, police, and armed forces as may be necessary to enforce world law and provide world security.

4) Other powers: We recognize that although some world federalists believe that such limited powers would be sufficient as a beginning, others are convinced that any world organization to be effective, even at the start, must have broader powers to bring about peaceful change in the direction of a free and prosperous world community. Such differences as exist between world federalists on this point are mainly questions of timing. There is full agreement that we should move as rapidly as possible to a world federal government with authority and power to legislate on other basic causes of international conflict.

*This statement was written and distributed by UWF in 1947.*

# Appendix 16

## UNITED WORLD FEDERALISTS STUDENT CHAPTERS

The (H) indicates a high school chapter, the (P) a preparatory school chapter, and the (C) a college chapter.

An asterisk beside C, H, or P, indicates that the chapter has fewer than ten members as of this date. Ten is the required number of members a chapter must have to be officially recognized.

*Alabama*
Birmingham-Southern College (C)
    Marilyn Cooper, Birmingham

Huntington College (C)
    Gene Gibbons, Montgomery

*Arizona*
Phoenix College (C)
    James Carroll, Phoenix

Russell Ranch School (P)
    Pitt Stonier, Tucson

Tucson Senior High School (H)
    Anthony Tery, Tucson

University of Arizona (C)
    William S. Lovekin, Tucson

*Arkansas*
Arkansas State Teachers College (C)
    James A. Andrews, Conway

*California*
Associated Claremont Colleges (C)
    Henry Anderson, Clark Hall, Pomona College, Claremont

Berkeley High School (H)
    Mrs. Heath-Walker, Berkeley

Berkeley Student Chapter (C)
    Thomas Moore, Berkeley

Palo Alto Chapter (H)
    Stanley Croonquist, Palo Alto

Pasadena City College (C)
    Martin L. Sandell, Wilmar

San Diego State College (C)
    Darrell Beers, San Diego

Sequoia Chapter (H)
    Jim Porter, San Carlos

Stanford University (C)
    Al Johnson, Palo Alto

Westwood Chapter (C)
    Charles Norris, Van Nuys

*Appendix 16*

Ventura Junior College (C)
    Donald H. Shaw, Ventura

**Colorado**
University of Colorado (C)
    Rhita Greenberg, Boulder

**Connecticut**
Connecticut College (C)
    Phyllis Clark, New London

Greenwich Student Chapter (H*)
    Larry Hardin, Greenwich

Hawley School (P*)
    Mary Pat Carroll, Newtown

Loomis School (P*)
    John Walber, Windsor

Norwich Student Chapter (H)
    Barbara Kaufman, Norwich

Pomfret School (P)
    Huston St. Clair, Jr., Pomfret

South Kent School (P)
    Neal Peirce, South Kent

St. Margaret's School (P)
    Gladys Granger, Waterbury

Trinity College (C*)
    Robert Obrey, Hartford

University of Connecticut, Storrs (C)
    Frank Dagostino, Storrs

Westover School (P)
    Harriet Veltman, Middlebury

Yale University (C)
    Jake Ewald, New Haven

**Delaware**
University of Delaware (C)
    John Broujos, Wilmington

**District of Columbia**
Washington Area Chapter (C)
    Donald Lief, Washington

**Florida**
Florida Southern College (C)
    George Thompson, Lakeland

Florida State University (C)
    Rufus Jefferson, Tallahassee

Orlando-Winter Park Chapter (H)
    George Saute, Winter Park

Rollins College (C)
    Marie Prince, Winter Park

University of Florida (C)
    William B. Holland, Gainesville

**Georgia**
Emory University (C)
    Ralph Jacks

Morehouse College (C)
    Willie Smith, Atlanta

University of Georgia (C)
    Marion Montgomery, Athens

**Idaho**
University of Idaho (C)
    R.E. Hosack, Moscow

**Illinois**
Bradley University (C)
    James Becker, Peoria

Eastern State Teachers College (C)
    Omer Tobias, Charleston

Joliet Junior College (C*)
    Lillian Eggers, Joliet

Lake Forest College (C)
    Robert Sharvy, Lake Forest

Principia College (C)
    Carol Keck, Elsah

Quincy Senior High School (H)
    Sue Keisker, Quincy

University of Chicago (C)
    Carl W. Reed, Champaign

*Indiana*
Ball State Teachers College (C)
  Lawrence Carlson, Muncie

Depauw University (C*)
  Don Finney, Greencastle

Earlham College (C)
  Robert Godsey, Richmond

Indiana State Teachers College (C)
  Robert Meurer, Terre Haute

Indiana University (C)(not officially recognized)
  Ruth Orton, Bloomington

Purdue University (C)
  Marjorie Ewbank, Lafayette

*Iowa*
Buena Vista College (C)
  Gladys Kuehl, Storm Lake

Central College (C)
  Don Bruggink, Pella

Cornell College (C)
  Richard Bishop, Mt. Vernon

Drake University (C*)
  Thomas Kelly, Jr., Des Moines

Ft. Madison High School (H)
  Betty Jo Shelley, Ft. Madison

Humboldt Chapter, (H*)
  Dick Fredericksen, Humboldt

Iowa State College (C)
  John Forsberg, Ames

Iowa State Teachers College (C)
  Willard Sayre, Cedar Falls

Pella High School (H)
  Melvin Hugen, Pella

Westmar College (C)
  Enid Schmickle, Lenars

University of Iowa (C)
  Bill Shuttleworth, Iowa City

*Kansas*
Arkansas City Senior High School (H)
  Walter Rickel, Arkansas City

St. John's College (C)
  John L. Dreher, Winfield

University of Kansas (C)
  Lois Beth, Lawrence

Winfield High School (H)
  Lois McNeil, Winfield

*Kentucky*
Louisville Collegiate School (P)
  Margie Helm, Louisville

*Maine*
Bates College (C)
  Raymond Sennett, Lewiston

Bowdoin College (C*)
  S.D. Spector, Brunswick

Gorham College (C)
  Barksdale R. Macbeth, Brunswick, Gorham

*Maryland*
Garrison Forest School (P)
  Dita Douglas, Garrison

Goucher College (C)
  Mary Hinrichs, Riderwood, Baltimore

Hood College (C)
  Jean Righter, Frederick

University of Baltimore (C)
  Floyd Flickinger, Baltimore

University of Baltimore—Night School (C)
  Stanley Sollins, Baltimore

*Massachussets*
Abbot Academy (P)
  Lee Booth, Andover

## Appendix 16

Beaver Country Day School (P)
  Patricia Hurley, Chestnut Hills

Cambridge School (I*)
  Diana Kirchwey, Weston

Dana Hall (I*)
  Blossom Appel, Wellesley
Groton School (P*)
  Donald Williams, Groton

Hingham High School (H)
  Arlene Reed, Hingham

Mt. Hermon School (P*)
  UWF Student Chapter, Mt. Hermon

Mt. Holyoke College (C)
  Leight Minturn, Mt. Holyoke, South Hadley

Northfield School for Girls (P)
  Nancy Chapman, East Northfield

Massachussetts Institute of Techonology (C)
  John Benjamin, Cambridge

South Hadley High School (H)
  Rosalie McInerny, S. Hadley Falls

Smith College (C)
  Erica Payson, Northampton

Tabor Academy (P)
  Norman E. Hunt, Marion

Tufts Chapter (C)
  William Gowan, Dorchester

Roxbury Latin Federalist (H)
  Jonathan Fine, Brookline

Wellesley College (C)
  Judith Dreifuss, Wellesley

Wheaton College (C)
  Amy Wright, Norton

Williams College (C)
  A. Richard Goodman, Williamstown

Winsor School (P)
  Eleanor Toumey, Boston

Harvard Student Feds (C) (not officially recognized)
  Mason Harding, Cambridge

*Michigan*
Ann Arbor High School (H)
  Ann Nelson, Ann Arbor

Albion College (C)
  Neil Blintz, Charlotte

Fordson High School (H)
  Von E. Knisely, Dearborn

Kalamazoo Student Chapter (H)
  Ruth Summerlott, Kalamazoo

Port Huron Junior College (C)
  John Rawley, Pt. Huron

University of Michigan (C)
  Irwin Robinson, Ann Arbor

Wayne University (C)
  Reinhardt Wilke, Detroit

*Minnesota*
Carleton College (C)
  Edgar Brenner, Northfield

Central High School (H)
  Lois Rosenblum, St. Paul

Sauk Centre High School (H)
  Lorraine Otte, Sauk Centre

Summit School (P)
  Nina Steefel, St. Paul

University of Minnesota (C)
  Bill Feller, Minneapolis

MacAlester College (C)
  Joan B. Langland, Minneapolis

*Missouri*
Clayton High School (H*)
  Henry Schweich, Clayton

Ferguson High School (H)
  Jacquelyn Cheney, Ferguson

Mary Institute Chapter (P)
  Eliza Rodewald, St. Louis

University of Missouri (C)
  Morran D. Harris, Columbia

Washington University (C)
  Burton Resnic, St. Louis

**Montana**
Montana State College (C)
  Betty Ruth Baldwin, Missoula

**Nebraska**
Univ. of Nebraska (C)
  Kenneth Purcell, Lincoln

**New Hampshire**
Dartmouth College (C)
  Richard Reed, Hanover

Keene High School (H)
  Joyce Stone, Keene

Phillips Exeter Academy (P)
  Stephen Petschek, Exeter

St. Paul's School (P)
  James D. Colt, Concord

**New Jersey**
Blair Academy (P*)
  Richard Orr, Blairstown

Bloomfield Senior High School (H)
  Anna J. Miller, Bloomfield

Boonton High School (H)
  John Ryder, Boonton

Beard School (P)
  Sheila Fey, East Orange

Kent Place School (P)
  Betty Sims, Summit

Newark Academy (P)
  Ken Baum, Newark

Oranges & Maplewood (H)
  Dick Chase, South Orange

Perth Amboy Student Chapter (H)
  Paul Breslow, Perth Amboy

Peddie School (P)
  William H. Dettmer, III, Hightstown

Pingry School (P*)
  Robert Rogers, Union

Princeton University (C)
  Bob Stevens, Princeton

Montclair Academy (P)
  Richard H. Sandler, Montclair

Hun School (P)
  Douglas Barr, Princeton

Rutgers University (C)
  Jack Ballan, New Brunswick

**New York**
Albany Academy (P)
  Douglas Landon, Schenectady

Adelphi College (C)
  John Shapiro, Garden City

Bennett Junior College (C)
  Carol Babcock, Millbrook

Brooklyn College (C)
  Margie Schonhaut, Lorraine Wallach, Brooklyn

Bronx Area Chapter (H)
  Stanley Weiner, Bronx

Brooklyn High School Area (H)
  Judith Passoff, Brooklyn

Buffalo University (C*)
  David Sprague, Buffalo

City College New York (C)
  Jack Monderer, Myron Weiner, Brooklyn

Colleges of the Seneca (C)
  Peter Marks, Hobart College, Geneva

*Appendix 16*

Columbia University (C)
    Donald McIntosh, Scarsdale

Cooper Union (C)
    Marilyn Wolfe, Englewood, New Jersey, Maxine Field, Brooklyn

Cornell University (C)
    Judy Van Fleet, Ithaca

Emma Willard School (P)
    Pam Taylor, Ramelle Ferer, Troy

Wendell L. Wilkie Chapter (H)
    Bernate Spaet, New York

Garden City High School (H)
    Barrie Keating, Garden City

Great Neck High School (H)
    Peter Adelman, Great Neck

Harvey School (P)
    Robert Pomeroy, Hawthorne

Hunter College (C)
    Sheila Leiman, Brooklyn

Isaac Young High School (H)
    J. Peter Singer, New Rochelle

Keuka College (C)
    Patricia Neeley, Keuka Park

Lawrence High School (H)
    Edythe Birnbaum, Cedarhurst, L.I.

Latin American Institute (C)
    Gunther Meyer, New York

Masters School (P)
    Sallie Watson, Dobbs Ferry

New Paltz State Teachers College(C)
    Henrietta Aschs, New Paltz

Nottingham High School (H)
    M.J. Hasbrouck, Syracuse

New Rochelle High School (H)
    Fred Levy, New Rochelle

New York University Heights (C)
    Bruce Grund, Bronx

Park School (P*)
    James Pincus, Buffalo

Pelham High School (H)
    Joyce Ferry, Pelham

Port Jervis Student Chapter (H)
    Harvey Cohen, Port Jervis

Pratt Institute (C)
    Grace Ball, Channing Gilson, Brooklyn

Riverdale Country School for Girls (P)
    Ann Regensburg, Bronx, Lucy Bunzl, Riverdale

Russell Sage College (C)
    Mary Deposati, Troy

Sarah Lawrence College (C*)
    Ruth Scheinfeld, Bronxville

Scarborough School (P)
    David Gamble, Scarborough

Skidmore College (C)
    Nancy Radack, Saratoga Springs

South Side High School (H*)
    Jerome Rubinstein, Rockville Centre

Syracuse University (C)
    Barbara Oken, Syracuse

Triple Cities College (C)
    Nissel Rose, Endicott

Vassar College (C)
    Eleanor Little, Poughkeepsie

Washington Square College, New York University (C)
    Seena Schwartz, Bronx

Wells College (C)
    Elizabeth Bloom, Aurora

White Plains High School (H*)
    Magda Eichenwald, White Plains

Briarcliff Junior College (C)
  Virginia Biddle, Briarcliff Manor

Long Island University (C)
  Murray Hirsch, Brooklyn

Thomas Jefferson High School (H)
  M.G. Cohen, Brooklyn

*North Carolina*
Atlantic Christian College (C)
  Bob Clark, Wilson

Asheville School (P)
  George Crouse, Asheville

Catawba College (C)
  Peter Cooper, Salisbury

Duke University
  Jack Matlock, Durham

Eastern Carolina Teachers College (C*)
  Noah A. Talen, Greenville

Davidson College (C)
  Clyde Tandy, Jr., Davidson

Greensboro College (C)
  Mary Clegg, Greensboro

Guilford College (C*)
  Alan Hamilton, Guilford

Lenoir-Rhyne (C)
  Harry Faggart, Jr., Hickory

Rocky Mount High School(H)
  Louise Esterling, Rocky Mount

Salem College C)
  Robert C. Gray, Winston-Salem

Salem Academy (P)
  Peggy Schwartz, Winston-Salem

University of North Carolina (C)
  Marie Wicker, Chapel Hill

Wake Forest College (C)
  Marcel B. Humber, Wake Forest

Warren Wilson College (C)
  Ed Scott, Swannanoa

Woman's College, University of North Carolina (C)
  Mimi Temko, Greensboro

*Ohio*
Antioch College (C)
  Eliot Fremont-Smith, Yellow Springs

Columbus Academy (P)
  George Bown, Columbus

Denison University (C)
  Marion I. Pascoe, Granville

Miami University (C)
  Robert Almy, Oxford

Ohio State University (C)
  Leon Resnick, Columbus

State College (C)
  Charles King, Wilberforce

Toledo Student Federalists (H)
  Alvina Littlefield, Toledo

Walnut Hills High School (H*)
  Marcia Harris, Cincinnati

Western Reserve Academy (P)
  Ben Kjellgren, Hudson

University of Dayton (C)
  Robert J. Funk, Dayton

University of Akron (C)
  Clarence Carlson, Akron

University of Toledo (C)
  Sally Wheeler, Toledo

College of Wooster (C)
  Mary Schweickhart, Wooster

*Oklahoma*
Phillips University (C)
  James Spainhower, Charles Huddleston, Enid

## Oregon

Linfield College (C)
  Jewel Wallen, Mcminnville

Pacific University (C)
  Yae Ono, Forest Grove

Reed College (C)
  Dale Merrill, Portland

Eugene Student Federalists (C)
  Jessie Becker, Eugene

## Pennsylvania

Allderdice Student Federalists (H)
  Allan Reuben, Pittsburgh

Baldwin School (P)
  Marianne Dennis, Bryn Mawr

Beaver College (C)
  Shirley Peters, Jenkintown

Bryn Mawr College (C)
  Margery Shaw, Bryn Mawr

Bucknell University (C)
  Myron Kronish, Lewisburg

Canton High School (H)
  Claudia Ottoson, Canton

Carnegie Tech (C)
  John Ewart, Pittsburgh

Friends Central School (P)
  Mary Gibbon, Marjorie Davis, Philadelphia

George School (P)
  Ann Yeomans, Morrisville

Haverford College (C)
  William Chapman, Haverford

Lancaster Country Day School (P)
  Marilyn Reigle, Lancaster

Lewisburg High School (H)
  Joyce Ziegler, Lewisburg

New Castle High School (H)
  Richard Stevens, New Castle

Mercersburg Academy (P)
  Frank Laimbeer, Mercersburg

Philadelphia High School for Girls (H)
  Charlotte Toll, Philadelphia

Shady Side Academy (P),
  Parker Berg, Pittsburgh

Shipley School (P)
  Nora Stone, Bryn Mawr

Swarthmore College (C)
  Paul Shoup, Swarthmore

Towanda High School (H)
  Gladys H. Pipher, Towanda

Troy High School (H)
  Evan C. Williams, Troy

University of Pennsylvania (C)
  Walter Ainsworth, Philadelphia

University of Pittsburgh (C)
  Margaret Martin, Caroline A. Bonnett, Pittsburgh

Washington & Jefferson College (C)
  Robert Carlberg, Oakmont

Westinghouse High School (H)
  Lemyra Gillis, Pittsburgh

Westtown School (P)
  Jean Russell, Westtown

Wilson College (C)
  Sue Law, Chambersburg

## Rhode Island

Brown University (C)
  Barbara Adler, Providence

## Tennessee

Southwestern-at-Memphis (C)
  Irvine Anderson, Memphis

*Texas*
Hardin College (C)
  Mrs. L. B. Lee, Wichita Falls

Southwest Texas State College (C)
  Will Gibbons, John B. Dodson, San Marcos

Texas Christian University (C)
  Ernest Miller, Ft. Worth

Texas Tech (C)
  Richard Erlich, Lubbock

University of Texas (C)
  Frank Armstrong, Jr., Austin

*Utah*
Brigham Young University (C)
  Robert L. Haman, Geri Kemsley, Provo

Ogden Senior High School (H)
  W.R. Thornley, Ogden

University of Utah (C)
  Dalmas Nelson, Salt Lake City

*Vermont*
Middlebury College (C)
  Elizabeth Chappell, Middlebury

Putney School (P)
  Karl Schuman, Putney

*Virginia*
Norfolk Division—William & Mary(C)
  Charles Crowe, Portsmouth

Sweet Briar College (C)
  Diana Dent, Sweet Briar

William & Mary (C)
  Robert Pace, Williamsburg

University of Virginia (C)
  George Stoner, Charlottesville

*Washington*
Broadway Edison Technical School (P)
  E.D. Jones, Seattle

St. Paul's School (P)
  Sylvia Sprout, Walla Walla

Washington State College (C)
  Claude McCormack, Pullman

Yakima High School (H)
  Betty Ann Roberg, Yakima

*Wisconsin*
Wauwatosa High School (H)
  John Walter, Wauwatosa

West Allis Central School (H)
  A.M. Jaecks, West Allis

University of Wisconsin, Milwaukee Extension (C)
  Pamela Rice, Milwaukee

*Wyoming*
Casper Junior College (C)
  Frank Bowron, Casper

University of Wyoming (C)
  John Fisher, Laramie

*Mimeographed chapter list circulated by the UWF Student Division headquarters, November–December, 1948.*

*Appendix 17*

## THE TALK OF THE TOWN, NOTES AND COMMENTS, DEC. 8, 1945

*The* New Yorker *Magazine*

Almanac to be hung by the wood box in the kitchen:

APRIL 26-Dr. T.V. Soong addressing the United Nations Conference in San Francisco: "If there is any message that my country wishes to give to this Conference, it is that we are prepared to yield if necessary a part of our sovereignty to the new international organization in the interest of collective security."

JUNE 13—Emery Reves in "The Anatomy of Peace": "As the 20th century crisis is a worldwide clash between the social units of sovereign nation states, the problem of peace in our time is the establishment of a legal order to regulate relations among men, beyond and above the nation states."

AUGUST 11—Dorothy Thompson in her syndicated column: "A political deduction as logical as the instinct of self-preservation can immediately be drawn from this greatest of all human discoveries: There must be a world state."

AUGUST 12—Robert Maynard Hutchins, Chancellor of the University of Chicago, in a broadcast: "Up to last Monday, I must confess, I didn't have much hope for a world state. I believed that no moral basis for it existed, that we had no world conscience and no sense of world community sufficient to keep a world state together. But the alternatives now seem clear."

AUGUST 16—Stephen King-Hall in the *National News-Letter,* London: "We must not be afraid to admit that world government is no longer an ideal limited as an objective to societies supported by enthusiasts and short of funds. World government has now become a hard-boiled, practical, and urgent necessity."

August 18—Norman Cousins in the *Saturday Review of Literature:* "Already he [Man] has become a world warrior; it is but one additonal step—though a long one—for him to develop a world conscience. He shall have to recognize the flat truth that the greatest obsolescence of all in the Atomic Age is national sovereignty."

August 18—Freda Kirchwey in the *Nation:* "A new conference of the nations must be assembled to set up a world government."

August 27—Michael Foot, British M.P., in the *New York Post:* "What is required is a deliberate resignation of sovereignty, at least on this supreme issue [the bomb]. The fundamental fact of San Francisco was, however, that no such concession would be required of any great state."

August 30—Charles G. Bolté in a letter to President Truman: "We must strive eventually to achieve a world order based on law, governed by representatives responsible to all the people and guaranteeing the rights of all men."

September 1—Cord Meyer, Jr., in the *Atlantic Monthly:* "In international society, there is no final authority to which the national states must refer their disputes for settlement. We should frankly recognize this lawless condition as anarchy, where brute force is the price of survival. As long as it continues to exist, war is not only possible but inevitable."

September 23—Editorial in the *Chicago Sun:* "The wise backers of the San Francisco Charter realized from the beginning that the world organization set up under it was but a stride in an essential direction. Today, the harnessing of the atom means that the course must be greatly speeded to world government: government with sovereign powers, to which all individual nations delegate sovereignty over the affairs which require world control."

October 16—A group of men and women assembled in Dublin, New Hampshire: "That in place of the present United Nations Organization there must be substituted a World Federal Government with limited but definite and adequate powers to prevent war. That a principal instrument of the World Federal Government must be a World Legislative Assembly."

October 20—Editorial in the *Saturday Evening Post:* "We have come to the point where nothing less than world government will suffice to tailor international politics to hitherto-undreamed-of resources of power."

OCTOBER 22—Ralph Barton Perry in "One World in the Making": The one world of which we fondly dream is not designed to satisfy the exclusive interest of any man or any group. It contains no masters' or servants' quarters. It serves each interest only by serving all interests. It rests on this widest and all-inclusive base and on nothing else. It is not an idle dream. It is not a mere playful exercise of the imagination but a project to which men are driven by practical necessity."

NOVEMBER 1—Professor Albert Einstein in the *Atlantic Monthly:* "Do I fear the tyranny of a world government? Of course I do. But I fear still more the coming of another war or wars. Any government is certain to be evil to some extent. But a world government is preferable to the far greater evil of wars, particularly with their intensified destructiveness."

NOVEMBER 8—Captain Harold E. Stassen at the annual dinner of the Academy of Political Science: "The world needed government on a world level before the atomic bomb. Now it has become an imperative."

NOVEMBER 22—Anthony Eden in the House of Commons: "Every succeeding scientific discovery makes greater nonsense of old-time conceptions of sovereignty."

NOVEMBER 23—Mr. Bevin in the House of Commons: "I feel we are driven relentlessly along this road; we need a new study for the purpose of creating a world assembly elected directly from the people of the world, as a whole. I am willing to sit with anybody, of any party, of any nation, to try to devise a franchise or a constitution—just as other great countries have done—for a world assembly."

NOVEMBER 24—Dr. J. Robert Oppenheimer in the *Saturday Review of Literature:* "It is a practical thing to recognize as a common responsibility, wholly incapable of unilateral solution, the completely common peril that atomic weapons constitute for the world, to recognize that only by a community of responsibility is there any hope of meeting that peril."

DECEMBER 1—Dr. Richard D. Present in *Free World:* "The problem is a much broader one than international control of atomic energy; all measures must be taken to prevent another war. Nothing less than world government can accomplish this."

*Distributed by Americans United for World Organization, Inc., 465 Fifth Ave., New York, New York*

*Appendix 18*

# PROMINENT SUPPORTERS OF WORLD GOVERNMENT DURING THE PERIOD BETWEEN 1943 AND 1953

Albert Einstein
John Saltonstall
Raymond Swing
Carl Van Doren
Walter Reuther
Mark Van Doren
Grenville Clark
Norman Cousins
Thomas K. Finletter
Cass Canfield
Vernon Nash
W.T. Holliday
Justice William O. Douglas
Boris Artzbyasheff
Stringfellow Barr
Robert Hutchins
Henry Cabot
James Carey
Charles Bolté
Edison Dick
Gov. Frank Graham
Prof. Albert Guerard
Isadore Lubin

Mrs. Robert Lehman
Douglas Fairbanks, Jr.
Bishop Bernard Sheil
Charles Pratt
Jerry Voorhis
C.M. Stanley
Chet Huntley
Elmo Roper
James Warburg
Edward M.M. Warburg
Prof. Frederick Schuman
Mrs. J. Borden Harriman
Edgar Ansel Mowrer
Abe Wilson
Randolph Compton
Thomas Dodd (Later U.S. Sen.)
Alan Cranston (Later U.S. Sen.)
A. Philip Randolph
Rex Stout
Clifton Fadiman
Leo Cherne
Justice Robert Jackson
Prof. I.I. Rabi

*Appendix 18*

Chester Bowles
Paul Hoffman
Lewis Mumford
Harold Urey
John Hersey
Russell Crouse
E.B. White
Erica Mann
G.A. Borgese
Prof. Mortimer Adler
Oscar Hammerstein, II
Cord Meyer, Jr.
Thomas Mann
Clarence Streit
Clare Boothe Luce
Mrs. Thomas Lamont
Emery Reves
Prof. Robert McIver
Bette Davis
Ingrid Bergman
Greer Garson
Fiorello LaGuardia
Christopher LaFarge
John Steinbeck
Sen. Claude Pepper
Sen. Joseph Ball
Sen. Wayne Morse

Sen. William Fulbright
Sen. Hubert H. Humphrey
Sen. Henry Cabot Lodge
Sen. Leverett Saltonstall
Rep. John McCormack
Rep. Emanuel Cellar
Dorothy Canfield Fisher
Dorothy Thompson
Louis Nizer
George S. Kaufman
Arthur Compton
Carl Sandburg
Walter Wanger
Beardsley Ruml
Robert E. Sherwood
Gov. G. Mennen Williams
Gov. Luther Youngdahl
Dean Paul Shipman Andrews
Scott Buchanan
Ely Culbertson
Frank Kingdon
Will Rogers, Jr.
Harold Stassen
Raymond Massey
Prof. Robert Redfield
Arnold Toynbee

*Appendix 19*

# THE CLARK-SOHN PLAN

*This brief outline covers the plan sketched in Grenville Clark and Louis B. Sohn's "Peace through Disarmament and Charter Revision—Detailed Proposals for Revision of the United Nations Charter."*

Powers: Disarmament, inspection of arms, peace-keeping with UN "Peace Force," monopoly of atomic power development and compulsory adjudication of international "legal" disputes. Revised Article 17 gives limited but real power to aid economic and social development. Yet elsewhere author says "Outside that field [of war prevention], it should have no authority whatever except to recommend." To these powers are added a vast range of advisory powers on almost all international matters.

Organs: A very powerful General Assembly (unicameral) with three constitutional committees or "Councils" (an Executive Council of 15 and less important Social and Economic Council and Trusteeship Council); an International Court for "legal" cases and an Equity Tribunal for non-legal disputes (with advisory power only); a Secretariat; military staff committee; special budget and taxation committee; and UN "Peace Force."

Membership: Every independent nation is a member without right of secession, every person a citizen. Nations can be suspended but not expelled.

Representation: In General Assembly: one per five million of population, including colonial territories, with a maximum of 30 from any nation. Thus, the General Assembly would number about 400. Representatives are not necessarily directly elected, though the constitution recommends it. The General Assembly elects the Executive Council on which the top six nations each have a guarantee of one seat. The Assembly can recall and replace the Executive at any time but must simultaneously elect a new Council. Powers of the Assembly and Executive Council are largely co-extensive. Action by the Assembly is by absolute majority; by the Executive, 11 votes.

Detailed Arrangements for Disarmament: United Nations Peace Force establishment; taxation (limited to 2% of value of world production); courts; privileges and immunities; and Bill of Rights (applying against the UN only) are to be embedded in the Charter in a series of annexes. This "constitutional legislation" is to be agreed upon in the comprehensive negotiation of world problems which Clark sees as an essential preliminary to the establishment of this constitution.

*The initial draft of this proposal appeared in Grenville Clark's "A Plan For Peace" in 1950.*

*Population and Votes in General Assembly (Some Examples)*

| Country | Population | Votes |
|---|---|---|
| Argentina | 16M | 3 |
| Australia | 8M | 2 |
| Belgium and colonies | 23M | 5 |
| Brazil | 48M | 10 |
| Canada | 13M | 3 |
| France and colonies | 118M | 24 |
| Germany | 68M | 14 |
| India | 342M | 30 |
| Italy | 46M | 9 |
| Japan | 80M | 16 |
| Mexico | 24M | 5 |
| Pakistan | 73M | 15 |
| Sweden | 7M | 1 |
| U.S. and territories | 154M | 30 |
| U.S.S.R | 194M | 30 |
| U.K. and colonies | 131M | 30 |

*Reprinted from* World Frontiers, *Vol. 2, No. 2, Summer 1954.*

# The Chicago Constitution

*1948 brought to the world a memorable document, the* Preliminary Draft of a World Constitution. *Conceived and written by an outstanding group of men,\* who represented various fields of study, the constitution was published after more than a year of intensive discussion and inquiry, which took place in Chicago, Illinois, giving the work its popular name.*

*It is interesting to note that this document, known for its far-reaching suggestions, was planned to include only the minimum needed to preserve peace throughout the world. But as the group continued their deliberations, they became increasingly convinced that "Peace is the effect of Justice," and their resulting proposals were drawn up accordingly:*

1. *A declaration of duties and rights* is made foremost.

2. *Grant of Powers* include:

   a. The maintenance of peace; judgment and settlement of conflicts and prevention of violence; origination and disposal of armed federal forces; limitation and control of weapons and national militias.
   b. The laying and collecting of federal taxes and establishment of budget.
   c. The issue of control of money and credit.
   d. Supervision of boundaries and migrations, including administration of territories not ready for self-government; decision on formation of new states; and vetoing immigration laws if in contradiction to world law but leaving nations the right to maintain standards of quality for admission.
   e. Regulation of commerical transportation and communication affected with federal interest.
   f. Establishment of agencies to aid the development of the earth's resources and to the advancement of physical and intellectual standards.
   g. The right to appropriate land for proper federal use, with reasonable compensation.

3. *Government structures:*

   a. A *Federal Convention* of approximately 2,000 delegates, one delegate for each million of population, directly elected by the people of all nations and subdivided into 9 Regional Electoral Colleges.
   b. A *World President* elected at the Convention for a six-year term.
   c. A *Council* of 99 members, as the principal legislative body elected by the Convention, 9 councillors being elected from each of 9 regions and 18 being elected at large.
   d. A *Planning Agency* appointed by the president, to prepare budgets and to pass upon plans for improvement of the world's physical facilities and production
   e. A *Grand Tribunal* of 60 Justices appointed by the President, subject to veto by two-thirds of the Council.
   f. A *Tribune of the People* as a spokesman for the minorities.
   g. A seven-man *Chamber of Guardians,* elected by the Council and presided over by the President, to control the armed forces.

4. *Existing national states* would survive and would retain local authority but would be deprived of those function and powers which are basic to world government.

The Committee has hoped that a *Founding Convention* would be held and that it would be called by the United Nations General Assembly. It has proposed that the constitution resulting from the Convention become effective after ratification by a majority representing two-thirds of the world's population.

*\*Committee to Frame a World Constitution:* Robert Hutchins, chairman, G. A. Borgese, Sec., Mortimer Adler, Stringfellow Barr, Albert Guerard, Harold Innis, Erich Kahler, Wilber Katz, Charles McIlwain, Robert Redfield, Rexford Guy Tugwell.

*Reprinted from* World Frontiers, *Vol. 2, No. 2, Summer 1954*

# Appendix 20

## WHAT ABOUT THE RUSSIANS?

*These pages, prepared by the Student Division of United World Federalists, represent an attempt to answer questions that often arise concerning Russia and World Government. They are in no way official policy of United World Federalists. Student Division, United World Federalists, Inc., 31 East 74th Street, New York 21, New York, Phone Regent 7–7380.*

*Is world government possible without Russia?*
In the long run, no. Some federalists believe that if an honest offer of world government were made to the Russian government as official U.S. policy, and if Russia turned the offer down, the best course would be to start without Russia, leaving the door open for her to join when she wished.

Other federalists insist that any "world" government not including Russia would be interpreted, and probably would become, a bloc against Russia. They point out that the present threat of war is between the U.S. and the U.S.S.R. and that any system designed to guarantee peace must include both nations.

Nearly all United World Federalists are agreed that primary efforts must be made: first, to convince the American public and the American government of the necessity for world government; second, to obtain Russian agreement.

*Has Russia given any indication of being favorably interested in world government?*
None. The Russian government has issued no official statement on world government, but the press and radio have commented occasionally, labelling the idea as provincial utopianism or as a Western imperialist scheme. In general, Russia seems not to take the idea very seriously.

It must be remembered, however, that no serious offer of world government has ever been made officially to Russia.

*This statement was distributed by the UWF Student Division circa 1948-9.*

*In view of the current anti-American propaganda campaign by the Soviet government, do you think cooperation between Russia and the United States in any plan is possible?*

Bitter exchanges of words have made the Russian-U.S. split more obvious but have not made solution impossible. Anti-American propaganda by Russia could be turned off in a matter of days, if more basic problems causing friction were solved. Anti-Russian propaganda in the United States would also taper off very shortly.

*Didn't the U.S. offer world government to Russia when she proposed the Baruch plan? And Russia turned it down.*

Not at all. The Baruch plan calls for inspection and an international monopoly of the potentially dangerous peacetime used of atomic energy. Atomic plants are to be distributed in a strategic balance throughout the world.

If, however, one nation were to be caught making atomic weapons secretly, or if one nation were to seize the atomic plants within its borders, the only action suggested under the Baruch plan is for the Security Council (without its Big Power veto) to request the other nations of the world to join forces against the violator, which would mean seizing the atomic plants within *their* borders. Such a plan would eliminate the danger of a surprise atomic attack.

The atomic arms race would thus be postponed, but the end result would be war between nations, not the arrest of individual criminals by a world police force, as would be the case under a world government.

Also, the Baruch plan takes no account of biological weapons or other weapons of mass destruction. Even if the plan had been adopted, the nations of the world still would have been allowed as many rockets, blockbusters, bacteria, and mechanized armies as they wished.

A world government, unlike the Baruch plan, would enforce disarmament and would also provide world law and world courts in which individual violators of world law could be tried.

*Doesn't Russia's refusal to limit the veto show that she would never join a world government?*

Not necessarily. The veto power is a logical and integral part of a system where all power is retained by sovereign nations and where each nation, large or small, has one vote. Russia cannot be expected to give up her veto in an organization where any two countries, however small, have more voting strength than she.

Much more thorough revision of the U.N. than that suggested by Secretary Marshall must be proposed to Russia before her refusal can be considered proof that she would never agree to a world government where she would have a voice proportionate to her actual power.

*What about Russian insistence on the "sovereign independence" of states? Certainly this is contradictory to the principles of world government.*

Is Russia interested in the independence of her small neighbors, or is she interested that they should throw off all American influence and sympathies? The answer, it seems clear, is that Russia is interested in "sovereign independence" only because it sometimes serves as a useful weapon in the current struggle for power with the U.S.

*But Russia and the U.S. have disagreed on almost every important matter now before the U.N. How can you expect them to agree in a world government?*

No one expects complete agreement ever, but United World Federalists ask that differences be settled peaceably under law rather than by force or the threat of force as at present.

Furthermore, many of the conflicts between the U.S. and the U.S.S.R. would vanish once the possibility of war was removed. So long as nations have the power to wage war, Russia and the U.S., as the two largest powers in the world, are potential enemies, and one's loss is the other's gain. Under such circumstances, each local problem (i.e., Trieste, the Ruhr, the Austrian peace treaty, Korea) has become part of a worldwide struggle for power with rational solution sacrificed in a scramble for political prestige and military position.

*What has Russia to gain from joining a world government?*

Like the rest of the world, Russia would gain a great deal. She would gain the security from aggression, obviously one of the main concerns of a nation that has been invaded twice in the last 30 years.

She would gain time to complete her reconstruction from the last war without having to prepare for the next one at the same time. The tremendous amounts of money, labor, and goods now spent on military preparation could be used, for the first time since 1917, in the production of consumer goods to raise the standard of living of the Russian people.

*Doesn't it look as if Russia were deliberately provoking another war, in the belief that she will win it and thereby rule the world?*

It is difficult to believe that either Russia or the U.S. would deliberately provoke a world conflict which neither would "win." Wars are desired when the victor has something to gain from them. An atomic war would leave both sides infinitely poorer than they are today.

Seven million Russians were killed in World War II, and 25,000,000 lost all their property. It is undoubtedly safe to say that the Russian people do not desire another war and that the Russian government knows another war would undo the work of every Five Year Plan Russia has had.

Both Russia and the U.S. accuse the other of provoking war. It seems much more likely that fear of each other is leading both nations to prepare for a conflict neither wants.

*But what about communism? Certainly the Russians want the whole world to be communistic.*

There is little question that Russia would like to see the world go communist, just as America would like to see it return to capitalism. However, it is extremely doubtful that the Russians mean to fight a war to get communism for other nations. Marxists believe that communism will inevitably come about through revolutions within each nation. Current Russian policy seems to be to stall until another depression brings what they believe will be the collapse of capitalism.

*Might it not be necessary for the United States to back anti-Communists with armed force and, if necessary, fight a war to eliminate the communist threat to our freedoms and our way of life?*

Certainly not. Communism is an idea and a way of life, and the only way to defeat it permanently is to show that the American brand of democracy is a better way of life. In a peaceful world, under a world government, this shouldn't be as hard as it is today. Totalitariansm has little appeal in anything approaching normal times.

The handful of communists in the United States are not a great menace as Communists. The danger lies, not in their ideas, unacceptable to most people in the U.S., but in the fact that they are a potential fifth column in case of war with the Soviet Union.

The greatest danger to American democracy is not the communist threat, but the threat of another war, preparation for which would bring governmental controls, restrictions of civil liberties, and restrictions of economic freedom such as America has never seen.

To prepare for modern war, the government would have to be empowered to force the decentralization of American industry, whether or not such decentralization were profitable to the individual owners concerned.

If an atomic attack upon the United States were impending—or begun— the military would have to have the power to act immediately, without consulting the people or the Congress.

Once the war had started, the power to make peace would have to be taken from the people, lest a demoralized populace surrender while scientists and technicians were on the verge of winning the war. The American Army would probably end up with the job of putting down civil disorders at home by those who wished to end the war.

The American nations might win a third World War, but it seems pretty certain that American democracy would die in the process.

*Can democracy and totalitarianism exist side by side under one world government?*

There is no reason to assume that they could not. The world government would deal only with matters requiring international action. National governments would continue to have full authority over internal policy.

When Switzerland first set up its federal government, some of the cantons were democracies, some oligarchies, and some had authoritarian governments.

In the United States, even in recent years, there have been differences in the extent to which various states have been democratic. The withholding of the vote from almost half the population of Mississippi has not limited the rights of the citizens of New York. The reign of Huey Long, generally conceded to be a dictatorship in most important respects, did not cause a similar state government to arise in California, nor did it cause Louisiana to withdraw from the union. Neither will Soviet governmental control of Russian newspapers under a world government necessarily result in a censorship of the American press by the U.S. government.

*Can capitalism and communism exist under one world government?*

For the next 10 or 15 years, yes. Regardless of economic systems, Russia and the U.S. are in excellent position to do business with each other. Russia is one of the few nations in the world well enough off to buy American products without extensive loans or gifts from America first. America is the only place where Russia can buy the machines necessary for her reconstruction and increased industrialization.

In the long run, one of the two systems, or perhaps a third system, would probably win out over the others. Americans believe that capitalism can outproduce and outsell communism. Russians believe that capitalism will soon collapse of its own weight and the world turn to communism. The British, the Scandinavians, and others offer their brand of socialism as a third alternative.

There will be rivalry and friction, but if the war scare were removed, as it would be under a world government, the struggle between capitalism and communism could be viewed in its proper perspective, as a competition between two economies. The test would be which system could afford the best standard of living, not which nation could command the most destructive armies.

*What should the United States do to bring about Russian agreement to a world government?*

The U.S. government should offer to the Soviet government to take part in strengthening the U.N. into a world government, asking the Russian government to join with us in the planning.

First, this offer should be made by no one less than the American Secretary of State, as the official position of the U.S. government.

Second, the offer should be made prior to and supplementary to international action in the U.N. itself, for at present, the U.N. is only a league of sovereign states. As such, it cannot "force" its members to do anything. It cannot give itself power. The power must be given by those who now hold it, the sovereign states, particularly the United States and Russia.

Once the U.S. and Russia announced their willingness to take part in a world government, there is little doubt that the rest of the world would join with them to strengthen the U.N.

Third, the offer must be accompanied by willingness on the part of both nations to compromise. In return for Russian agreement to a world government, the U.S. would have to make certain concessions. Peace is not free.

Most important of American concessions required would be the willingness to take part in and give power to a United Nations where she would have less influence than she has today. Whatever the reason, the U.N. position today usually parallels the U.S. position and opposes the Soviet view.

It is unrealistic to expect Russia to surrender her power to an organization where such a situation is likely to continue indefinitely.

*What are the reasons Russia might not accept an American offer of world government?*

Such reasons are many. 1) The Russian government is profoundly suspicious of anything offered by America, feeling that such offers are only "capitalist plots to drive Russia from the U.N." Efforts must be made to allay such suspicions.

2) If convinced that the offer is sincere, Russia will then suspect that America plans to dominate the world government. Again, America must show that such suspicions are unwarranted, by inviting Russia to help draw up the original plans, by providing careful limitations of power and checks and bal-

ances so that no one nation can dominate the world government.

3) The Russian conception of the state as merely an expression of economic relationships will make it difficult for Russia to envisage a common government over two economies. The fact that the Russian government, itself, is totalitarian, that it controls the total economy of the nation, will add to the difficulty in imagining a government with powers strictly limited to matters of security. We must make it clear that the world government we propose would not have the power to interfere in internal economic affairs in any nation.

4) It is also possible that Russia considers war or the threat of war as an instrument to increase her political and economic power in the world. However, the increasing realization that modern war is so destructive as to be no longer practical as a means to *any* end will help to overrule Russian objections to the only system that can prevent war.

5) The last possible reason why Russia might refuse to take part in a world government would be that she was bent on a course of world conquest and world rule. If this is the case, world government—and peace—are impossible. We cannot assume that this is the case, however, until we have offered world government to Russia, shown our willingness to submit to world law, and made every effort to prove that distrust of our motives is unwarranted.

*What if all these efforts are made, and Russia still refuses?*

It may then be necessary to start without Russia. Such a course would be justified, however, *only* after every effort had been made to secure Soviet participation.

A world government could be formed without Russia if a majority of the nations of the world, including nations on every continent and a substantial majority of the world's population and industrial strength, agreed to federate. Russia's initial decision to stay out might change if she saw such a union functioning effectively and if the door were always left open for her to join.

Such a federation would be better equipped to build its common defenses while waiting a possible Russian change of heart, as it would be better prepared to defend itself if it should be attacked.

*Appendix 21*

# Suppose You Had No Cop on the Corner

Suppose you had no law in your city or your country; no government in your state or at Washington? No laws and no police, no traffic regulations, no obligations to pay debts or uphold contracts, no punishment for burglary or murder. No legislatures, no executives, no courts!

Would the strong respect the rights of the weak? Would order and peace be possible? How long would you and your family be safe?

Suppose all your governments were leagues like the present U.N. Congress, your state legislature, and the city council could then only make "recommendations" that certain laws be obeyed. Motorists caught speeding could be given tickets only if they agreed they wanted to go to court. In court, certain people of power, even if convicted of murder, could not be sentenced unless they, themselves, agreed with the judge.

Sound ridiculous? Yet this is the condition of world affairs today.

There is no government above the national level. And until there is, there can be no real world law, no world police, and no permanent peace. The United Nations is a step forward. It should be supported and its present powers used fully. But it lacks the powers of real government. It cannot make binding and enforceable law.

Join those who seek to transform the U.N. into a federal world government with limited but adequate powers.

Peace is not merely the absence of war, but the presence of justice, of law, or order—in short, of government and the institutions of government; world peace can be created and maintained only under world law, universal and strong enough to prevent armed conflict between nations and having direct jurisdiction over the individual in those matters within its authority.

United World Federalists, Inc., is conducting an active campaign to awaken the American public to the need for a greatly strengthened U.N., which will make laws, interpret laws and enforce laws, binding on all people.

Through films, radio, and press—world government publications, pamphlets, and advertising—mass meetings, study groups, and speaking tours—every effort is being made to arouse public opinion on this, the most important issue of our time. The choice is "World Law—or World War!"

*Official organizing folder of the United World Federalists, 1949.*

*Appendix 22*

# ON THE ROAD: STUDENT CARAVAN REACHES WASHINGTON

Student federalists from 11 states, the District of Columbia, Alaska, Brazil, and Sweden participated last month in the National Student Caravan for World Government. Starting from San Francisco in mid-June, the Caravan reached its destination, Washington, D.C., after two weeks and 3,200 eventful miles.

Caravaners were often feted by local chapters of United World Federalists in towns through which they passed and found time occasionally for picnics and recreation. But the dominant mood was sober determination to spread the world federalist message from coast to coast as best they could with their limited time and resources. The students had fun, but the fun was incidental; the Caravan was no joy ride.

John and Virginia Meloney perhaps best exemplified the serious attitude of all the caravaners. They left Fairbanks, Alaska, in April, traversed the Alcan Highway, and spent six weeks helping Washington state federalists campaign for Initiative 174 before joining other caravaners at San Francisco.

At towns and cities along the route, the procedure was for caravaners to gather at the city limits, where they met local federalists—and often motorcycle police escorts—who piloted a parade through town to whatever function had been scheduled. These included public rallies, press and radio interviews, and luncheons.

World Government News, *August 1950*

*Appendix 23*

## Participants in 1950 Student Federalist Caravan

Phyllis Barnhill, New York, New York
Edgar Brenner, New York, New York
Lucy Bunzl, New York, New York
Charles Butterworth, Lansdowne, Pennsylvania
Bob Byrd, Duke University, Greensboro, North Carolina
Dave Caulkins, Cleveland Heights, Ohio
Jacquelyn Chaney, Ferguson, Missouri
Nonie Clark, New York, New York
Mary Coleman, Charleston, Illinois
Manoel de Sa, New Haven, Connecticut
Ralph Fleming, Portsmouth, Virginia
Murray Frank, New York, New York
Bill Friedlander, Berkeley, California
Ira Haupt, Asbury Park, New Jersey
Bob Jackman, Oak Park, Illinois
Estelle Jasper, Washington, D.C.
Joan Kirchner, Lake Hiawatha, New Jersey
Pete Lederer, Indianapolis, Indiana
Solveig Lilja, New Haven, Connecticut
Harry Lustig, University of Illinois, Urbana, Illinois
Henry McClure, Kirkwood, Missouri
Leroy Montague, Chicago, Illinois
Don Neisser, East Orange, New Jersey
Pete Novick, Jersey City, New Jersey
Don O'Brien, Bronxville, New York
David N. Ong, Cleveland Heights, Ohio
John Parker, San Francisco, California
Richard N. Pierson, Jr., Cold Spring Harbor, New York
Marilyn Probe, Ladue, Missouri
Richard Roberts, Sunnyside, New York
Larry Stone, Lambertville, New Jersey
Pat Thompson, Kirkwood, Missouri
Barbara Turlington, Chevy Chase, Maryland
Ellen Waldron, Toledo, Ohio
Ted Weiss, South Amboy, New Jersey

*Appendix 24*

## Wallerstein's Resignation from UWF

Imanuel Wallerstein
1325 Concourse
New York, 52 NY

February 23, 1951

Mr. C.M. Stanley
115 Sunset Drive
Muscatine, Iowa

Dear Max,

It is with a sense of the deepest personal regret that I feel I must resign from the National Executive Council and such of its committees as I may be a member. I do this not primarily because of the many policy issues that have split UWF nor because of some of the recent administrative and program decisions. I am resigning because of my conviction that UWF, as presently constituted, is not capable of doing any effective work to achieve it goals.

There are two main tasks, it seems to me, essential for federalists to undertake today. One of these, which is and has been UWF's prime concern, is the immediate redirection of U.S. foreign policy along more constructive lines. It seems to me that herein UWF has impossibly limited its scope and will not succeed in what it is attempting to do. It would seem far more effective to constitute a mere committee of 100 top-level men to pursue this particular goal, men who are reasonably homogeneous politically and willing to comment often and meaningfully on a fast-moving world situation.

On the other hand, UWF seems to me to have no serious inclination to undertake the other task, the long-range and more important one. This is the task of providing a doctrine, a new ideology, which can rehabilitate a sick world, the task of proclaiming a doctrine of one world, which is a manifest heresy today, and a readiness to accept the inevitable consequences and recriminations.

In short, I believe that in what UWF is trying to do, it is not being effective. In what it is not trying to do, it is committing a serious error of omission. In any case, for either of these tasks to be accomplished, the structure, the premises, and the membership of UWF would have to be radically altered.

I have lost faith in UWF because I believe UWF has lost faith in itself and its idea. I shall remain a member of UWF because I am sympathetic with its goals and curious as to its progress. But I no longer believe it is the significant organization I once thought it was.

Sincerely yours,
Immanuel Wallerstein

cc: Alan Cranston, Thomas Robertson, Jr.

*Appendix 25*

# The Wallerstein Credo: A Supplementary Credo for the Student Division

Our time has seen a radical shift in the traditional roles nations have played within world society. The peoples of Asia, the Middle East, and Africa have decided to be free. To these people, however, freedom means more than political self-determination. It means also eliminating foreign economic control while attempting at the same time to raise swiftly and substantially their living standards. It means a cultural rebirth and a realization of their essential dignity as human beings. Any national policy which stands in the way of this movement is unwise, unjust, and dangerous. Any national policy which does not foster this revolution for freedom is doomed to failure.

Western man is faced with a situation where he and his power are no longer supreme. Adjustment is hard, and harder still unless it is recognized that an adjustment is needed.

The leadership of the Soviet Union is dominated by a crusading and perverted idealism seeking to exploit the world's difficulties to their own ends, which, wittingly or not, are now brutal ends that deny the essence of freedom. The success of the Soviet Union is based upon the special role it plays in the world's uneasy balance. Half underdeveloped and half industrialized, half in Europe and half in Asia, it knows the problems of both areas and can capitalize on the strong points of both positions.

And the tragedy of all this is that it occurs in a framework of world anarchy, whereas the institution of law historically has been the only structure which can promote peaceful change.

As Americans, as student federalists, and as citizens of the world, we believe:

   a. The significance of the world revolution for freedom must be brought to the attention of the American youth community; and that we must place into this perspective the power struggle between the United States and the Soviet Union.
   b. That we must support the just struggle of two thirds of the people of the world to achieve freedom.
   c. That we must depose from any leadership in this movement for freedom the Communists whose methods would destroy freedom.
   d. That we must preserve and expand freedom at home, combatting tendencies to limit traditional liberties in times of crisis.
   e. That we must support the United Nations and its specialized agencies and seek the development of the UN into a world federal government.

[Note: The original Wallerstein draft also contained the following four program objectives, which were deleted in the final draft.]

Toward these ends we shall work immediately to achieve:

1. An expanded, multilateral program of technical assistance and world economic development.
2. The elimination of racial and religious discrimination throughout the world.
3. Negotiations of differences between nations through the United Nations, combining compromise with devotion to fundamental principles, while recognizing the limitations of negotiations in a lawless world.
4. A wider understanding of the need for world federal government.

*6/20/52 I. W. [Immanuel Wallerstein]*

# Appendix 26

## REVOLUTION AND ORDER
### by Immanuel Wallerstein

> *"There are today social revolutions sweeping the world . . .*
> *Any world order, whether it be a series of alliances of world federalists or world government, which sought to limit or curb these revolutionary aspirations would be doomed to the same failure as Metternich's Holy Alliance."*
> —William O. Douglas

One fundamental problem the world faces today is the existence of anarchy in a world containing two large power-blocs and of technological advances that make the prospects of war enormous in scope and potential destruction. World federalists have an answer to that problem. They say that until nations submit themselves to the rule of law, there is no possibility of achieving permanent peace. World government lays the groundwork and gives us hope for a peaceful solution to our conflicts.

But there is another problem that faces the world today and which is at least of equal importance with the first problem. It is the fact that "there are today social revolutions sweeping the world." This problem is distinct from the other though the course of world events leads each to have an enormous effect on the other.

The relationship and contrary interests between revolution and order is, I think, worthy of more attention than federalists have been wont to give it. The problem, stated succinctly, is this: Will the nations undergoing national and social revolutions be willing to renounce their right of revolution and accept the rule of world law, without some concrete assurance that the problems underlying their revolutions will be dealt with adequately? The glib answer, often given, is that of course world government will be flexible enough to allow for peaceful change within its framework. But I'm not sure that is a satisfactory answer.

The question is not one of how much power a world government will have. The question is whether the two thirds of the world undergoing revolution will have confidence in any sort of government, enough confidence to surrender their major weapon in their struggle for a better life. I am suggesting, in short, that unless there is some assurance and confidence *beforehand* that the needs of the revolution are being met, or at least substantially on the way to being met, the peoples of Asia and Africa are not going to be willing to talk about world government even if the West is ready.

No government can countenance violent revolution within its territory. A federal government will even suppress violence that is wholly within the boundaries of a constituent unit. In the United States, in 1893, President Cleveland sent in federal troops to deal with a strike, over the protest of the governor of the state. President Cleveland was not adhering to the spirit of federalism although he found legal premises on which to act. There seems little reason to think that a world federal government would do otherwise. Surely a civil war in China would never have been permitted even if there were absolutely no outside interference. From a political, if not a legal, point of view, the civil war would have been seen as worldwide in its implications.

A world government means a disarmed world. This includes the Vietminh and the Hukbalahaps as well as the British Navy and the Red Army. But if a disarmed Vietminh means the continuance of the Bao Dai regime, why should the Vietminh disarm? Do we really think it will disarm? The peoples of Asia have fought for 400 years to regain indepedence from the West. They will not lightly surrender this independence on the basis of Western promises that world government will be "flexible." They are not persuaded by the argument that a world government is necessary to allow the Soviet Union and the United States to peacefully coexist. Rather, perhaps they are persuaded of the truth of this argument, but it is more immediate and more important to them to know what will be the effect of the establishment of a world government on their problems, the abolition of misery and feudalism.

It is not only that two thirds of the world are concerned with misery and feudalism. It is that they do not believe that the other one third is also concerned with these evils. There is a legacy of hostility, suspicion, fear, and wounded dignity that the Western world has bequeathed to Asia and Africa. And few of our actions since 1945 have been designed to remove these fears and suspicions. Unless definite action is taken now to remove this legacy, then all our talk of world government is not likely to be received very favorably.

Because entry into a world government is so full of dangers for the United States, we often do not realize that the dangers are as great, if not greater, for other countries. Federalists, to be sure, have to fight isolationism, unenlightenment, national pride here at home. But, whereas the United States is strong and hence could be expected perhaps to be generous, much of the world is weak and can ill afford to trust lightly promises to be fulfilled in the future.

Justice Douglas in his address to the UWF Convention said: "The question is not whether revolutions will take place throughout the world. They are as certain as time. The question is: Who will direct these revolutions? Will they follow democratic lines or will they be under totalitarian auspices? Through history all attempts to suppress them eventually have failed. In recent years the powers that allied themselves with decadent vested interests against revolutions in Asia lost the friendship of the peoples. The powers that allied themselves with the people's struggle for independence have constantly gained in favor."

The Soviet Union has, by and large, very effectively allied itself with the people's struggle for independence. It seems to me that this fact is of prime concern to federalists. It is not enough for us to urge that American foreign policy have a defined aim of world government as the solution to the American-Russian struggle. We must also urge that American foreign policy have a defined aim of assuming some leadership in the struggle for a better life throughout the world. Thus, I would say, there are at least two problems, not just one, with which world federalists should be concerned.

To urge land reform and tax reform in Asia, to urge concern with the minimum of social security indispensable to a decent life, is no doubt peripheral to the abolition of anarchy, peripheral though essential. But is is not peripheral to the central problem of most of the world, the revolt against the shackles of an outmoded social and economic structure. If we American federalists hope to induce the world to renounce the weapon of revolution and accept the path of law and of order, then we must first demonstrate a deep, personal concern with those problems which most of the world faces. A bird in the hand is worth two in the bush. The power of revolution is in the hand. World government lies in the bush. A restoration of confidence in the West's interest in the problems of social revolution is a prerequisite to the interest of the underdeveloped areas in world order.

The United States, being a prosperous and a free nation, is a conservative nation. Justice Roberts once told a group of student federalists that he worked for a world government in order that he might get back to being a good conservative again. This statement applies to the problem of social revolution as well as to that of anarchy. We must call to the American people as Thomas Carlyle once called to his contemporaries: "O my conservative friends, who still specially name and struggle to call yourselves 'conservative,' would to heaven I could persuade you of this world-old fact, than which Fate is not surer, that truth and justice alone are *capable* of being 'conserved' and preserved! The thing which is unjust, which is not according to God's law, will you, in a God's universe, try to conserve that? It is so old, say you? Yes, and the hotter haste, ought you, of all others, to be in, to let it grow no older! If but the faintest whisper in your hearts intimate to you that it is not fair,—haste, for the sake of conservatism itself, to probe it rigorously, to cast it forth at once and forever if guilty."

Federalist Opinion, *May 1951*

## Appendix 27

### THE MEANING OF REVOLUTION

*An editorial published in* World Frontier *in 1952 under the direction of Editor-in-Chief Shane Riorden.*

Communist propaganda has succeeded over a time in so denaturing certain words that our language of politics is becoming increasingly tongue-tied. Peace, Democracy, and Revolution are perhaps the best examples of such abused words. In the language of a recent campaign slogan, we say, "Don't let them take it away."

The word Revolution is, we believe, a useful one with no adequate substitute, and so we here propose to state what it means to us.

First perhaps, is our belief that revolutionary ideas should be heard. Such ideas are, almost by definition, unpopular ideas, and yet if history teaches us anything it is that such ideas are the very seed of the body of human progress. It is also true that vital ideas cannot be suppressed, and the attempt to do so only corrupts the suppressors. We believe that the genius of constitutional democracy is its discovery that the free expression of ideas leads not to disunity or "disloyalty" but to the deepest sense of a people united in freedom and tolerance.

To argue that radical ideas are often foolish ideas is to miss the entire point of the philosophy of free expression in a constitutional democracy. A radical idea cannot be acted upon in such a system because action requires acceptance of the idea by many people. When this happens, the idea is no longer truly radical.

The democrat faces a real problem when he sees that the proponent of an idea palpably knows that what he says is untrue or deliberately uses words which he knows will convey a different meaning to his audience than to himself. Senator McCarthy and the American Communists come readily to mind. The democratic solution is more pragmatic than logical. Let them talk, and let their opponents talk; the truth will become manifest. The solution is far from infallible but the alternative—suppression and conformity—is infinitely worse.

Following from these beliefs is our belief that the idea of world federal government being a revolutionary one has a right to be heard. And it should be heard because we believe that world government is the most important revolutionary idea of our time—revolutionary because it revolts against the nation-state as the ultimate organization of mankind, important because it is the only solution to world war and world anarchy. One of the purposes of this publication is to serve that end. Parenthetically, let us add that this idea has been mistakenly, and often viciously, associated with another revolutionary movement, world communism. Their principal similarity is their attack on American nationalism, but their difference, which is profound, is that one merely substitutes Russian nationalism while the other suggests a whole new worldwide level of political allegiance, not as a substitute to love of country, but an addition to it.

The third meaning of revolution for us lies in our interest in those countries in the Middle East, Asia, and Africa where a dual revolution is now simmering or boiling. The first part of this upheaval in time is the revolt for national independence. The second (which in many cases may come only after the success of the first) is the struggle for equality. The United States is only incidentally responsible for the revolutionary conditions there. The attitude which the United States takes toward these revolutions will, however, determine to a great extent the history of the next hundred years. As Americans and democrats, it is easy for us to accept, in theory at least, the first of these revolutions—the fight for national independence—for our own country was born of such a rebellion.

As believers in constitutional government and humanitarian solutions to problems, we find it harder to understand and sympathize with the second. For this revolution whose goal is the social and economic transformation of these countries will often involve violent upheaval, bloodshed, and their typical aftermath, totalitarian government.

If we recoil automatically from revolution, we shall, with respect to revolutionary ideas and the revolutions for independence, be untrue to our historical experience. With respect to the revolutions for equality and transformation of the state, we shall be unable to act intelligently.

The second revolution poses for us the greatest dilemma. Our more conservative compatriots have already recoiled from even its most passive and law-abiding examples, merely because reforms were undertaken under the banner of socialism. And similarly, some of our most humanitarian compatriots have recoiled from revolutions where violence and authoritarian methods have been used. For most of us, the fact that socialism is one of the revolutionary goals is not unduly alarming, nor do we wholly abandon hope for good results merely because violence has been used.

Yet in the events that are to come, our hopes for enlightened and democratic and thorough-going peaceful reform are going to be rudely shaken. In some countries there is a foundation for democratic change—for example, India. In other countries there can be violent, authoritarian, but nevertheless valuable reform under a strong national leader—for example, Egypt. In still other countries, unfortunately, there seem to be no substantial alternatives between reform and revolution as espoused by the local communists, and the unyielding power of the landed class which now rules. The landed class may be found on the side of independence, but unalterably opposed to the more fundamental second revolution.

It was a familiar shibboleth of well-meaning Americans as recently as six years ago that the United States should promote a "third" or liberal party in China, since the communists on one hand and the Kuomintang were both bad for different reasons. More realistic observers, even at this time, pointed out that this third force in China was largely a mirage. China is an especially valuable example of the problems we face because our policy there was disastrous to Chinese-American relations from any point of view. For a long time liberals went along with our government's half-hearted support of Chiang Kai-Shek because they were looking for that ephemeral third party as a possible successor to Chiang, or they kidded themselves with the idea that the Chinese Communists were not really communists at all. While the weakness of the liberals was day-dreaming, the weakness of the conservatives was miserliness and bombast. They really wanted the Kuomintang to stay in power. They were far from willing to do what that long and expensive job involved. The result was that we intervened feebly in behalf of Chiang and we earned the reputation of imperialist meddling without realizing any of the profits of being imperialistic. It was probably physically possible for a really large-scale American intervention to prevent a Communist victory, but no one, least of all the Republican howlers, was willing to do anything of the sort. The administration was apparently too inept or craven to point out to the country what the realistic alternatives were.

In several Asian countries, we are now where we stood in China in 1946. In those situations we must weigh the facts in each case and take the main chance: either get in or get out. In many other places, the facts do not call for such a decisive step and are really so diverse that they defy generalizations of policy. Perhaps the best procedure would be to state several propositions and apply them to the particular cases:

1. Recognize the existence and inevitability of the dual revolution.
2. Encourage and help those revolutions where possible (which in some cases might mean a strictly hands-off policy, in others active economic and political aid).
3. If there is no realistic alternative to indigenous communist leadership of the second revolution, we must choose between outright intervention and a friendly policy looking hopefully to Titoism.

We have here stated three meanings of revolution, but in a sense they are one. Revolutionary acts—the creation of a world government, the achievement of national independence, and the attack on economic and social injustice—must go hand in hand, and all must and will be furthered by the free expression of revolutionary ideas.

*Shane Riorden, Editor-in-Chief, William Friedlander, Donald McIntosh, Gilbert Jonas, Associate Editors,* World Frontiers, *Vol. 1, No. 3, Winter 1952-1953*

## Appendix 28

## NATIONALISM: GRAND ILLUSIONS AND POLITICAL FACT
by Gilbert Jonas

*During 1953 the student federalists, under the aegis of WORLD, launched its first campaign against colonialism. In so doing, they found it necessary to explain the relationship of nationalism to capitalism.*

The recent General Assembly debates on North African independence contained a good deal of nonsense, as well as enough sense to justify their existence. It would be naive to assume that the debates themselves changed any of the delegates' minds; undoubtedly it was the influence of the United States which led the traditionally anti-imperialist Latin American bloc to present an "innocuous compromise" (in the words of the *New York Times*). Even the most casual observer could see the United States delegation trying not to "lose" either the French or the Arab-Asian bloc. In the end, the alleged needs for French cooperation in NATO and the European Union persuaded the United States to adopt a position which not only defied American tradition, but also alienated the anti-colonialist world.

At the same time, Mr. Acheson's success in persuading the Latin Americans to initiate and support a "compromise" illustrates the new kind of political control characteristic of the 20th century. Small nations can no longer maintain their political independence even though they may retain their territorial integrity; the sheer size and economic power of the greater states, if only by coincidence and accident, tend to draw the lesser nations toward one sphere or another for their own survival. Economic power of the kind the United States possesses in relation to other nations, including those of Western Europe, is likely to be the deciding factor in the really critical political issues, if only through the tacit possibility (or explicit threat) of withholding economic aid. This pattern may not be imperialism of the 19th century variety, but it has the same net effect, even if its methods differ from the institution glorified by a Cecil Rhodes or a Theodore Roosevelt.

As to the substance of the General Assembly debates on the question of Tunisian and Moroccan independence, both sides relied on a point of international law. The pro-French bloc, including Ambassador Jessup, argued that international treaties (of Algeciras and Fez) give to France the responsibility of determining the foreign affairs of both Morocco and Tunisia. Within this bloc some of the colonial powers, including South Africa and Great Britain, maintained that the UN, by virtue of Article 2, paragraph 7 of the Charter, does not have jurisdiction in colonial (i.e., domestic) affairs.

The General Assembly majority clearly rejected this position by voting to place the matter on the agenda for discussion and then by actually coming to a vote on a resolution. The Arab-Asian nations, together with Guatemala and Mexico, argued that the same international treaties guaranteed the sovereignty of the Moroccans and Tunisians notwithstanding the French responsibilities under the Protectorate Agreements. Although as recently as August 1952, the International Court of Justice upheld this position regarding American claims for equal commercial rights in Morocco, the Court, of course, cannot enforce such decisions. Since each nation remains the final authority for interpretation and enforcement, any argument based on international law tends to be a rationalization of a predetermined political position.

## Implications of the Debate

The real significance of the debates lies in a broader context. In the final voting, the Arab-Asian and Soviet blocs, a clear majority in terms of population, were slightly outvoted by a coalition of colonial powers, the United States, and a collection of reluctant Latin American nations. The Soviet bloc is once again riding the wave of the 20th century revolutions of mankind, symbolized by the Arab-Asian bloc. These revolutions are, to varying degrees, an extension of the democratic, nationalist, and social revolutions of the last two centuries. The forces in opposition stand for a *status quo* in which their wealth and their past colonialist exploitation are significantly conspicuous.

The history of imperialism in the last few decades has demonstrated the hopelessness of any attempt to maintain control of a colonial area once a full-fledged independence movement is under way. From their own point of view, the only realistic course for the metropolitan powers is to withdraw, gradually if there is time, rapidly if there is none. For an interim period, political control can be maintained, of course, by their military power, but the cost will be prohibitive, especially as the continued struggle gradually wrecks the economic wealth of the colony. In areas such as these, only full political self-determination will satisfy the native peoples.

Although self-rule cannot be denied these people, we must recognize the falsity of the once unquestioned belief that a peaceful and prosperous world order can be built on the principle of national self-determination. The principle assumes that national groups can be determined along some combination of racial, linguistic, or ethnic lines and can be geographically defined. The fallacy of this premise has been demonstrated by the history of the last 50 years; not only has it been next to impossible to separate groups along national geographic lines, but assuming its possibility, the net result would be an incredible balkanization of the world. The experience of the numerous multi-national states like Switzerland, Canada, Russia, and the United States illustrates that the ideal of national self-determination has never been fulfilled and is not a prerequisite for peace or order.

The principle further assumes that national groups have rights which can be fulfilled only by political self-determination. It is important to remember that only individuals, not nations, have rights. These rights—political, social, and economic—were thought during the 19th century to be most securely safeguarded by the achievement of national self-determination. Not only did the very contrary—progressive limitation of individual rights—prove true, but as this nationalism became aggressive, it became clear that the "rights" of one nation pursuing its "place in the sun" infringed upon those of other nations.

Some people mistakenly conclude, therefore, that even full-fledged indigenous independence movements—such as exist in Indo-China, Malaya, Tunisia and Morocco—should be opposed because the benefits of national self-determination are illusory. This would be to oppose the inevitable. On the other hand, it would be equally mistaken to conclude that once these peoples have achieved independence, their troubles will be over. In the modern world, small nations cannot remain independent, either economically or, at least in areas affected by the tensions of the world power struggle, politically. If the nations in the colonial world do not enter among themselves into political and economic combinations of some kind, they will find that they will have escaped from the old imperialism only to fall into the clutches of the new *de facto* control exercised through economic pressure.

There are signs that groupings of nations, independent of Moscow and Washington, may emerge. Ironically, the actions of the Western nations in the

Moroccan dispute served to encourage such third force tendencies. The road to any effective unification, however, will not be an easy one, largely because the same nationalistic forces which have forced the colonial powers out make all but the most informal cooperation with other nations very difficult.

In most of colonial Africa, political self-awareness has not developed sufficiently to give rise to strong nationalist movements. However, continued colonial exploitation and suppression will inevitably drive the colonial peoples to look upon complete national self-determination as a panacea for all their troubles. Here is a chance for the colonial powers to adopt a far-sighted and practical policy. If cultural autonomy, local political participation and decent living standards are granted before full-fledged nationalist demands have a chance to grow, the transition of these areas from colonies to equal members of larger groupings will be made immensely easier. Two examples of this would be the proposed Caribbean Federation and the gradual inclusion of the Gold Coast as an equal member of the British Commonwealth. Another realistic possibility may be UN trusteeship administration of all colonial areas as a step toward supranational world integration, in which each of these areas will have proportionate representation.

**Design for the Future**
The future of all nations lies in the direction of political and economic integration. The very survival of smaller groups dictates it. The gradual extension of human rights is based on it. Wherever it is necessary to fulfill promptly the demands of national self-determination, this fulfillment must be viewed as a phase in the development of greater political integration, if the welfare of these peoples is to be served. In the same light, wherever nationalist demands are not yet full-fledged, the phase of national independence can be circumvented by an integration which achieves the human benefits that national self-determination promises but cannot deliver. Ultimately a realistic policy must recognize that the extension of individual rights in a given area is the only criterion for determining which should be supported at a given time—national self-determination or greater political integration.

World Frontiers, *Vol. 1, No. 4, Spring 1953*

# Appendix 29

## MOROCCO AND TUNISIA—A RESOLUTION

*This WORLD Board resolution represents the first concrete political attack against colonialism by the student federalist movement.*

French rule in Morocco and Tunisia has denied the people of those lands:

1. Free political institutions and practices
2. A just share of the economic wealth of their lands
3. Protection under law and order consistent with civilized standards
4 The right to govern themselves as they deem fit.

The people of Morocco and Tunisia have come to realize that, under French rule, they cannot achieve ultimate fulfillment of their own dignity as human beings and have therefore embarked upon a concentrated movement for ultimate national independence.

The French government, under pressure from French colonists in North Africa, has refused even to discuss real restoration of sovereignty to the Moroccan and Tunisian people and has, in its efforts, been supported by the few remaining colonial powers and the United States. Meanwhile in order to maintain their power, the French have resorted to coercive measures and outright violence which has resulted in the death of hundreds of Moroccans and Tunisians, as well as of Frenchmen, and the jailing of thousands of nationalist leaders.

Realizing that this situation involves many complex factors, such as the certainty of some French economic losses, we nevertheless believe that past French gains more than compensate for these losses and that the basic justice of the Moroccan and Tunisian independence cause must be the primary consideration.

In view of these facts, and recognizing that the desires of the Moroccan and Tunisian people are part of the worldwide surge for the betterment of their lot on the part of the downtrodden, predominantly colored, and poverty-afflicted people of the world.

Convinced that the rejection of these hopes and desires will drive the Moroccans and Tunisians, and eventually all other oppressed peoples, down the path of violence and anarchy and into the arms of an even worse and perhaps more final tyranny;

Determined to participate in the creation of a just and peaceful world community based on human dignity, political equality, and economic justice and the establishment of a federal world government in which all these basic rights of man are safeguarded and in which each man counts as one;

We therefore urge the United States, through its citizens and representatives, to support in the framework of the United Nations the desires of the Moroccan and Tunisian people by endorsing their requests for UN-supervised negotiations between the French and the legitimate leaders of the Moroccans and Tunisians for

—Democratic home rule with sovereignty residing in the people of Morocco and Tunisia, guaranteed by a constitution freely arrived at and a representative government

—Guarantee of a just share of the material resources of Morocco and Tunisia for the people who live there, together with guarantees of legitimate French economic interests which do not conflict with those of the Moroccans and Tunisians; and,

If necessary, an interim period of political tutelage for self-rule under United Nations jurisdiction

*Approved by the WORLD National Board, Dec. 20, 1952*

# *Appendix 30*

*The leaders of WORLD produced this document as part of a nationwide information campaign in support of Morrocco's independence struggle throughout 1953.*

# FACT SHEET ON MOROCCO, 12/4/52

### The Issue of International Law

*Facts*: Moroccan independence and sovereignty are guaranteed by the Treaty of Algeciras (1906) and the Treaty of Fez (1912), both of which the French signed. Moroccan sovereignty was reiterated by a decision of the International Court of Justice in August 1952, when the Court upheld the rights of Americans trading in Morocco.

*Conclusion*: French refusal to grand de facto independence and sovereignty to the Sultan of Morocco is a violation of at least two international treaties and of international law as it is traditionally understood. Asian-Arab insistence of UN Assembly jursidiction in the Moroccan problem is a step forward in the evolution of law from the international order to supra-national order.

### The Issue of Political Self-Determination

*Facts*: Prior to 1912, the Moroccan people enjoyed over 1,000 years of uninterrupted political indepedence and cultural identity. After 1912, the French gradually assumed direct political control, predominantly by force of arms, denying the Moroccans both participation in their own government and adequate political tutelage as preparation for eventual self-government.

Conclusion: French rule in Morocco is the denial of the right of self-government to a legitimate national and cultural entity with a definite continuous history.

**The Issue of Economic Justice**
*Facts*: The French rule, by its imperialistic nature, has transformed the Moroccan economy so that it is linked to and dependent on that of France as a market for raw materials and a producer of manufactured goods. French political control has ensured French monopolies in economic development, resulting in an unjust distribution of Morocco's wealth, the larger share being drained from the economy by the French, the smaller share being insufficient to produce an adequate, much less rising, standard of living for the Moroccans. After 40 years of French rule, the Moroccans are still poor, disease-ridden, and illiterate. In some cases, their lot, linked to a money economy since 1912, has actually deteriorated. The French colonists meanwhile have monopolized most of the good land, most of the political control, and almost all of the beneficial effects of modernization, such as hospitals and schools, both of which are paid by from taxes on the Moroccans. The French have, in addition, created an artificial feudal system, binding the Moroccan peasants to the land with extortionate taxes and laws and further depriving them from a just share of the fruits of their toil.

*Conclusion*: By its very nature, French imperialism in Morocco is based on economic injustice—the denial to Moroccans of a just share of what they produce—and, insofar as this denies freedom, French imperialism is counter to human dignity.

**The Issue of Human Dignity**
*Facts*: One of the justifications of French rule in Morocco has been the assertion of the concept of racial supremacy. Moroccans have been subjected to all the indignities and humiliations of a subjected people.

*Conclusion*: Moroccans have come to identify themselves with the darker skinned peoples who have been traditionally subjected by the white European West. Their cause has been taken up by the Asian-Arab bloc in the UN who historically suspect the West of racist feelings. Much of the tensions in these areas is directly traceable to opposition to Western racism. Insofar as people in the underdeveloped areas identify themselves with Moroccan independence, a strong factor is inescapably that of anti-racist tendencies.

**The Issue of Civil Liberties**
*Facts*: Prohibition of freedom of Assembly, press, and speech have marked French rule, especially since the declaration of siege in 1940, which has yet to be rescinded. The Arab press is censored. All trade unions but the communist-controlled C.G.T. are prohibited. Moroccans are required to carry special passes and visas to travel from one part of Morocco to another. Since the abolition of Islamic law, Moroccans have none of the safeguards of law which would then guarantee a fair trial, the right of habeous corpus, etc.

*Conclusion*: French rule has all the earmarks of a totalitarian state in Morocco. Suppression of these facts in the United States, moreover, leaves a strong flavor of suspicion that American civil liberties are not unaffected by the denial of civil liberties in Morocco.

*In sum*, we condemn French rule in Morocco as a denial of human dignity, economic justice, and political equality for the Moroccan people. We urge the establishment of political self-determination for the Moroccan people because legitimate nationalism is a prerequisite for responsible internationalism. The creation of an independent Moroccan state is necessary for the growth of a just and peaceful world community. French adherence to her treaty obligations is part of the process of the evolution of international law, which together with an emerging world community, and the creation of equal nations based on legitimate national aspirations, will combine to produce the conditions necessary for the formation of a world federal government, upon which the ultimate peace, justice, and freedom of the human race depend.

*Distributed by WORLD to its chapters, members, and the press, December 1952*

*Appendix 31*

*Student federalists in Illinois produced a lively and thoughtful periodical,* Federalist Opinion, *under the editorship of Harry Lustig. As the decisive meeting in Des Moines approached, Lustig and his colleagues offered these guidelines to the UWF delegates.*

## A Guide to Des Moines

The questions to be faced by delegates to the UWF General Assembly at Des Moines will be critical, complex, and often confused. Thus we felt that we could provide a service by giving a brief, non-partisan description of the issues and referring wherever possible to fuller expositions of the points of view cited. We also hope that those who first read this editorial after Des Moines will find it helpful in evaluating the results of that Assembly.

Perhaps the most fundamental programmatic issue which will come to the fore is the debate between the "grass-rooters" and the "top-level boys." Those who advocate spending more time, effort, and money on education at the community level will point to the failures and retrenchments suffered by UWF during the past year and will argue that it is a useless endeavor to try to change U.S. foreign policy by working among a few Congressmen for the passage of a world government resolution, when the spirit of the American people is still in large measure narrowly isolationist and fiercely nationalistic. This viewpoint is developed in Max Awner's article "Let's Make UWF a People's Organization," in this issue of *Federalist Opinion*. The top-level point of view is developed in the article, "Basic Reorientation Voted by UWF Leaders," in the January 17, 1951, issue of *For Your Information*. A defense of the top-level approach, however, may not be further attempted; instead, the argument will probably be advanced that the present UWF program is a well-balanced one and the best that can be carried out with the funds available.

Most of the grass-roots critics will probably attack the administration on two more counts: the withdrawal from cooperation with World Government News and the firing of Vernon Nash. Both of these measures, it will be claimed, constituted attempts by the national leadership to silence critics of its policies and to prevent the spread of dissenting opinions among the membership. To this, the present administration will reply that a house organ was necessary for the effective dissemination of information among the members and that the release of Dr. Nash was a regrettably necessary economy measure.

Another issue which will be discussed is whether UWF's program should be concerned solely with advocacy of world government or whether this is the time to stress other short-range steps to peace and progress. The division on these questions of "functionalism" and "taking stands" will be along the same familiar lines. Minimalists will object to the thinning of our resources and to the possible creation of dissension within our own ranks through the taking of stands on controversial foreign policy questions and through the support of "side issues." Maximalists will urge that UWF lead the way with an imaginative short range peace program and that it demonstrate its concern with world economic and social problems by lining up a good share of its resources and energy behind the Stringfellow Barr proposals. The first viewpoint is perhaps most closely represented in Dale Hiller's article in this issue of *Federalist Opinion;* for an exposition of the second, we recommend the articles by Harris Wofford and Harry Lustig in our February issue.

The argument of universal versus partial federation, so predominant at last year's General Assembly at Washington, will probably still be with us, especially since the convention is being held—from the universalists' point of view—in the lair of the enemy. It is the Iowa delegation which has always claimed that world government can be sold to the American people only on a strong anti-Russian line.

But the question which may well engender the greatest heat this year is the composition and method of election of the National Executive Council. So great is the concern that a special "Members Committee for a Representative National Executive Council" has been formed weeks in advance of the convention. Its sponsors decry the present method of election of the organization's governing body as unrepresentative and claim that the convention requirement of voting for a complete slate of 30 nominees deprives the voting delegates of the opportunity of casting their ballots for only those nominees of whom they approve. As evidence of the alleged unrepresentativeness of the National Executive Council, they cite the reversal, by the present Council, of some of the policies adopted at the Washington Assembly. They advocate the creation of a National Council whose members will be elected by the State Branches and, in small measure, by the Student Divison. The administration replies with the claim that the present Council makeup is the most effective and that many valuable and important members would not be elected under the new plan. Recently, a committee of the present National Executive Council evolved a so-called compromise proposal. It is fully described and defended in the May issue of *The Federalist*.

So much for the problems facing UWF as a whole. If these questions are important for the continuing health of the organization, the answer to the questions which are facing the Student Division are keys to the survival of a student federalist organization in this country. The Student Division of UWF simply cannot go on, as it is presently constituted, for reasons which will become apparent upon reading the articles concerned with this problem. There are three ways out, short of completely abandoning every attempt of spreading the federalist idea among students in the United States. The first is the complete dissolution of the Student Division and the integration of its members and chapters among the remainder of UWF, without any special recognition of the special program interests by the students. Although it is concerned with a somewhat different question, Charles Melchior's article in our May issue perhaps comes closest to being in sympathy with this solution. Secondly, there exists the hope of influencing the policies of UWF as a whole to such an extent at Des Moines and of electing an administration so friendly to the students that the Student Divison could essentially maintain its present structure but would enjoy enough programmatic autonomy and financial support to carry out its educational activities. What minimum changes in administrative policy would have to be made on the national level is clearly explained in the article by H. Gay in this issue of *Federalist Opinion*. Finally there are those who believe that the only solution lies in reverting to a completely independent student federalist organization, responsible for its finances as well as for its program and policies. Gil Jonas expounds such a viewpoint in this issue in his Letter to the Editors.

These, then, are what we believe to be the most important problems which we as federalists will have to wrestle with at Des Moines. We have chosen not to express an editorial opinion but have preferred instead to state our views, in some cases, in individual, signed articles in this and previous issues of *Federalist Opinion*. And no doubt we will chip in, in the debate at Des Moines. There is one problem, however, on which we would like to memorialize our readers. At every UWF convention, after many hours of debate on a particularly controversial issue, there is some individual who gets up and says, "I don't know what all this argument is about; all I know is that I am for world government." or words to that effect. The temptation is strong, after long and bitter wrangling, to cheer the astute apostle of peace and to adopt a meaningless or contradictory "compromise" resolution. We hope that this will not happen at Des Moines. The issues are important enough that they must be settled once and for all. The organization must know where it is going.

Federalist Opinion, *June 1951*

*Appendix 32*

# THE INTERIM COMMITTEE OF AMERICAN FEDERALIST YOUTH

*This was the official call to federalist and other American youth to found a new student organization in 1951.*

The Interim Committee of American Federalist Youth invites you to support freedom, peace, and justice by working for a world federal government which will insure order and promote justice for all men working for those measures which will create such a world community by:

- Supporting the struggle of men everywhere for freedom and for economic and social justice.
- Supporting an expanded world development program and technical aid.
- Supporting oppressed men throughout the world in their efforts to end colonialism.
- Opposing at home the abrogation of civil liberties and the imposition of thought control on our citizenry.

Come to the founding convention of a new youth world government organization in Philadelphia the weekend of October 19-21. The convention will be held at the YWCA, 2027 Chestnut Street.

**What ICAFY Is**
The Interim Committee was established by the UWF Student Convention which met at Des Moines in June. That convention—faced with a rapidly

declining student membership, decreased financial support, and marked apathy—considered how we could rebuild an effective youth federalist movement.

Because of policy and program differences with UWF, it seemed impossible to carry out within UWF the kind of program the delegates had outlined. The Interim Committee was elected and given the responsibility for organizing a convention to establish a new organization.

**What ICAFY Has Done**
Committees have prepared over the summer drafts on policy, program, and structure, which will be submitted to the convention, recommending:

- A broader policy than any world government organization in the U.S. now has
- A program which will emphasize education and field work and the training of leaders
- The publication of a magazine which will help to build in the United States strong, creative public opinion in favor of measures necessary to create a free, just, and prosperous world community
- Great chapter autonomy

**What the Convention Will Do**
The Convention will begin Friday, October 19, at 9 A.M. Registration will begin Thursday night, October 18.

The Convention will use ICAFY's reports as a basis for its discussions. To encourage participation by all delegates in the debates, the convention will break down into small groups, each of which will consider policy, program and structure. Each discussion group will elect representatives to policy, program, and structure drafting committees. These drafts will be submitted to the convention for adoption. The Convention will make the final decision about the nature of the new organization.

**Delegates and Votes**
ICAFY is sending invitations to many present and former youth members of federalist organizations and a few other selected youth leaders. However, representation will be based upon individuals present at the Convention, who have been invited, not upon already existing federalist chapters. Any individual who will signify his intention to work with the new organization will

be accredited as a voting delegate, provided that not more than ten delegates are accredited from one school or university, or community, whichever is smaller. In addition, all delegates coming to Philadelphia from points further than 1,000 miles will receive two votes; from points further than 2,000 miles, they will receive three votes. All other delegates, including the original 21 members of ICAFY, will receive one vote. In cases of conflict, the Convention Credentials Committee will have final jurisdiction.

**How You Can Come**
Send the registration blank below to ICAFY, 448 Sixth Avenue, New York City, together with a $3.00 registration fee. Most of the delegates will stay at the Whittier Hotel, 15th and Cherry Streets. Rooms for two or three occupants will cost between $2.00 and $2.83 per person per night. Single rooms are available and are more expensive. Each delegate who wants ICAFY to reserve a room for him must send with the registration blank a $3.00 room deposit, which will be credited toward the total hotel bill. First registrations received will receive preference in allocation of rooms. If you want to be sure of one of our reserved rooms, return this blank to ICAFY by October 12.

There will be a Convention Banquet, which will cost about $2.00 per delegate. Check registration blank if you wish a ticket reserved for you.

ICAFY will send you information about the agenda and where and when to register.

REGISTRATION BLANK
NAME _____
ADDRESS _____
SCHOOL _____
MAILING ADDRESS _____
I wish to be a (Delegate( Observer
( Enclosed $3.00 registration fee.
Please reserve a room for me for 3 nights—October 18–20.
( Single( Multiple
( Enclosed is $3.00 room deposit.
( I will arrange for my own accommodations.
( Reserve a banquet ticket for me.
( I cannot attend, but would like to receive a report of the Convention and more information about plans for the new organization.
*Return to:* Interim Committee of Federalist Youth
448 Sixth Avenue, New York City

## Appendix 33

## WORLD—a Youth Organization for a Just World Community under Federal World Government

*"WORLD is doing precisely what our student generation badly needs."*
—Albert Einstein

### WORLD Statement of Beliefs

*We believe* in the creation of a just and peaceful world community based on human dignity, economic justice, and political equality.

*To this end, we propose the establishment of a federal world government and the taking of certain related interim measures.*

We strive toward a world community in which all men:

Will be free from the threat of war
Will enjoy a decent measure of health, comfort and security, and will have an opportunity to better their standards of living
Will enjoy the friendship and respect of their fellow men
Will have an opportunity to develop to the fullest their human capacities
Will enjoy the widest possible amount of personal freedom
Will control their governments and the societies in which they live

We are convinced that men everywhere are striving toward these goals. Yet today we live in a world where:

There is widespread poverty, starvation, and sickness
Millions of people are victims of prejudice and hatred
People are bound in ignorance and near-slavery
Men are kept in oppression by foreign rule, feudalism, and dictatorship
Everywhere men are striving to abolish these injustices.

In this ungoverned world community, nations are spending vast quantities of human and natural resources, preparing to settle their differences as they always have—by force. Once more all men are threatened by the devastation of war.

To achieve the just and peaceful world community we desire, we will work to improve social, economic, and political conditions and to create a federal world government. By government, we mean an organization with institutions responsible to the people, and with power to make decisions and enforce them on its individual citizens, without infringing on the basic human rights of individuals. This government must have power beyond mere police power in order to cope with problems of worldwide concern. Yet we believe many of these powers will not and should not be used if, through their national governments or otherwise, men find just and democratic solutions to their problems.

We believe the creation of a world government will accelerate the progress toward a just and peaceful world community. Conversely we are also deeply convinced that the possibility of achieving an effective world government, and with it a just world community, depends to a great degree upon practical measures of economic and social reform which can be undertaken now both at home and abroad.

*Therefore:*
1. We support all attempts to establish a just and democratic world government, whether by transformation of the United Nations through revision of its Charter, in a world convention of directly elected representatives of the people of the world, by adoption of a constitution prepared by a world convention of parliamentarians, or by any other lawful and reasonable means.
2. We support enlarged programs of social and technical assistance and world economic development. These programs should be under international control whenever possible.

3. We support peoples of the colonial and trust areas in their endeavor to win political self-determination. Subject to their wishes, we believe that the United Nations should have some interim role in the administrative control of these areas, unless they are now ready for independence.
4. We support the right of all peoples to control their own resources and economies. Men have the right to freedom from economic exploitation and the assurance of a just share of the fruits of their labor.
5. We support efforts to increase world trade among all nations and to remove unreasonable restrictions on that trade.
6. We support the elimination throughout the world of all forms of discrimination and inequality, whether for political, racial, national, or religious reasons.
7. We support efforts to preserve and extend civil liberties everywhere and support the principles of the Universal Declaration of Human Rights. We emphatically oppose the present attacks on civil liberties in the United States.
8. We support the work of the United Nations and its specialized agencies and commissions in their efforts to remove international tensions and improve the conditions under which men live.

*Adopted at WORLD's first annual convention, Philadelphia, 1951. Revised at WORLD's second annual convention, Urbana, Illinois, 1952*

*We will act* to give the youth of America the clearest possible understanding of the problems facing the world and our country, to urge young people to work out constructive solutions to these problems, and to suggest ways in which young people can work together to put such solutions into effect.

*To carry out this program:*

1. WORLD publishes a quarterly thought magazine, *World Frontiers,* which serves as an outlet for that segment of thinking Americans youth which is both freedom-loving and world-minded.

"*World Frontiers* is an attractive and interesting publication. And I wish it and your organization all success."
—*Associate Justice William O. Douglas*

2. WORLD recognizes the direct relationship between a just and lasting world peace and a universal acceptance of the intrinsic value and dignity of all human beings. We oppose all forms of discrimination and, through a program of education and social action, work to implement the provisions of the Universal Declaration of Human Rights. We support efforts to preserve and extend academic freedom and student rights on American campuses.
3. World disseminates information on work opportunities for young people in social and economic development programs, especially for underdeveloped areas. We support the efforts of the International Development Placement Association (IDPA) to recruit, train and place qualified young technicians in such work.
4. As another method of building the just world community we desire, WORLD will work to register Americans as world citizens, thus accepting the responsibilites of world—as well as national—citizenship. We will also urge and aid local communities to take similar steps by declaring themselves "world territory."

*WORLD's local chapters* have combined dynamic thought with action. For example:

1. The Washington, D.C., chapter in 1952 took part in a peaceful demonstration before the South African embassy in the national capitol to protest the discriminatory policies of the South African government. It was timed to coincide with the beginning of the widespread non-violent resistance of South Africans against the racist policies of their government.
2. In defense of academic freedom, the University of Minnesota chapter in 1952 led a mass student protest against the dismissal for his unorthodox political views of a Minnesota professor.
3. The University of Chicago chapter in June 1952 planned and was host to WORLD'S annual National Policy Institute, where young people met to discuss problems of U.S. and foreign policy and international affairs.
4. Other WORLD members and chapters have in the past led campaigns to send wheat to India, vigorously fought the inclu-

sion of loyalty oaths on campuses, organized protests against outbreaks of racist violence in the United States and collected funds for their victims, campaigned for student governments to send delegates to the Rome Congress for World Government, and cooperated with local social welfare organizations to eliminate local conditions of poverty, ignorance, and disease.

**What We Are**
WORLD is a national, non-profit organization for young people, 30 years of age and under. Persons over 30 may join as associate members with all but voting privileges.

The policies, program, and officers of WORLD are determined at an annual convention of the membership. All members receive a monthly newsletter and *World Frontiers.*

WORLD is affiliated with World Student Federalists, the international student world government movement, located in Amsterdam. We also cooperate with other student and adult groups whose programs are similar to our own. WORLD was formed in October 1951.

**You May Join WORLD**
If you indicate support of our policy statements, you may join WORLDas an individual member or a member of a chapter.

Chapters may be formed by *five* members in high schools, colleges, and communities. WORLD chapters are free to work for the goals outlined in WORLD's policy statement in ways which they deem most advisable. The national organization has, however, established certain critieria for organization of chapters. This information and application forms may be obtained from the national office.

**Finally, It's Up to You**
It's up to you because it's your world.

It's up to you because no one else will do it for you.

From here on, you take over. You are the leaders of tomorrow's world. The future of the world is in your hands.

## Officers

Gilbert Jonas, Columbia University, Chairman
Virginia Lastayo Riorden, Executive Director
Harry Lustig, University of Illinois
Alan J. Upin, Albert Lea, Minnesota, Vice Chairmen
Shane Riorden, Bristol, Pennsylvania, Editor, *World Frontiers*

## National Board

Thomas Caldwell, University of Illinois
Anne Elmendorf, Stanford University
Murray Frank, New York School of Social Work
John Grifalconi, Cincinnati, Ohio
Bernard Heinzen, Carleton College, Minnesota
Kenneth Kurtz, Columbia University
John Logue, University of Chicago
Donald McIntosh, Columbia University
Loucille Melander, University of Minnesota
Frank Miller, Carleton College, Minnesota
Pete C. Novick, Dartmouth College
Shane E. Riorden, Bristol, Pennsylvania
Virginia Lastayo Riorden, Bristol, Pennsylvania
Immanuel Wallerstein, New York, New York
Ed Wolff, Washington, D.C.
*Office of the Chairman, 24 East 97th Street, New York 29, N.Y.

( I wish to enroll as a member of WORLD (membership includes to subscription to *World Frontiers* and continues for one year from date of joining).
I enclose:
( $3.00 regular ($5.00 associate(over 30)
( $4.50 couple ($7.50 couple (over 30)
( $2.00 high school
( I am interested in WORLD and would like more information.
*Name* _____
*Address*_____
*School and Year of Graduation*_____
*Permanent Address* _____
Return to:WORLD,RFD#2,Bristol,Penna.

*Appendix 34*

# WHERE WE STAND

by Don McIntosh

*As the cold war deepened and the fighting in Korea became more bloody, Americans increasingly abandoned the struggle to organize a lasting peace. WORLD board member Donald McIntosh sought to explain the student federalist dilemmas.*

This article is an attempt to define the point of view of those who have created WORLD. WORLD's policy is a synthesis of two streams of federalist thought which before now have been unable to agree completely. I will call them the "constitutional" and the "functional" approaches to world government. There are, of course, variants of each viewpoint; in each case, I will discuss the variant which I think most valid.

Federalist organizations have in the past usually adopted the constitutional approach, which argues as follows: The present nation-state system cannot solve the two main problems facing mankind today—the control of war and the allocation of the world's economic resources to obtain better satisfaction of mankind's needs. Control of war through balance of power, the most effective method within a nation-state framework, works only under special conditions which do not apply today. All that the balance of power can offer us is a perilous short-run stability with no prospect of long-run improvement. Meanwhile, world economic problems become ever more acute. With the major nations spending most of their energy maintaining their position in the power struggle, there is no hope that these problems can be solved. Attempts to do so within the nation-state system are a waste of time because such attempts will run counter to the dictates of national survival. A shaky holding operation is all that can be undertaken. Only the establishment of a federal world government can pull the world out of its ever-deepening crisis and enable mankind to move towards the solution of its major ills.

Those who hold this point of view differ as to the nature of the proposed world government. I believe they are on their firmest ground when they call for a federal government, democratic in nature, possessed of a preponderance of force and considerable economic powers.

While constitutionalists seek to move from world anarchy to world government, functionalists think the main problem is rather the transition from the world society to world community. The important distinction between society and community will emerge from the following description of this second stream in federalist thought.

During the past century, the world's economic and political systems have increasingly become a single intertangled network. This does not necessarily mean that a single economic and political system is emerging, but it does mean that each of the existing systems has such close ties with the others that any important event has global repercussions. I need not summarize the steps by which most economics have become world economics and most politics, world politics. We sum up this state of affairs by saying, "The world society now exists."

The only place where the world is not a unit, the functionalist argument continues, is in the minds of men. It is the sense of unity that is lacking. In a world as small and tightly knit as ours is becoming, international problems and conflicts will naturally arise. In this situation, men today seek at best their national welfare, which they usually consider to be antithetical or irrelevant to the welfare of other nations. The nation-state system is a system of cooperation, in that the nations trade with each other, and form more or less temporary alliances, and it is a system of struggle, in that when a conflict arises, each nation considers solely its own interest. Since appeal cannot be made to a sense of common interest, international conflicts can only be settled by force, threat of force, and propaganda. Issues are decided not by who is right, but by who is the strongest.

The functionalist considers this an undesirable state of affairs. He points out that all the great ethical systems affirm the central position of the doctrine of human equality. From this point of view, to act as if the welfare of one nation were more important than the welfare of another is immoral. This immoral state of affairs must be expected to continue as long as the largest unit with which the individual identifies himself is the nation-state. "The national interest" is the dominant value in the world today. When it is necessary to the national interest, the property, liberty, and the life of the individual must be sacrificed. Only when enough people have shifted their highest value from the nation-state to mankind itself will it be possible to move towards the solution of the world's problems on a moral basis.

The functionalist does not object to "power politics" in itself; he objects to the value (nationalism) which present-day world power politics serves. The use of force is not itself immoral; what is immoral is the use of force for the sake of the national interest. He would consider force perfectly moral if its use were the only way to further the interest of mankind. In this respect, functionalism naturally leads to federalism, for only government should use force for the sake of the community when force is justified.

The functionalist concludes that the time has come for the transition from the world society to the world community. The world society, an economic, political, and social network, exists already. The problems generated by the world society cannot be solved until a world community exists, that is, until a significant number of people feel obligated to act for the interest of the whole. For this, at bottom, is what defines a community—a sense of obligation to the welfare of the group. There must, of course, be some agreement as to what the welfare of mankind consists of. If we look around us, and remember the heritage of our civilization, these values are not hard to find. They can be expressed in three general terms: liberty, equality, and security. Together they spell one word: freedom.

Human welfare can be more concretely defined today by such words as human rights, political democracy, land reform, the end of imperialism, control of world cartels, social security, reduction of extremes of income. Perhaps even more fundamental reforms than these are needed.

The key fact about WORLD's position is that it has poured a functionalist content into a constitutionalist framework, thereby eliminating many of the weaknesses of both positions.

For example, the "orthodox" federalist point of view has always suffered from an inability to translate its policy into a program that has any concrete application to the world today. The task of convincing people of the need for a world government whose structure is dimly defined, and whose ideological content is totally neglected, is perhaps a worthy one. However, it is precisely the main obstacle to world government that is ignored by these omissions. United World Federalists, for example, has on this basis probably convinced everyone it is going to convince, and this is a considerable number. But where do they go from there? Attempts to amend the U.S. Constitution, obtain resolutions from Congress, or amend the U.N. Charter are worse than useless. To combat the very real ideological forces of nationalism with empty federalist formulae is like firing blanks at an enemy equipped with live ammunition. If you make enough noise, he will arouse himself sufficiently to destroy you with a single salvo.

If the goals which a world government is designed to serve are worth struggling for, they are worth struggling for now. Such struggles, if carried out correctly, can help build the world community on which world government must be based.

To take the other face of the coin, casting the functional approach into a federalist form adds a whole new dimension to the current fight for human justice. The isolated battles occurring all over the face of the globe can now be seen as the parts of a single struggle. World government at once symbolizes and embodies the goals of this struggle. Symbolically, it is the political expression of the basic ideal behind the fight for human justice—the brotherhood of man. These goals are embodied by world government because its establishment would be the greatest single stride towards their fulfillment. Only from a federalist point of view can the frontiers of human endeavor be seen in their true relationships to each other, and a grand strategy of battle be worked out, so that the operations on the various fronts will concentrate, rather than dissipate the energy of men of good will.

Thus is solved the old dilemma, "Which comes first, community or government?" The realization of each involves the other. The birth of a child provides an analogy. A period of development within the womb is necessary before birth can occur. The act of birth enables the growth of the infant to continue on a new level. The establishment of a world government will mark the birth of the world community, but for the birth to occur, the world community must develop for some time within the nation-state system. Nor will the world community reach full growth at the birth of a world government. Birth is simply a crucial and necessary event in the process of growth.

The policy of WORLD is an advance on previous federalist thinking, not because it is new, but because it consolidates ideas that have been developing for some time. Now that we have built an organization on these ideas, it is possible to start putting them into action. We do not claim to know any final answers to the great problems facing the world society, but we do hope, and believe, that armed with this point of view, we will be better able to attack these problems.

World Frontiers, *Vol. 1, No. 1, Spring 1952*

*Appendix 35*

# A Globalist Glossary

*From Paris, AMIP (newsletter of the Agence Mondialiste de Presse), discussing the movement for world federation's internal strife of the past year, reported a cynical definition.*

"A world federalist is a man who loves all men except the other world federalists of his country."

Some other definitions that were provoking self-conscious chuckles among federalists last month:

*Maximalist*—one who knows what would be good for the people of the world better than they do.
*Minimalist*—one who knows what the people of the world will accept better than they do.
*Partialist*—one who wants to have a federation even though nobody else is in it.
*Universalist*—one who believes that no nation should join a federation until all other nations have done so.

World Government News, *January 1952*

# Appendix 36

## INTERNAL SECURITY IN AMERICA

by Robert Redfield

*By 1952 the proponents of McCarthyism had begun to intimidate many of the nation's prominent thinkers and reformers. Prof. Redfield felt compelled to oppose the tide of witch hunts.*

The necessity to take special measures in time of special peril against enemies who are themselves something unpleasantly special must, of course, be recognized. The necessity in such a critical time to prevent a truly disloyal man from getting into a position of power is beyond question, and the laws and procedures with regard to espionage and treason need to be strong and effective. On the other hand, there seem to me five respects in which our efforts today to make ourselves strong within go beyond these necessities and turn the blows we strike for our own defense inward against our own breasts.

(1) We have deceived ourselves into thinking that we have acted effectively when much of our action has been in fact ineffective. We have cumbered the nation with a weight of security regulations that do not make us secure. No small amount of the nation's energy and human anxiety goes into the questioning, the enquiring, and the provings of innocence of Communist intention and connection. Asked to advise a Federal agency on some quite theoretical and non-political matter, a scientist is required to fill in forms and submit himself and his friends to long interrogations that yield nothing relevant to the task he is to perform. One questionnaire sent an American who was invited merely to lecture to a government agency was in fourteen closely printed pages and included the question, "Are there any unfavorable incidents in your life not mentioned above which may be discovered in subsequent

investigations, whether you were directly involved or not, which might require explanation? If so, describe."[1] Thousands of us spend hundreds of thousands of hours altogether on these efforts.

Some Americans, the improperly challenged and the wrongly suspect, find their productive and honorable activities brought to a halt for months while they are challenged and questioned. I could cite not a few cases known to me personally. The procedures to which such Americans must submit themselves violate deeply cherished principles as to the relationship between an American and his government. They are either public trials of a man's reputation, without legal safeguards, before the press and at the challenge of legislators who do not act as legislators but as prosecutors. Or else they are secret investigations before administrative loyalty boards, civil or military, with the power to deprive a man of his job with much of the effect of a conviction for crime. This is government by men and not by laws. Citizens who have been cleared are in some cases in substance ruined, for the mere fact that they were investigated makes the next employer reluctant to hire them. I know such men.

We might pay these high prices for security if these measures did in fact give us security. But they don't. They do not stop the traitor or the spy. By these means the real enemies are rarely caught. One does not detect espionage through a questionnaire or find treason in a textbook. The oath demanded of a secret enemy of the country will not protect us from that enemy; he will swear gladly. The oath demanded of a faithful public servant is an affront to him; he will not serve the better for submitting to its compulsion.

The real injury done to ourselves by these futile measures arises from the self-deception which they accomplish. We confuse ourselves by thinking that by these acts we have made ourselves safe. The oath demanded of a public servant deceives him who demands it. It is an incantation by proxy. It is a piece of primitive magic, like a charm recited by a savage to keep the tigers away. The charm recited, the savage may sleep less uneasily, but the tigers can only catch him the more readily.

(2) We have allowed bad men and bad acts to pass, granting them a measure of public approval, and so have weakened the principles of good conduct which have long strengthened and guided us. It is common to say of Senator McCarthy that one does not approve of his methods, but his ends—to attack

---

[1] Martin, Kingsley in Letters to the Editor, *New York Times*, June 22, 1952.

Communists—are the right ends. But the bad means are not sanctified by the good ends. Lying and bullying are bad and require to be constantly condemned, and there is no reason whatsoever for granting even tacit and qualified approval to lying and bullying when it is done for apparent self-interest. The discovery of how many proven Communists in high places can be soberly credited to Senator McCarthy? *The New York Times* says not one. And how many loyal Americans have been intimidated into ineffectiveness by what he and others like him have done? We can only weaken ourselves when we are silent before an anti-Communism that is an obvious cover for demagoguery. And when we say that a man's ends are good but we don't approve his methods, and then do nothing to stop the methods, we are acting just as many Germans did when Hitler began to bully and to lie under the claim that he would make Germany strong and free. They went along because they thought the ends were good.

We make a related mistake when we overvalue the advice and testimony of old-time recanted Communists. Because they attack Communism vigorously, we tend now to accept whatever they say, although we would not have accepted it when they were Communists. We forget that their present anti-Communism does not relieve us of the duty of judging how clearly and justly they think today. If we looked at them more critically, we would see that some of them—but of course not all—have that kind of mind which sees everything as white today and black tomorrow. They are, in the phrase of Eric Hoffer, inveterate True Believers. This being so, the testimony they now bring forward should be judged according to the demands of our reason.

If we did use our reason, we would not fall into the confusion to which True Believers of many political origins are prone, the belief that the world is divided into two kinds of people—Communists and anti-Communists. This just isn't so; the assumption ignores a third of mankind, most of them Asians. Moreover, one particularly distressing form of this dichotomizing of mankind that we hear now, and even applaud, divides the world into Communists and Christians. One or the other, we are told, must prevail. It is melancholy to hear this in a country where Jews, Buddhists, and Moslems are free to practice their religions and to receive political honor and support; the expression of this idea is a fine way to lose friends abroad; and it is another oversimplification with which to stifle our powers of rational thought.

This same confusion of which I now speak is most obviously shown in the acceptance of guilt by association. Again like savages, we have come to think that any two people or any two ideas that have been together have the qualities of each other—or at least the political intentions of each other. We have allowed a reasonable principle for catching criminals to grow into another sort of self-deceiving magic. If we are looking for a bank robber and find that the night watchman secretly consorts with bank robbers, we have good cause to enquire into the possibility that it was the night watchman who robbed the bank. But we have recently extended this principle into a fantastic network of secondary linkages by which any American can be proved guilty by association with somebody or something. If a man attends cocktail parties where members of left-wing organizations were present, we suspect the man's loyalty, whereas maybe he just likes cocktails. We find ideals and reforms guilty by association. When a federal investigator asks you or me about the efforts of a friend in working for Negro rights, it is because Communists apparently work for Negro rights too and our friend's efforts raise a presumption of guilt by association. Even our words are guilty by association. I really believe that if today Americans form any organization with the word "peace" in its name, they become subject to possible investigation. We have let the Russians poison the word "peace" for us. Recently I read that General Eisenhower was rebuked by some religious organization for coming out for the brotherhood of man. Didn't he know that was what the Russians were working for?

(3) We have allowed ourselves to become involved in fighting the battle that is over instead of the one that is before us. Men who ten years ago advocated measures which were not unreasonable then we now harass or exclude from public service because in the light of what we have all learned since, those measures would be unreasonable if adopted now. When General Marshall tried to get Chinese of several political kinds to cooperate in running China and in fighting the Japanese, he was a loyal and a reasonable man. In the light of what all of us then knew, in the face of the battles we had then to fight, he was neither wicked nor stupid. And the many Americans, in government or out of it, who worked to the same ends in the light of the same facts with the same honest intentions, were neither wicked nor stupid. Yet today many of us brand them as one or the other of these things because in the light of what we know today what they did then might have been pleasing to the Communists. Some of us impugn the character or the judgment of those who testified on behalf of men known now to have been perjurers or worse, although the witnesses could not have known it then and did their American duty in declaring the truth as to what they then knew.

All this turns our attention away from the place where it now belongs: on the present situation, the current problem. We have allowed ourselves to be caught up in a wasteful controversy as to whether what particular men did or said ten years ago with regard to China would or would not have affected the outcome in China. We also waste our energies by fighting Communists we used to have at home. In fact, the Chinese problem has changed utterly since 1942. In fact, the power and influence of Communists inside the United States is much less now than it was. A Washington correspondent summarizes the present situation as follows: "Communists are now all but powerless in the trade unions; in the intellectual and educational, world they lead isolated, ineffectual lives; and the handful who may still hold government jobs must, in order to remain concealed, abandon all political activity."[2] Yet many of us keep trying to say what ought to have been done ten years ago, while the danger of war and of seizure of power by Stalin abroad remains terribly great.

(4) We lost important friends abroad by these domestic demonstrations of irrationality. Many an Englishman looks with puzzled alarm at what he sees in this country. In his own country, spies have been caught and promptly punished without any considerable restraint upon freedom of opinion and discussion. You can make a speech for Communism in England, even from the vantage point of a cathedral or a university chair and, though you may thus show your own surprising foolishness, you are not stopped. What is more important, the next Englishman is not intimidated from speaking his mind on solid issues. For men who in their own country find sensible conditions for combining security and freedom, much of what goes on along this line in the United States is worse than foolish; it has an unpleasant odor of what goes on in Russia. From our side we know that the difference between the slavery in Russia and the relatively minor pressures now exerted in America to bring about political orthodoxy is very great, but to many a European, what they see happening here suggests what goes on among the Soviets. The refusal to let American scientists go abroad to attend scientific meetings on grounds mysteriously hidden under the phrase, "It would not be for the public benefit," and the many denials of admission to our country of European or Asian scholars, artists, and other people brought about because the McCarran Act makes the consul who must grant the visa fear he may get into trouble if he admitted

---

2 Rovere, Richard H., "Communists in a Free Society," *Partisan Review*, May—June, 1952, p. 343.

the man—these things look, to many a European, like the same sort of evil, though a much smaller one, that he sees in Russia. There seems to be a curtain to the west of him also, though it is certainly not of iron, but perhaps of lightweight polished chromium. And the pursuit of Communists or people thought to be connected somehow with Communism through American government bureaus and teaching staffs seems, to not a few thoughtful Europeans, to deserve no milder name than "political purge." The Feinberg Law of New York State leaves to the school board authority to discharge any teacher which the board thinks to be subversive, leaving it to the board to determine what is subversive. Mr. Justice Douglas declared that this law inevitably turns the school system into a spying project. Thinking of occurrences in this country of which the Feinberg Law is far from the worst, Kingsley Martin, editor of the British weekly *The New Statesman and Nation*, wrote: "To threaten those whose job is to think independently with loss of employment if they do not conform to a prescribed pattern of thought is to penalize integrity and ability, to put a premium upon mediocrity and conventionality. It is a most surprising development in a country which stands in the eyes of the Old World as the very symbol of the individual's right to reject authority."[3]

Mr. Martin's words express my fifth assertion: We, Americans of all people, have become, to some degree, timid and passive. We accept conformity, even demand it. We relax our grip on a first American principle: individual responsibility for government. There is evidence that Americans are becoming afraid to speak out. The National Opinion Research Center is finding it notably harder than it was to get people to answer questions on political or social issues; they would just rather not. I meet men who say that nowadays they would rather not be quoted on such matters for fear of being criticized or of losing their jobs. I meet government employees who have lost courage and the will to work by reason of the anxiety that hangs constantly over them. My university colleagues increasingly hesitate to put their names to this protest or that declaration of opinon because others on the list of signers are suspect and they fear to become suspect too. And we Americans have been passive at the growing government by silence, at the authority given government bureaus to withhold information, at the refusals of the State Department to disclose reasons for its decisions to deny a passport or to cancel a grant. It seems

---

3 Martin, Kingsley, *Ibid.*, p. 343

that we are ready to accept, in our government bureaus, the view that "papa knows best." And the drift toward safe conformity is reported outside of the field of political opinion. Scientists I know are now concerned over the growing disposition on the part of young scientists to take only "safe" subjects for investigation, problems which are not venturesome, which no one will criticize. And the distinguished playwright, Arthur Miller, has recently described playwriting in America today as characterized by timidity, by "an atmosphere of dread." Looking at the artists of our country, Miller says, "Guardedness, suspicion, aloof circumspection, these are the strongest traits I see around me, and what have they to do with the creative act?"[4]

These things are true, but they are true only in some degree. The main current of American tradition is against them. If one European, Kingsley Martin, sees this country as today demanding conformity in ideas, another, Joyce Cary, sees our people as still "much more profoundly democratic and individual than any other people in the world."[5] And so we are. It is only that in our unintelligent anxiety over internal security we have allowed ourselves to act out of character. The drift to timidity and passivity is unAmerican. A failure to assume personal responsibility for government is unAmerican. To turn our faces away from the threat before us and to dispute amoung ourselves as to the blame for losing an old battle is unAmerican. To act with such unreasonable suspicion of our good friends in foreign countries that they wonder what Russia-like darkness has come upon America, the asylum of political refugees, is highly unAmerican. These are the things that committees on unAmerican activities should really be investigating.

It is our good sense that, in a difficult time, has gone temporarily astray. We have plenty of courage, but it is not always intelligently directed. We have good purposes, but some of the measures we take defeat our purposes. We know that Communism is an immense evil and a great danger. We know too what Stalin wants to accomplish. He wants two things: to seize power and to confuse us into weakness. To resist his attempts to seize power abroad, we take suitable measures; to resist his attempts in our own country, we catch spies and prevent his agents from getting into offices and jobs that hold power. But to resist his evident attempts to confuse us, we too often respond by becoming confused. In the matters I have mentioned, we react so irrationally to

---

[4] Miller, Arthur, "Many Writers: Few Plays," *New York Times*, Auguest 10, 1952, Sect. II, p.1.
[5] Cary, Joyce, "the Sources of Tension in America," *Saturday Review of Literature*, August 23, 1952, p.3.

his attacks that the confusion follows from our reactions rather than from his actions.

Why do the devil's work for him? To prevent the Communists from confusing us, we can stop confusing ourselves. We can submit our courage to the demands of reason. To protect ourselves from Communists within, we can choose instruments that fit the purpose. These are strong laws and energetic action against treason and espionage. We can direct our energies to the real dangers by limiting our loyalty proceedings to men and women considered for critical jobs. These proceedings are wasteful, distracting, and intimidating when they are applied to thousands of teachers and minor employees of government or business. We can abandon the oath, a piece of primitive self-deception, as a test of loyalty. We can observe in its original Holmesian simplicity the measure of those dangers which call for restrictions in civil liberties; the danger must be clear, not just the product of our naturally enhanced general anxiety about the dangerous state of the world, and it must be present, not last year's danger. We can repeal those provisions, among others, of the McCarran Act which prevent good and helpful men and women from coming to our country to help us. We can insist on public procedures, with safeguards of due process, for challenges of exercises of administrative discretion performed away from the view of the public or performed under legislative immunity. We can elect legislators who behave soberly as legislators getting the facts about the laws they are to enact and who are not running their campaigns from the committee room by bullying witnesses and destroying reputations. We can refuse support to such men, in whom in the words of Tacitus, "malignity wears the false appearance of honesty." And we can speak out on all public matters as to which we feel strongly but always strive to speak from a generous heart and an informed intelligence. He is secure who is clear as to good purposes, and clear as to the measures that will really serve these purposes.

*Robert Redfield, chairman of the Department of Anthropology of the University of Chicago, was a member of the Committee to Frame a World Constitution and the National Executive Council of United World Federalists. This is part of an address given at Occidental College, Los Angeles, California, October 22, 1952, reprinted from* World Frontiers, Winter, 1952–53

*Appendix 37*

# THE WIGGINS CASE:
## ACADEMIC FREEDOM IN JEOPARDY

by Alan Jay Upin and Maurice L. Copeland
*"Founded in the faith that men are enobled by understanding.
Dedicated to the advancement of learning and the search for truth.
Devoted to the instruction of youth and the welfare of the state."*
—*The University of Minnesota*

It shouldn't have been a surprise—the non-reappointment of Dr. Forrest O. Wiggins as a philosophy instructor at the University of Minnesota. There were indications that this was a definite possibility. The administration set the precedent a year and a half ago when, with the unvoiced approval of the entire state, it dismissed Dr. Joseph Weinberg of the physics department after he was cited for contempt of Congress. Dr. Weinberg was subsequently acquitted of the charge, but this made little difference to University officals, who refused to reinstate him.

On December 12, 1951, Dr. Wiggins received formal notice that his contract would be terminated at the end of the present academic year. In line with University tenure policy, no reasons were given for the termination, but the letter stated that the action was taken on the recommendation of Dr. E.W. McDiarmid, newly-appointed dean of the College of Science, Literature, and the Arts. It was not until Wiggins's announced his non-reappointment to his classes that the now controversial issue was given public recognition.

It is necessary to point out at once that Dr. Wiggins is both a "radical" and a Negro. All of the groups protesting Wiggins' dismissal made it known very early that they were convinced that his being a Negro had nothing to do with the case. That he was the most outspoken "radical" on the faculty was generally accepted as having a great deal to do with it. In fact, shortly after the action was made known, Wiggins charged in an interview that the administration's failure to renew his contract stemmed from legislators' disapproval of his poltical views. That same day, Dr. George P. Conger, chairman of the philosophy department, stated that he and the members of the department were "unanimous" in recommending Wiggins's retention. It was revealed that, in November, when recommendations for promotions were in order, Dr. Conger had requested, as he had several times before, that Dr. Wiggins be advanced to the rank of assistant professor. Dean McDiarmid deferred action on this request.

After having made known his position, Dr. Conger suggested to Dr. Wiggins that he write a personal credo which could be presented to the Dean. Wiggins complied with this request, but after McDiarmid read this paper, he asked Dr. Wiggins to show how his position differed from that of the Communist Party. Wiggins immediately objected that, since he was not a Communist, he could not tell where the points of difference were. He further took exception to the attempts to test the political beliefs of an instructor.

The University adhered to its policy of silence regarding Wiggins's non-reappointment until three members of the Minnesota legislature announced that they had urged University officials to remove Wiggins. It should be pointed out that during the 1951 Minnesota legislature, a copy of a speech entitled "The Ideology of Interest," which Wiggins had presented before a group of students, was placed on the desk of every legislator. In this speech, Dr. Wiggins severely criticized United States foreign policy, especially in regard to Russia, relating our motives to the interest principle of the free enterprise system.

Some felt that the legislature's decision to cut the University's budget was based on disapproval of the views expressed in that paper. Many predicted that Dr. Wiggins's days at the University were numbered.

One legislator said, "Academic freedom, of which we hear and read so much, is not to be preserved at all cost—for it has its limitations." This legislator claimed that Dr. Wiggins had been "a source of embarrassment to the University, humiliation to the citizens of the state, and confusion to the student body."

When these remarks were made public, Dr. J.L. Morrill, University president said, "Any recommendation made by Dean McDiarmid or any action on my part was taken without reference to any comments or representations made by any members of the legislature."

Following an executive session of the University Board of Regents, President Morrill stated publicly that the Regents, "saw no reason" to reconsider the administration's decision. He stated unequivocally that Dr. Wiggins was dropped because Dean McDiarmid does not consider him "competent." He read a letter from the Dean which said, "Dr. Wiggins continuance is not justified on the basis of his scholarship record or his potential contribution to the philosophy department."

Immediately thereafter Dr. Conger, with the unanimous consent of the philosophy department, issued a documented statement demanding the reinstatement of Dr. Wiggins. He pointed out that Wiggins's academic preparation for his position was "entirely satisfactory." In this paper, Dr. Wiggins's scholarship and teaching ability were endorsed in flattering testimonials from various colleagues and students.

Dr. Conger affirmed Wiggins's competence when he said, "I wish to stress the great value to our department of his abilities as a teacher." The charge that he had failed to give evidence of creative scholarship was effectively challenged when it was pointed out that he had introduced six new courses in as many years.

Dr. Conger wrote, "On the eve of my retirement, I can sincerely say that if I can feel that I have left behind me a group of students who feel a fraction of the admiration and respect for me that these students have expressed for Dr. Wiggins, I shall retire a happy man."

It is evident that the view of Dr. Conger and that of the administration were diametrically opposed. The students were concerned, therefore, as to just who was the better judge of Dr. Wiggins's competence, the University administration or his colleagues in the philosophy department.

The students, after forming an organization to protest the dismissal, obtained more than 2,300 signatures (even though it was during final week) on a petition that "requested the University administration to clarify the grounds on which Dr. Wiggins had been considered incompetent." This was done because the administration had offered no specific evidence in rebuttal of Dr. Conger's paper.

Dr. Morrill, when presented with the petition, stated that he was "unimpressed" with either the content or the number of signatures. In his answer to the petition, Morrill said he had "documentary evidence of grave doubts of (Wiggins's) scholarship."

The students protested that his answer "did not clarify the grounds on which Dr. Wiggins was judged incompetent as requested. (it) mostly repeats and elaborates the denials, generalizations and insinuations which characterized Dr. Morrill's first statement."

The students (and the outside community, which finally began to express objections to the University's decision) were therefore hampered by the paucity of evidence to support a very serious charge. This led the student committee to conclude: "We have serious doubts that incompetency is the real issue; we cannot conclude that the principles of academic freedom are not involved, and we are not convinced that the University did not accede to outside pressures." For what other conclusion was there to be drawn from the facts which had been made known to the public?

Since it felt that Dr. Wiggins had not been proved incompetent, the student committee prepared to present to the Board of Regents a petition which called upon the administration to reinstate him. This petition had been overwhelmingly endorsed by a voice vote at a mass rally attended by an estimated 1,000 students. After the students' intention had been made public, Morrill said that "no documentary evidence" bearing on the case would be made public. The Regents refused, the next day, to reconsider the case and voted unanimously "to reaffirm the action taken on December 15." Thus, the disturbing implications raised by Wiggins's dismissal were to go unanswered.

And so the case stands today.

As far as the future is concerned, Dr. Wiggins told the writers that he had written letters of application to various universities and that none of the replies was encouraging, which seems to indicate that the case at Minnesota has hurt his chances of getting another job as an instructor. Wiggins believes there are three factors hindering his receiving an appointment at another university. These are the fact he is a Negro; the drop in university enrollments; and the fact he is a radical. Dr. Wiggins regrets that he underestimated the audacity of the reactionary element. He said, "The country has gone farther along toward fascism that I thought it had." People have drawn different conclusions from the issues presented by the administration, students, the public and Dr. Wiggins himself. Someone has said, "Those who control education have been made sufficently aware that the people are becoming concerned over the inroads on academic freedom." Though this is certainly true to some degree, we think that for us as young people a far more sobering conclusion must be drawn.

It seems to us that we must realize that the state universities are, in the final analysis, under the control of the people of the various states and by their representatives in the legislatures. These representatives, and the people themselves, do not, for the most part, understand either the facts or the implications in cases such as this. This seems to be true not only because conservatism is a dominant adult attitude, but also because of the limited political education most people have received. We must realize moreover than an almost hysterical fear of communism completely dominates the adult thinking of our nation today. Unless we can effectively combat this hysteria, academic freedom is seriously threatened.

*A senior in the University of Minnesota, majoring in Philosophy, Al Upin has been a federalist since 1948, is now president of the Minnesota WORLD council, and of the University WORLD chapter. He is a National Board member of WORLD. Maurice L. Copeland, a Journalism major, is the former articles editor of the University of Minnesota magazine, SKOL, and former staff member of the Minnesota Daily. He is a correspondent for the Chicago Defender and a veteran of World War II. From* World Frontiers, Spring 1952

*Appendix 38*

## Point Four: Another American Tragedy?
### by Gilbert Jonas

*Point Four was the first American post-war initiative which offered the promise of economic development to the non-European world. However, its potential was handicapped by its recruitment to help fight the cold war.*

The U.S. government is engaged in the Point Four Program of technical assistance primarily because it believes that Point Four will help stop Communism. Many liberal Americans have agreed that Point Four will aid our containment policy. After more than a year of Point Four, however, some American experts have begun to reconsider this belief. Other experts, principally interested in raising the living levels in the underdeveloped areas, have reiterated their stand that Point Four is not a solution to the economic ills of two thirds of the world and can even intensify those ills.

Whatever the strong points and shortcomings of the technical assistance idea in general may be, the American program of Point Four has produced its own unique difficulties, which can make this program harmful to the goal of increased living levels in the underdeveloped areas as well as futile in halting Communism.

Most of the dilemmas our Point Four administrators now face can be traced to certain political, economic, and social attitudes held either by Americans or by the recipients of Point Four. The failure to understand each other's attitudes has already led in some places to a likelihood of the very thing the program was designed to avoid—Communist ascendancy. Our negative containment policy leads us to oppose generally whatever programs Russia advocates. But many of these programs would improve the welfare of the people.

By opposing them, we weaken our own position and hurt Point Four. Many Americans further err by thinking that anyone who agrees with any of Russia's policies, or opposes any of our own, is automatically an enemy.

The overwhelming problem that most of the human race faces is poverty. Poverty means empty stomachs, curable diseases, primitive housing, stultifying ignorance, and the political instability which these conditions perpetuate. This suffering is the fate, but not the choice, of the poor. A successful technical assistance policy recognizes this and proceeds with both sympathy and understanding to help the poor of the underdeveloped areas to help themselves.

The U.S. policy-makers, while at times nominally recognizing these facts, are primarily interested in halting Communism. The Communists, however, have been loudly advocating policies that promise to alleviate poverty. And where they have gained a foothold, the Communists are often carrying them out. The land reforms they have instituted in China and North Korea, in sharp contrast to the "paper" reforms of the U.S.-supported regimes, are obvious examples.

Communism flourishes on the very conditions that now exist in the underdeveloped areas. Communism is not likely to gain a total victory, however, until the people in these areas are convinced that it is an alternative to their oppression or until their oppression becomes unbearable. "Point-Four-to-halt-Communism" is bringing about both these conditions. In many places, the Communists are convincing the people that they have a real alternative. We are not.

This problem is further complicated by another dominant U.S. attitude: that military might is everywhere the best way to stop Communism. But military aid does nothing to alleviate the economic problems of the underdeveloped areas. Indeed, U.S. military aid to governments which have done little or nothing to eliminate the poverty of their people, as in China and South Korea, entrenches these regimes in power, and thereby perpetuates or increases the poverty, nullifies what little economic aid we have given, precludes any peaceful change, and drives the people closer to the only alternative we have failed to wipe out—the Communist alternative. Meanwhile, the people identify us still further with the interests that are opposed to their welfare. And by insisting on joint preparedness, we have increased the economic strains, and, consequently, the political instability of the somewhat more democratic governments, such as those of the Philippines and Thailand.

The underdeveloped peoples, of course, see their own poverty as their main problem. They are not interested in the Cold War—or a hot one for that matter. The Asian leaders see in a Third World War and present preparations for it only a diversion of resources from more productive channels. More important, they have at present little desire to choose sides, since neither side offers any real help in relieving their poverty. Many Asians maintain that both the U.S. and Soviet camps are essentially Western, more like each other than Asians; that neither ideology offers them a solution; and that they must search for their own answers. From the Asian view, the small amount of economic aid that the U.S. is willing to offer in exchange for military allegiance in no way compensates for the dangers of involvement in a new global conflict. They will not accept economic aid hinged upon either the acceptance of military aid or the affirmation of political loyalty. Recently, the Indonesian parliament rejected U.S. economic aid because of the military strings attached. This act was symptomatic of the Asians' desire to steer clear of the U.S.-Soviet power struggle. Yet rejection of economic aid means perpetuation of the same miserable conditions upon which Communism breeds freely.

Even acceptance of the small sums of Point Four aid which the U.S. does grant can often make matters worse. Americans greatly exaggerate the extent to which technical assistance can solve the economic problems of the underdeveloped areas. We tend to deify our own "know-how" and to minimize the cost of applying it. The $35 million Point Four allotment, equal to the annual budget of a medium-sized American city, has become a salve for the disturbed consciences of well-meaning, but ill-informed, American liberals. Especially when compared with the billions we spend for rearmament, this sum fails to make much of an improvement in material welfare or an impression in the minds of the underdeveloped peoples. For example, technical aid is usually first applied in raising medical and health standards. This almost immediately reduces the death rate in areas where the birth rate is extremely high and insensitive to change. The rate of population increase soars upward, so that many more people must live at a subsistence level, unless starvation wipes them out. Any increase in agricultural productivity is eaten up by a new population increase. Indeed, the Indian living standard has been falling gradually in the past 20 years, partly because the application of this kind of aid has greatly increased its population. This is but one example of how technical assistance, when parcelled out in tiny sums, can intensify, rather than alleviate, poverty.

The underdeveloped peoples are intensely conscious of skin color. They and their ancestors have been subjected to centuries of oppression and indignity based on the myth of white supremacy. U.S. support of the colonial powers together with the wide-spread propaganda about racial discrimination in the United States has made it very difficult to convince these people that we are "the leaders of the free world" or that our world is truly free. Even in our administration of Point Four, we have shown attitudes of racial or cultural superiority. This is especially bad in a time when a surge of racial and cultural pride is sweeping the underdeveloped areas.

These people resent charity and dislike being used as pawns in global power politics. They see that containment of Communism comes first for us and that a genuine desire to help them comes second. They fear that any ties to U.S. policy may involve them in a future war.

For these reasons, it is not difficult to understand why they are suspicious of U.S. aid. Any unilateral aid we offer, if accepted, will only be taken with many reservations—reservations which the American Congress finds difficult to approve. Unilateral aid has outlived much of its effectiveness, partly because few nations will accept aid with strings attached and partly because those that do will use it for purposes other than the benefit of the people. Unilateral aid, moreover, tends to work against the international coordination necessary for the most efficient use of the scanty resources of the underdeveloped areas. Whether or not the underdeveloped areas achieve their economic goals depends upon how closely they cooperate with each other. In countries where the slightest waste results in the loss of more human lives, the prevention of waste and the most efficent coordination of economic development are mandatory.

Another major handicap is our antipathy towards Socialist and "left-wing" governments. From our actions, one would think we preferred the most corrupt and vicious regime to a Socialist one. The Socialist governments of the underdeveloped areas are involved in a life-and-death struggle to get the most out of their primitive methods of production and their small ratio of resources to people. This ratio rules out the possibility of their going through the wasteful trial-and-error stages of 18th and 19th century western capitalism. They must make immediate use of the vast store of knowledge already accumulated in the West. Only planned economic activity on a large scale can make the most efficient and rapid use of this knowledge. We cannot dismiss their efforts merely by calling them "Socialist." Socialism, in its many forms, is here to stay, is not necessarily totalitarian or pro-Russian, and cannot be eradicated by attaching political strings to Point Four.

Our fear of anything "left" has made us support the "safe" regimes of the extreme right, such as those of Syngman Rhee, Bao Dai, Ibn Saud, Franco, and Chiang Kai-shek. None of these regimes has started the sweeping reforms required to alleviate their people's poverty. Many of them have used our technical assistance to create small, extremely wealthy and powerful ruling groups. Our aid has thus widened the gap between rich and poor and increased the Communists' chances.

Point Four, moreover, has been coupled with a propaganda campaign, carried on through the U.S. Information Service and the Voice of America, that has failed to match the successes of Soviet propaganda and has often backfired. We have, in the main, described the high living standards of the U.S. and implied, if not actually stated, that these levels can be attained by the underdeveloped peoples if they join our "holy crusade against Communism." According to numerous travellers in Southeast Asia and India, this propaganda has created as much envy and subsequent disillusionment with unfilfilled American promises as it has created new friends. A few pilot projects set up in the midst of increasing squalor also serve to raise the hopes of the millions not benefitting from these projects. When, after a few years, these hopes are disappointed American propaganda merefy intensifies the differences between the "haves" and the "have-nots." An Asian peasant need not be a disciple of Karl Marx to comprehend the differences. And there is a growing comradeship emerging among the "have-nots" who now desire to have. Interestingly enough, the average Indian farmer classifies the Soviet Union among the "have-nots."

When the welfare of the people is held first, revolutions are sometimes highly desirable. Because historical change has been speeded up by modern communications and transportation, these revolutions will occur sooner than most of us realize. Whether they take a violent form depends on how much aid we send and how quickly we can get that aid to the underdeveloped nations. Whether these revolutions are Russian-oriented (and a violent revolution is not necessarily Russian-oriented, as Indonesia and Burma demonstrate) depends to a great degree on how we expend that aid and to whom we give it. If we attempt to Americanize the underdeveloped nations, we shall force them from our sphere and possibly into the realm of the Russians. If we insist on unilateral aid, as we have so far, the underdeveloped areas, already suspicious of most things Western or American, will continue to look upon this aid as another effort of "western imperialism."

We must abandon our "free enterprise" obsessions as far as the underdeveloped areas are concerned. Gargantuan sweat-shops based on vast supplies of cheap labor, the mass-production system, and Western capital have earned the West a back-log of ill-feeling in colonial and semi-colonial areas. A misused Point Four will simply repeat these experiences.

In sum, a successful Point Four program must be based on a desire to increase the living levels of the majority of the underdeveloped peoples. It must be administered with humility, tolerance for the different means of achieving the goal, understanding of the various cultures, and firmness in insisting upon expanding democracy and honest government. If we can do these things, the defeat of Russian Communism in the underdeveloped areas will take care of itself.

World Frontiers, *Vol. 1, No. 1, Spring 1952*

# Appendix 39

## TO TRAIN THESE HANDS

*An early organizing brochure of the International Development Placement Association (IDPA) which arose from the student federalist movement.*

**Train These Hands**
Here is a program of human assistance for the underdeveloped areas.

In our shrinking world, two great groups of humanity are coming together. The one third of the world's people who are adequately fed, and the rest who live in hunger, poverty and disease, are becoming next-door neighbors.

"The City of the Poor"—the "underdeveloped areas" of Asia, Africa, and Latin America—at one time had little voice in the world's affairs. Now these peoples are emerging as independent nations whose plight affects all humanity.

Both groups are now in possession of a great truth. They know that modern science has the power to lift the age-old blight of poverty from the entire earth.

The International Development Placement Association was founded to bring to the underdeveloped countries, on a person-to-person level, the skills we as a developed modern society possess and they need. In response to each country's request, IDPA supplies trained persons for development programs, who contribute their skills and who train others to carry on the programs to their goal. IDPA's field workers return with a greater understanding of the peoples of these countries and their needs.

**A New Program**
Each underdeveloped country has its own problems and requirements for technical assistance and economic development. Through the U.S. Technical Assistance Program and the UN Technical Assistance Board, many of these countries have received the initial aid of highly skilled experts in their overall development programs.

But to carry out such programs a country needs more than just "top experts." Teachers are needed, and nurses, and nutrionists, and engineers, and child welfare workers—not "top experts" but trained and educated younger people who are available in a developed industrial society but almost unobtainable elsewhere.

This scarcity of trained persons is an obstacle which many countries could not overcome because they cannot afford to import these persons from the West at Western wages.

IDPA channels the forces to bridge this gap. Many trained and skilled Americans will work for a year or two in the underdeveloped nations at *local* wages, to give and teach their skills and help the people in their own effort to rise from poverty.

IDPA locates and selects non-profit government and community welfare development programs in the underdeveloped countries which desire the assistance of trained personnel. It selects the best of its many applicants as field workers, counsels and orients them for their experience abroad, and provides grants when conditions warrant.

Scores of opportunities are opening for the placement of IDPA field workers throughout Africa, the Middle East, and Asia. Special trips to these areas by IDPA staff representatives are bringing a widespread response from governments and community welfare development programs.

In America, over a thousand persons have made application to IDPA. Those selected have either been placed or are awaiting placement as field workers.

**Spirit and Vision**
IDPA, through the efforts of its field workers, brings *human assistance* to these nations, of whatever kind they need and request.

Because the heart of its program is the personal training and skill of field workers willing to work in the underdeveloped areas at local wages, IDPA gives substantial assistance in the critical phases of important development programs, attaining great tangible results at modest cost. It is a non-profit agency, whose plan has captured the imagination of Americans and has been enthusiastically welcomed abroad.

It depends entirely on voluntary support for its success.

From the world's richest country, IDPA field workers go into the poorest areas of the earth, where their knowledge is beyond price, to do the work of progress, hope and peace in the name of every person who believes that human dignity and values have no boundaries. We ask you, as a private American citizen, to help them do this task.

## Here Are Some IDPA Workers in the Field

*Teacher in Nigeria*
Don Eberly of Boston, Massachusetts, is finding his position at Molusi College in Ijebu-Igbo, Nigeria, a challenge to his best abilities and skill. He is the first science teacher on the faculty of the new college, one of six being established by the government in its program of social and economic development. In a letter of deep appreciation, the college thanked IDPA for "responding to our SOS and sending Mr. Eberly all the way from your beautiful America." Don has been put in charge of establishing the entire science department of the college, while helping with his own hands and ideas in the building of the college and its frontier-like facilities.

*Physicist in Indonesia*
The new Republic of Indonesia did not have a single nuclear physicist. Now they will have one—Bill Dickinson of Los Alamos, New Mexico. Recommended to the government of Indonesia by IDPA in response to their request, Dickinson will conduct teaching activities and research at the University of Indonesia. With his assistance, the University will build up its facilities for advanced study in modern physical science.

*Social Worker in India*
William Rowe of Alhambra, California, is doing basic education work in Sevagram, India. Receiving minimum subsistence without wages, Bill Rowe is bringing his knowledge to the development program of what Gandhi once called "one of the poorest villages in the poorest section of India." Ralph Blackwood of Sterling, Kansas, a teacher, and Marian Solomon of Spring Valley, Minnesota, a nurse, are with him at Sevagram as IDPA field workers.

With their active participation, Sevagram is becoming a model for Indian village-level community development.

## Officers

Clifford C. Dancer, Chairman
Herbert Eisenberg, Vice Chairman
Albert Ettinger, Secretary
Eugene G. Schwartz, Treasurer
Peter Weiss, Executive Director

## Board of Directors

Jean Alexander
Stringfellow Barr
Thomas C. Callahan
Ellen Camnitzer
Earl Eames
Jonathan Ezenekwe
James Farmer
Murray Frank

William Friedlander
Sanford Kravitz
Kenneth Kurtz
Robert R. Nathan
George Overton
Frank Parker
Arthur Pratt
Robert West

## Advisory Board

Roger N. Baldwin
Scott Buchanan
Dr. Frank G. Boudreau
Rev. Donald Harrington
Mordecai Johnson

Reinhold Niebuhr
Clarence Pickett
Robert Redfield
Jerry Voorhis
Gilbert F. White

*International Development Placement Association, Inc., 345 East 46th Street, New York, New York (circa 1954)*

# Index

*Note:* Page numbers in **bold type** reference non-text material

Abrams, Ivan, 20
ADA, 131-32
Adler, Mortimer J., 23, 34
Alexander, Jean, 92, 110, 120
American Association of the U.N., 62
American Civil Liberties Union (ACLU), 81
American Legion, and global armed force, 41
*Anatomy of Peace* (Reves), 28
Andrews, Bill, 83
Asheville compromise, 44-47
Asheville meeting, 42-43
Association for Education in World Government, 100
*Atlantic Monthly*, 21
Atlee, Clement, 40
Atomic weapons, 19, 41

Bache, Harold, 23
Baldwin, Roger, 120, 123
Baldwin, Russell, 68
Ball, Helen, 23, 33, **39**, 42, 46, 48, **52**, 61
Ball, Joseph, 6, 9
Bargman, Abe, 48-49, 53, 59, 69, 76, 92
Barkley, Alben, 76
Barnhill, Phyllis, 59, **60**, 81, 92

Barr, Stringfellow, 34, 40, 97, 120-21, 123
Barth, Alan, 97, 125
Baruch Plan, 50
Bauman, David, 20, 33
Beech, Virginia, 24
Benedict, Steve, **12**-13, 22, 27, 48, 60-61, 70
Bennett, Robert, 33
Berg, Elliot, 125
Berger, Lewis, 48
Bergman, Ingrid, 18
Berman, Eugene, 61
Beveridge, Sir William, 55
Biffle, Leslie, **77**
Blaine, Anita McCormick, 117, 120, 124
Blaine, Nancy, 123-24
Blake, Mildred, 47, **55**, **72**
Blumenstiel, Margaret, 9
Boeke, Richard, 103
Bok, Derek, 99
Borgese, G. A., 34
Bowles, Chester, 6, 46
Boyd Orr, Lord, 55, **71**
Bozell, Brent, 61
Brady, Kirk, 90
Brenner, Ed, 68, 89, 103, 104, 107

Buchanan, Scott, 120
Buel, Anna, 59
Burns, James, 61, 68
Byrd, Robert, 89, 105

Canfield, Cass, 55, 61
CARE, 90
Carney, Fred, 49, 53, 70
Carrington, Walter, 122
Carter, Dick, 117
Carter, George, 122
Chadwick, Steve, 12, 21, 23, 26, **30**, 33, 48
Cherne, Leo, 23
Churchill, Winston, 1, 3
CIA, 111
Clapper, Mrs. Raymond, 23
Clark, Grenville, 23
Clark, Joan, 72, 114
Clark, Nonie, 89, 97, 100, **102**-3, 110
Cleveland assembly, 73
Cold War, 76, 115-33
Coleman, Mary, **87**, 110
Communism, alternative to, 88
Communist parties, 43
Compton, James, 49
Compton, Randolph, 23, **55**
Concord meeting, 20-24
Corcos, Gilles, **19**, 53, 61
Cousins, Norman, 40, 46, 101, 106
Crane, Wilder, 12, 17, 22
Cranston, Alan, 70, 76, 96, 118
Cross-country caravan, 75-76
Crozier, Emmet, 13
*Cry the Beloved Country* (Paton), 130
Cullum, Mary Louise, 68, 73
Cutler, Bruce, 125

Dailey, Louis B., 106
Dale, Helen, **122**
Dancer, Clifford, 120
Davenport, Russell, 23
Davis, John Shelton, 59
DeConingh, Virginia, 125, 128, 131
Defenestration, 65
Delano, Bill, 122
Denitch, Bogdan, 123

Des Moines, showdown at, 101-2
Dodd, Thomas, 61
Douglas, William O., 46, 123, 132
Duke, Diane, 48
Dumbarton Oaks conference, 15
Dummit, Ralph, 81

Eagleton, Clyde, 62
Eagle, Vernon, 124
Education, 24-25
Einstein, Albert, 26, 60, 98, 123
Eisenberg, Herb, 92
Ellison, Ralph, 126
Eshman, Aaron, 17, 18
Ettinger, Al, 92, 120
Evans, Upshur, 53, **55**

Fadiman, Clifton, 23, 40
Fagan, Myron C., 78-79
Farmer, James, 120
Farrar, Curt, 23, 25, **29**, 34, 40, 42, 48, 68, 92
Farr, Tom, 49
*The Federalist*, 106-7
*Federalist Opinion*, 86
Federation of Atlantic Democracies, 3-5
Fine, Jonathan, 72
Finletter, Thomas K., 23, 46, 65
Fleming, Ralph, **67**-68, 70, 105
Fox, Katherine, 48
Frankhauser, Bill, 72
Frank, Murray, **67**-68, **72**-74, 81-82, 89-91, 103-4, 119-20, 122, 131
Fraser, Dee, 97
Fraser, Jack, 103
Friedlander, William, **77**, 79, 82, **88**, 92, 97, 100, 103, 113, 120, 125
Fuchs, Larry, **36**, 38, 48-49, **55**, 59, **60**, 68, 83, 89, 103, 122
Fulbright, William, 6, 46

Garinger, L. D., 12
Gaston, Gloria, 122
Glascow, Dick, **36**
Goodman, Richard, 68
Granik, Ted, 13
Gromyko, Andrei, 50

# Index

Haddad, Bill, 122
Hammerstein, Oscar II, 97
Hanna, Charlotte, 59
Hanson, David, 105
Harrington, Donald, 120
Harrington, Michael, 123
Harrison, Gil, 124
Hart, Norman J., **71**
Harvard Law School, 34
Hastings, Courtland, 106
Hastings, England Congress, 66
Hatfield, Mark, 99
Heinz, John, 6
Hennessy, Bernard, 73, 81, 92, 97
Herblock, 51
Hiller, Dale, 89, 100, 103, 105
Hockenberg, Harlan, 68
Hoffman, Harrison B. W., 104
Hoffman, Paul, 46
Holbrook, William, 68
Holliday, W. T., 46, 65
Holt, George, 106
Holt, John C. II, 104, 119, 125
Hoover, J. Edgar, 105
Houser, George, 125
House UnAmerican Activities Committee (HUAC), 76
Howell, Ernest, 91, 113
Hughes, Tom, 4, 6-7, **12**, **14**-15, **17**-18, 22, **31**, 33, 121; "Challenge to the Elder Statesmen," 11-13; "Marxism and Federalism," 35
"Humber Resolution," 39
Humber, Robert Lee, 46
Humphrey, Hubert, 6, 121
Huntley, Chet, 78
Hutchins, Robert, 123

IDPA, 120-22
Interim Committee of American Federalist Youth (ICAFY), 103-4, 107-10
International Development Placement Association, 117
International Union of Students (IUS), 34
*The Invisible Man* (Ellison), 126
Irion, Donald, 59, 61
*It's Up to Us* (Wofford), 19, 25

Jackman, Bob, 105
Jackson, Robert, 46
Jashchke, Melvin, 59
Johnson, Ernest, **39**
Johnson, Mordechai, 120, 123
Johnson, Priscilla, 72, 83
Jonas, Gil, **98**, 100, **102**, **122**
Judd, Walter H., 62

Kaye, Alvin, 20
Kaye, Steve, 20
Kelley, Doug, 92, 117, 120
Kelton, Richard, 61, 128
Kemeny, John, 72, 83, 106
Kennedy, John F., 6, 121
Kimball, Pat, 23, **39**, 49
Kimpton, Laurence, 99
Klein, Elaine, 92, 97, **102**-3, 105, **111**
Knoerr, Donald, 59, 61
Koppenaal, Richard, 59
Korean War, 115
Kravitz, Sandy, 92, 120
Kreveld, Gerrit, 126
Kurtz, Ken, 92, 117-20, 123
Kyle, Alastair, 70

Landau, Rom, 125, 128
Landy, Eleanor, 110
Langmuir, Irving, 46
Lapidus, Mrs. Milton, 106
Law, Lucy, 128-**29**
Lesserman, Philip, 61
Lessey, Samuel, 34
"Let's Join the Human Race" (Barr), 121
Levering, Sam, **55**
Levine, Donald, 61
Levin, Sandy, 131-32
Levy, Tom, 119
*Life* magazine, 30
Lindgren, Clare (Emmy Lou), 4-5, **12**, **14**, **16**, 18, 22, 33, **39**, 46, 48, 54-56; education programs sparked by, 24-25
Logue, John, 59

Look magazine, 18
Lord, Harold, 61
Lowenstein, Al, 110, 113, 117
Loyalty Oath, 80
Luce, Clare Booth, 2, 16, 37
Luce, Henry Robinson, 37
Lustig, Harry, 72, 100-101, 103, 117, 119, 127, 131
Luxembourg Convention, 38
Lynch, William, 33

Magee, Chris, **12**
Margolin, Jesse, 128
"Marxism and Federalism" (Hughes), 35
Masaryk, Thomas, defenestration of, 65
Matlock, Jack, 59, 68
Matthews, Z. K., 130
McCarthy, Joseph, 80
McIntosh, Don, 20, 23, 61, 68, **88**, 125
McIntosh, Laura, 20, 23
McLaughlin, Mrs. Ronald, 104
McMurray, Howard, 11
Melchior, Charles, 107
Melony, John, 75
Melony, Virginia, 75
Meyer, Cord Jr., 18, 21, 23, 46, **55**, 70, 89, 124; and the CIA, 111; named UWF president, 53-54, 97
Miller, Ann, 126
Miller, Jerry, 7, 13-**14**, 15
Minot, Steve, 48
Montell, Sherwin, 48
Montreux conference, 53-54
Moore, Harry, 123
Morganthau, Hans, 125
Morocco, 128-30
Movement for World Federal Government, 38
Moynihan, Daniel Patrick, 23

NAACP, 74, 81, 120
Naffziger, Joy, **12**
Nathan, Robert R., 120
National Organization of Veterans, 26
National Social Welfare Council, 74
National Student Council (NSC), 47

Nelson, Charles, 23
New Deal Fair Deal, 28
*The New Republic*, 124
Newton, Quig, 75
*The New Yorker*, 24
*New York Herald Tribune*, 13
Niebuhr, Reinhold, 120
Niles, Cushing, 23
Norris, Charles, **39**
Novick, Peter, 72

Osos, Toby, 110

Palace, Bonnie Shaner, 90, 92, 97, **102**
Parker, Frank, 120
Parker, John, 82
Parmalee, Foster Jr., 23, 26, 34, 38, 49
Parsons, Neil, 102, 104, 105
Peace Corps, 122
Peck, Garvan, **30**, 33, 49
Phillips Exeter Academy (New Hampshire), 24
Pickett, Clarence, 120
Pierson, Dick, 103, 106-7, 110
Poitier, Sidney, 130
Pomona College, 25
Potter, Fran, 110
Pratt, Arthur, 120
Prentice, Colgate "Coke," 22, 33, 37, 46, 61
Priest, Paul, 61, 83
Purdy, Mary Ellen, 14, 20, 23, **52**

Quayle, Oliver III, 104

Racism, 73-75
Rebellion of the students, 85-114
Redfield, Robert, 34, 89, 99, 120, 123, 125
Reisin, Sy, 81
Reukberg, Ben, 105
Reuther, Walter, 123
Reves, Emery, 28, 40, **52**
Reynolds, Edith, **30**
Riorden, Shane, 20, 53, 61, **98**, 119, 124
Riorden, Virginia Lastayo, 19-**20**, 22, 35, 38, 41, 46, 48-49, 53, **102**, 103, 110, 118-19, 126

## Index

Roberts, James, 83, 92
Robertson, Thomas "Duke", 89, 91, 96-97, **102**, 104, **111**
Roberts, Owen J., 9, 18
Robinson, Irwin, 72
Rogers, Natalie, **36**, 59, **63**, 66, 68-69, 73, 83
Rogers, Will Jr., 6
Rollins College (Florida), 24
Romulo, Carlos P., 40
Roosevelt, Eleanor, 6, 98
Roosevelt, Franklin Delano, 3, 9; death of, 18
Roper, Elmo, 23, 40
Ruml, Beardsley, 40
Ruopp, Phil, 49

Saeta, Phil, 80
Scarsdale group, 3
Schacter, Ruth, 113
Schneider, Eleanor 23, 25, 40, 49, 53
Schneider, Trudy **26**, 53
Schuman, Frederick, 70, 123
Schreier, Elliot, 80
Schwartz, Gene, 91-92, 110, 120
Schwebel, Stephen, 23
SDA, 131-32
Shaner, Bonnie, 73
Shapiro, Richard, 23, 33, 38
Sheil, Bernard, 123
Shepherd, George, 59
Siegal, Rheta, 72
Smith, Gerald L. K., 16, 77-78
Sohn, Louis, 34
Southern Institute (Florida), 25
Soviet Union, 21, 38; expansion of, 43, 64-65
Stalin, Joseph, 105
Stanford federalists, 80-81; and the Rome Congress, 97-100
Stanley, C. M., 96
Stanley, David M., 105-7
Stassen, Harold, 9, 18, 63, 65
Stimson, Henry, 46
Stockman, Jim, **30**
Stout, Dorothy, 69
Stout, Rex, 23

Straight, Michael, 124
Streit, Clarence, 2, 3-4, 11, 13, 23, 40
Strode, Hildreth, 83
Student Federalist Movement: becoming a national organization, 11-31; birth of, 1-9; Concord meeting of, 20-24; cross-country caravan of, 75-76; and the international arena, 15-18, 25-27; maximalist position of, 27-30; unification of, 41-43; volunteer organizing, 66-68
*Student Federalist* newsletter, 8-9, 64, 89
Sullivan, Donald, 91
Sutter, John, 72
Swift, Wesley, 77-78
Swing, Raymond, 23, 46

Taft, Robert A., 65
Taylor, Edmond, 123, 125
Temple, Shirley, 17
Tenney, Jack, 77
"Third Force in Asia" (Wofford), 124-25
Thomas, J. Parnell, 76
Thomson, Henry, 72
Thygeson, Fritjof, **30**, 33, 61, 68, 89, **94**, 103
*Time* magazine, 15-16, 37
Toynbee, Arnold, 49
Truman, Harry S, 64, 115
Tucker, Ed, 75
Tucker, Gerald, 12

UNESCO, 90
United Nations, 15, 18, 28-29, 41, 49; and the Baruch Plan, 50; powers of, 105; and world government, 49-57
United States, 21
United States National Student Association (USNSA), 1, 40, 66, 117
United World Federalists, 44-49, 53; membership plummets, 68-69; and racism, 73-75; right-wing efforts to silence, 79-82; severs relations with *World Government News*, 93-96; tensions between students and adults, 69-73, 82-83, 85-114; Wallerstein resigns from, 96-97
University of Chicago, 25, 30, 34; Wyoming Union of, **35**

Upin, Al, 103, 125
Usborne, Henry, 54

Van Doren, Carl, 46, **48**, 62
Van Doren, Mark, 23, **52**, 123, 125
Veterans, 18-20
Volunteer Organizing, 66-68
Voorhis, Jerry, 102, 120

Walker, Robert, 70
Wallace, Henry, 9, 64
Waller, Ted, 104
Wallerstein, Immanuel, 73, 85-86, 88-89, 91-92, **95**, **102**-3, 104, 110-**11**, 113, **126**; resignation of, 96-97
Warburg, James, 123
Watt, Robert, 46
Weichel, Dorothy, 97
Weiss, Herb, 73, **87**, 91, 97, 102-3, 110-**11**, 113, 125
Weiss, Peter, 92, 120-21, 125
Weiss, Ted, 73, 103, 110, 113, 119
Wellesley College, 24
West, Rob, 90, 92, 120
Wheeler, Joseph, 20, 23, **29**, 49, 66, 70-**71**
White, Walter, 74-75
Wiley, Steve, 89, 103
Wilkins, Roy, 75
Williams, Lee, 68

Willkie, Wendell, 9
Wilson, Abe, **55**
Winant, John, 46
Wisner, Frank, 111
Wofford, Harris Jr., **2**-6, **14**, 16-**17**, 20, 23, 33, **37**, 46, 48, 54-56, 68, 92, 120, 128; farewell address of, 11; *It's Up to Us*, 19, 25; and the Peace Corps, 122; speaking tour of, 7-9; "Third Force in Asia," 124-25
WORLD (World Order Realized through Law and Democracy), 116-33
World Assembly of Youth (Way), 74, 82, **108**, 110-14
World Congress for World Government, 92, 97-100
World federalism, endorsement of, 18, 68
World Federation of Democratic Youth (WFDY), 34, 65, 74
*World Frontiers*, 124-25
World government, 49-57; petition for United States support of, 63-64
*World Government News*, 89, 93-96
World Youth Festival, 50
Wright, Anna, 73

Young Adult Council (YAC), 82-83, 90-91, 111-12
Youngdahl, Luther, 123

Zamorsky, Lou, 59

Printed in the United States
87541LV00003B/68/A